Wetherell of
H. M. S. *Hussar*

Wetherell of
H. M. S. *Hussar*
The Recollections of an Ordinary Seaman of the Royal Navy During the Napoleonic Wars

John Wetherell

Wetherell of H. M. S. Hussar The Recollections of an Ordinary Seaman of the Royal Navy During the Napoleonic Wars
by John Wetherell

Published by Leonaur Ltd

Text in this form is copyright © 2008 Leonaur Ltd

ISBN: 978-1-84677-514-7 (hardcover)
ISBN: 978-1-84677-513-0 (softcover)

http://www.leonaur.com

Publisher's Notes

The opinions expressed in this book are those of the author and are not necessarily those of the publisher.

Contents

1803: Impressed!	7
1803: Sailing Under a Tyrant	26
1803: The Dutch Indiaman	42
1803: The *Revenge* 64	52
1804: Striking the Saints	65
1804: The Open Boats	77
1804: Prisoners of War	87
1804-9: Prisoner of the French	111
1810: Napoleon Passes By	130
1810-13: The Allies Invade France	151
1813-14: Driven by the Gendarmes	168
1814: To the South	195
1814: Perfect Paradise	220
1814: We Meet the British Army	244

Chapter 1
1803: Impressed!

February 28, 1803. I was at this time a seaman engaged in the merchant trade. Our time rolled round and the ship *Jane* was shortly expected to be ready for sailing, her crew partly engaged, her cargo nearly all on board. My things all ready to take on board any time required.

March 8, 1803. We had a rumour that set all Shields in an uproar. The ship *Desdemona* came in with the woeful news that two large frigates lay in the Swin impressing every man protected or not. This was a bitter pill but I had to swallow it. Away to my dear girl I directly ran with those cursed tidings. We consulted what course to take. Whether to go by land or water to London. Father wished me to go over to my owner and have his advice, which accordingly I did. Mr. Makepeace advised me to take the carpenter's affidavit for the ship as she always protected one and gave me a letter to the captain. I returned to Shields and gave my father and his daughter my answer from Mr. Makepeace. I told father I thought to go up to London by land; however he and Betsey both thought my offer in the ship was best. I took the birth, bid *adieu* to my greatest pride and on the 11th of March left Shields with wind N.W. We had light winds and on the 19th at daylight in the morning clearly saw two frigates and several boats making towards us. Shortly after one of the boats fired at us. We hove too, they came on board, gave orders to send every body aft. A grim looking fellow took up the ships articles. Turning to Nicholson 'Where is your carpenter?'

'There Sir, at the helm.'

'Relieve him and put his things in the boat.'

'Why sir, he is protected.'

'That is the reason we want him in our carpenters' crew. Come, make haste. Coxswain bundle his things in the boat.'

'All ready Sir.'

'Here, drag this fellow along and bundle him in the boat.'

This was all in five minutes transacted, away they bore me on board the *Hussar* frigate. In a little while Captain Nicholson anchored the ship and came on board after me but it was all in vain; he had to return to his ship and leave me. I was called aft to be stationed and told truth that I was no carpenter; they put me in the top.

In a little time gave me to understand that I was now entering on my first adventures and must consider myself under the martial laws of my country and must use every means to obey my superiors, attend to my duty, all calls and orders, to be sober, silent and submissive, and above all to curb your tongue and temper was what I soon found a golden rule. Another great comfort attends a young man on board one of those inquisition Bastille prisons; that is, not to have any learning whatsoever: and only very little knowledge, if you have the luck to be born dumb and have quick ears, and eyes, you are the boy for those sort of destructive engines ... however here I am, therefore must make my time as light as master mates, boatswain's mates and shipmates will permit me.

A boy comes to me. 'What is your name? Sir Wm. Smithson desired me to enquire.'

I informed the boy what was my name and the place of my birth etc. Mr. Smithson was a native of Stamford and acquainted with all my family. He was very friendly to me and did me many little favours. I took his coat up and down, hung it up etc. In his letters to Stamford he mentioned me and often has said it would be a great pleasure to him to be transferred to any other ship and many other things which I shall not relate at the present. However night drawing on apace the hammocks were piped down and being on the gang way with mine, on the word being given pipe down, the crowd made a rush and drove me and my hammock headlong into the waste of the ship. Obriant, a master's mate, flew at me and in great triumph dragged me and my dunnage aft under the sentry's charge to wait the hammocks being all off the deck.

After the bustle was over I was ordered aft on the quarter deck as an unruly villain. However the midshipman of the main deck proved to be my friend Smithson; he came up and said he saw me drove down off the gangway with my bedding in my arms. The boatswain's mate of the deck also came up and spoke in my behalf and by those two friends to humanity I had the good fortune to escape at least two dozen. I was set at liberty and felt very happy at so narrow an escape. I thanked both my friends for their humane kindness and turned in. Next morning wash decks etc., loose sails and exercise them, up and down top gait yards.

Our first lieutenant, would smile and say, 'Those North country carpenters are the very boys fitting for H.M. Navy. They are mechanical mariners and we must not let one go past us.'

Yet he was much mistaken; to my own certain knowledge many of my acquaintance went past.

March 19. Mr. Wallace the first lieutenant smiling at me says you collier carpenters are the very boys we want on our tops, as we were all convinced yesterday by Barney Appleby. This Appleby had sailed on board the *Defiance* of 74 guns with the gunner and boatswain only fifteen months back. He was carpenter of the *Neptune* of Shields, and the gunner being in the boat when they boarded the *Neptune* finding Barney Carpenter and knowing him perfectly well he steps up to him.

'Well old ship mate,' says he, 'you have been very smart in learning your trade since we were paid off, however the *Hussar* is a fine ship and you have not quite forgot old times, so put your dunnage in the boat.'

Thus it was that through Barney the first man called for at first boarding was the poor unfortunate fellow who had the misfortune to be protected carpenter (and thus it was Captain Wilkinson used to say he could work his top with mechanics equal to any ship with their able seamen). Our topmen were mostly young men from the northward. In the main top out of thirty-six men twenty-four were imprest from those unfortunate affidavits which in the late war was the strongest protection granted. We shall leave them inventing some other trap for poor men.

March 21. This day H.B.M.S. *Antelope* commanded by Sir Sidney Smith joined us and anchored in Horsley Bay. Made a signal for our boat. Also the *Athelion* frigate's boat, she being the frigate in company with our frigate, the *Hussar,* as before reported.

Our boats at this time had all been manned with imprest men and were called sea boats' crews, and the old peace established crews the land or harbour boats' crews. Our boat was manned to answer the signal with our sea boats' crew, it was my lot to be one of the number. Ran down to the commodore, lay along side some time, spoke to several acquaintances had shared the same fate as myself, got our instructions returned back and hoist in boats all well. Several sail of colliers in sight, out all our boats and board them. Caught a number of three year servants all young men. It happened that the news reached the north concerning carpenters. This made them try three years indentures which equally proved as great a trap as the carpenters' protection.

March 29. In the course of this day the three ships tore away from the fleet in passing near 150 men. Sent their Lord Mayor's men on board of those vessels they had distressed by taking their hands, to assist them up to the Nore, and there they must be delivered on board the guard-ship. Their manner of picking their crew on board the *Hussar* was thus . . . on the first entrance on board a man was questioned, how long he had followed the sea in what employ etc. He was then stationed and told where he had to do his duty and to start the moment he heard his part of the ship called or all hands etc. In fine weather loose and furled sails two or three times per day, up and down top gait and royal yards, morning noon and night. Exercise guns every day at four bells at the same time the captain and officers were marking every man they took a fancy to and the rest was sent up to the Nore.

April 1, 1803. In this manner they obtained their ships' crews. On the first of April early in the morning our orders were to have our boats ready to go on shore after breakfast, harbour boats' crews; accordingly three boats from our ship, three from the *Athelion*, and four from the *Antelope* all started for the shore, having orders to fetch every man on board that was able to serve his King and country. They laid under the land till evening and then in great pomp made their landing good in Harwich.

They commenced their man-plunder as I term it. The market house was to be their prison, where a lieutenant was stationed with a guard of marines and before daylight next morning their prison was full of all denominations, from the parish priest to the farmer in his frock and wooden shoes. Even the poor blacksmith, cobbler, tailor, barber, baker, fisherman and doctor were all dragged from their homes that night and without the least timely notice as on former meetings. All assembled in private to hold a nightly meeting in the market house. The assembly started round in terror and confusion at the sight of their president and lieutenant and his attendants the marines.

'What means all this fun?' says one.

'Holy Father!' cries the parson.

'We are all enchanted,' says the blacksmith.

'Why, the devil never wears arms,' says the cobbler.

'I think,' says the barber, 'there has been some invading enemy or some Algerine landed on the coast and intends to drag us all from our families and our homes and use us as their slaves.'

'I should like to take a stitch in him,' says the tailor; 'he is certainly a magician; don't you see those red fiends all round him?'

Poor Jack chanced to be taken in the same snare. For some

time he sat pensively listening to their various tales. At last he hailed the quarter deck as he termed it.

'Yo hoy, you scab necks do you mean to keep a poor fellow here and give us no grog?'

'Stop, my man,' says Lieutenant Barker, 'till you go on board then you will get your grog twice every day.' Barker then addresses his hearers as follows. 'My friends, you must understand it is orders from government to man a fleet immediately against our inveterate enemy France, therefore to murmur is in vain. Be of good courage; you will soon be questioned and regulated. Those that are entitled to be set at liberty will be released, and those fit to serve their country and rush their threatening invader must fly to their standard and like true patriots protect that small garden, the residence of our first parents. Besides there is reason to believe this present dispute between us and France will be decided in a month or six weeks. It cannot be otherwise; we are all certain France has no navy at this moment and her merchant ships are mostly out at her colonies in the west Indies. This will be a grand opportunity for our seamen; they will fall in with them on their return to France, so cheer up my boys, this is the time you may make your fortunes and gain great laurels.'

In midst of this lecture all attention was paid to Barker's oration; daylight made its way through the shattered roof and once intended windows of the market house. A crowd of women soon assembled round the prison and their business was quickly made known. Wives demanded their husbands, children their fathers, and aged parents their son perhaps their only support.

April 2. The first salute was a shower of stones at the door and roof of Lieutenant Barker's castle. All the other officers at this moment were in their glory outside the town.

Some of them, good disposed men, sat down and eat their breakfast with the peasants and disdained to put them to the least trouble or alarm. Others full of self presumption took every harsh unfeeling means to perplex and terrify every living soul in their direction, dragging away fathers and children and sending them down to the market house under a convoy of marines. Lieutenant Barker finding his castle surrounded by an inveterate enemy and having a very poor guard was in a pitiful state and after a little reflection came to a parley, putting his head out through a hole formerly a window very mildly addressed his besiegers in the following style:

'My good people, you no doubt feel greatly alarmed at this unexpected visit we have paid your town and its vicinity, a visit to you very rare and to us very unpleasant but as our orders are from the admiralty we dare not refuse to obey their command. However, good people, I will give my word and honour that by this day noon your husbands fathers and children shall be restored to your arms again, only such as are entitled to serve their king owing to their being able seamen or gain their living by the salt water such as fishermen etc. Every other will be liberated as soon as the rest of my brother officers can all meet here, which I know must be shortly. Such is their particular orders, to assemble here at noon.'

This short story of our trembling son of Mars caused the besiegers to cease firing and for a little while the castle remained unmolested.

At last the wished for visitors began to muster from their various stations; a most welcome message to the besieged governor, he very seriously made known the serious attack that had been made against his castle and the determination of the foe was to release all prisoners under his charge. He also related his parley with them from his observatory and the articles agreed on between him and his adversaries etc. etc.

Being all assembled and the marine officers gave in report of all their men being present, Lieutenant Leftwidge of the commodore's ship gave orders to embark all imprest men on board the boats under the guard of marines, and should any person make the least objection or attempt by any means to effect their escape on their way from the market house towards the boats, or from the boats after having embarked, with intent to gain the shore, that man was to be fired at by the marines there present, and any marine refusing to obey such orders was to be tried by the martial laws of his country, and thus by parties of twelve or fifteen they marched all those unfortunate men down to the boats and left the shore crowded with heart broken wives and parents. One brave young man, William Wright, the fisherman, whose courage was daring sprang from the boat as she left the strand and ran with the swiftness of a deer pursued by a number of marines firing at him most furiously but all in vain; he crossed a mud bank and gained the other bank of a large inlet where he stood and waved his hat in defiance. Thus he was once more at his own liberty on shore. The marines and officers returned to the boats all mud and dirt, swearing vengeance against the next man that made attempt to desert.

April 3. Having all embarked again orders were to make the best of our way for the *Antelope*, Sir Sidney's ship, which we gained by sunset; lodged all our strangers on board that night and all boats returned to their respective ships. Next day was appointed as regulating day on board the commodore, the *Monkey* brig and a small cutter, to attend orders and receive on board such as were pronounced able to serve by sea. All such were crammed on board the *Monkey* and set up to the Nore there sent on board the guard-ship and by the sloop cutter. Those not able to serve were sent directly back to the shore, thus we past our time. Old Andrew McCarthy can not be forgot by me he was aged and made cooks mate being a lord mayors man as we term it; entered on the peace establishment, drinking a little ships beer or pursers swipes rather freely; after his work was done some enemy reported him to the quarter deck. He was taken aft put in irons all night to ruminate on his past frolic.

At daylight next morning this unfortunate mortal was called on deck and ordered to be lashed up in the fore-rigging and salt water to be poured down his throat through the help of a funnel, which was done and repeated several times, until the water passed through him as clear as when administered. He was then left in the rigging way they termed a spread eagle. This proved to be one of those cold sleety mornings quite frequent in the North Sea accompanied with a N.W. wind and very severe. After remaining in this horrid situation nearly two hours orders came to cut him down and make him scrub the coppers every morning for one month. When placed on the deck he was nearly at death's door being nearly chilled to the heart his messmates took him below and nursed him up so that in a little while he returned to his duty. As the treatment on board this noble ship proves at present to strike my memory more strongly than in general I will make it my present study.

Bob Moody had the misfortune to taste pursers' swipes rather freely. Being made warm and quite palatable it is a common practice on board men of war while in harbour; every evening numbers meet in the galley and make what they call hot nog, and over this they relate old stories and sometimes chance to have the misfortune to make too free and perhaps one looses his master; his doom is the brig (the irons), another makes too much noise, go in the brig. Others begin to dispute and fight. However we can not forget Bob Moody; it was in some of those galley meetings poor Bob was led too far, and was sent on board the brig reported drunk next day he was made fast to the spanker boom by his hands his feet placed in buckets and salt water administered to him through the aid of a funnel until passing through him. The buckets prevented any wet falling on the deck. Glorious good usage.

April 21. John Markins, another patient, had to pass through the mill. Not pleasing Dennis Obriant the master's mate while at work washing decks, Dennis calls old Cole the boatswain's mate, ordered him to take Markins forward and give him a good starting.[1] At this time Mrs. Markins was on board with her husband, and before Cole commenced his exercise poor Jack set up a horrid roar. This in one moment brought Sally on deck, and seeing her husband taking those nauseous bitters, knowing by his

---

1. 'Starting' was corporal punishment, often administered with a rope's end, petty officers often carried a 'starter' with them.

grinning and dancing they were not pleasant, Sally flies to the cabin door squalling out, 'Captain they are killing my husband.'

The sentinel drove her away not until she had roused the great mogul who sent for the officer of the deck, learnt the whole, and gave orders to put Markins in irons. This done at seven bells, 'all hands to witness punishment.' Markins was brought forth ordered to strip down his pantaloons, and then lashed him to a gun. Made Sally stand by his side until he had six dozen lashes on his bare posteriors. Great.

April 27. The first Lieutenant Mr. Wallace, a poor little diminutive creature, but considering himself sprung from the race of Cornwallis, was by far the largest man on board H B M S *Hussar*.

On the 27th of April in the morning being nearly calm our brave and bold commander desired the barge to be got ready to convey his grace on shore to Harwich the place of his nativity. His father kept a small barber's shop in the town known by old Wilkinson the barber. This great brave tyrannical cross unfeeling coward was his son and heir Sir Philip Wilkinson captain of H.B.M. frigate *Hussar* of 38 guns. The captain now being on shore the command must fall into the hands of our undaunted Wallace. His first attempt was what he most delighted in, impressment. After breakfast down boats and let them be manned with the sea boats crews. The weather being moderate numbers of vessels were in the Swin, colliers, coasters, fishing smacks and numbers of Dutch galliots etc.

Away goes our expedition a man hunting and sea robbing, distressing parents, robbing wives, and making widows and fatherless children. It was on one of those inhuman acts our hero sent his young blood hounds (midshipmen) to rob overhaul and drag away. In the course of the day several unfortunate men were dragged on board and had silently to bear such treatment. We shall refer to a circumstance both inhuman savage and horrid, on a young lad they took from one of the Harwich smacks. This boy was about seventeen years of age (and at this time we had a small tender used to attend our ship from the shore with letters, beer, soft bread, water etc.). The master of this smack or tender was a neighbour to the mother of the boy we refer to; this old fellows name was Lancaster and as the tender was to lay all night anchored near us this unfortunate boy thought if he could get on board of old Lancaster he would be conveyed safe to his dear old mother he being her only support.

His resolution was fixed and some time in the night he made his escape overboard and swam to the tender being convinced when there he was safe. Poor boy. To his astonishment on gaining the vessel his only supposed friend Lancaster put him in irons and on the following morning took him back on board the *Hussar*. His young sighs, tears and lamentations were all unheard by Lancaster; he was taken on board the frigate, put both legs in irons to wait the return of the grand judge Sir Philip Oh, this was the moment, revenge sparkled on the brow of each friend to humanity, ah, Lancaster had we dared to show our feelings, that day had been thy last!

April 30. This evening our captain returned on board and the very planks appeared overladen with his wretched frame; his weight of abominations were enough to sink him ship and crew all in the boundless deep. Sodom and Gomorrah were destroyed for their wickedness and Wilkinson ought to have been in the midst of them.

He was not long on board before his prime-minister informed him what had transpired during his absence, and on the following morning this boy was brought forth to suffer for attempting to gain that liberty that every imprest seaman strives to enjoy either in his mind or actions. All hands were called to be once more aggravated to take revenge. The marines all placed on the gangways and front of the quarter deck all under arms to protect the bloodthirsty monster in his barbarous tortures. However, let him proceed to work. Old douse-the-glim[2] presented himself to the altar of pollution (the quarter deck) reporting the prisoner ready.

---

2. 'Douse-the-glim' was the ship's master-at-arms, head of the ship's police. The last words the sailor would hear at night would be his command for the lights to be extinguished.

'Seize him up', answered the son of thunder; 'and as for you boatswain's mates do your duty or I will see your back bones. So go on.'

Another boatswain's mate, 'Go on.'

'Oh captain for the sake of my poor mother have mercy on me and forgive me.'

'No Sir, if I forgive you I hope God will never forgive me. Go on boatswain's mate.'

'Master at arms how many has he had?'

'One dozen and five Sir.'

'Go on boats mate'—he faints.

'Stop!' says the doctor.

'No Sir he is only acting. Go on, I say.'

He lay as still as any dead man. Poor fellow, that was the time every heart not made of stone whispered revenge: and had not the *Antelope* and *Athelion* both laid so near our ship, vengeance would have rose its horrid head and dashed the standard of cruel tyranny under foot, and in its stead planted the conquering flag of generous humanity. No, that blessed moment was not yet at hand. We had to grin and bear it may the Almighty direct us in what he thinks best.

By this time he had received two dozen, another boats mate had orders to go on—not any signs of life was to be seen in him. The Doctor felt his pulse and ordered him not to have any more lashes at present, he being entirely insensible of what was transacting.

'Well Sir,' says Wilkinson, 'Your orders shall be obeyed in that respect, by mine shall in another. Mr. Hill (the master-at-arms) take that fellow forward, and you boatswain's mates Make him fast with a rope and heave him overboard. I know how to bring him to his senses again.'

Accordingly his orders were obeyed. They hove him three times over board and then hove him on the deck, not any signs of life in him. Doctor Graham ordered him below and to be wrapped up in a blanket. In the course of an hour they let blood from him, he began to groan, and afterwards cry out for his mother. On the following day he with some more unfortunate men was sent on board the *Monkey* and up to the Nore. On board the guard-ship this was the last account we had of poor Henry Wilson.

That evening Lieutenant Barker or in other words the bold Jack of Clubs made a visit on board the *Athelion*. As we had just arrived alongside with the barge, Wilkinson ordered the barge to attend on Mr. Barker. In he tumbled, half drunk as usual. Away we go helter skelter, got on board, had our orders to wait alongside; we accordingly left a boat-keeper in her and the rest of us went on board the *Athelion*.

At last eight o'clock; set the watch and lights etc. We sat down on the forecastle with some acquaintances we found on board, found a little grog to kill grief; we then related different acts of cruelty committed on board the *Hussar* every day.

Says one, 'I cannot bear it much longer.'

'Ced Nor either will I,' says another.

'Well, but,' says a third, 'we have to bear it all, and by what I understand of his usage to the crew of the *Hermione* we shall grow worse and no better.'

'Well what is best to be done?' says Jack Waddell, a wild daring fellow.

'I don't know,' says one.

'Nor I,' says another.

Thus the consultation passed around in private amongst us. (At this time not one of us twelve had entered nor would we although made the sea boat's crew.)

'Well, my boys,' says Waddell, 'our only way to make our escape is a very quick one. Requires a firm resolution and to be done courage sincerity and to be bound on the sacred Bible to stand true to each other.'

'What way do you mean?' was every man's desire.

'Brothers,' says Waddell, 'will you all swear on this holy book never to reveal my proposals if you do not like to unite in with us in search of liberty?'

We then all swore to be true to each other, to use our utmost exertions in endeavouring to effect our escape and to defend each other as long as we were able to stand. All being duly swore and resolved to proceed Waddell observed to us, 'Now men all we have to do must be done privately and in haste. We must endeavour to accomplish our design without taking life.

'Our only means at present to escape from that cursed ship is on our return back with the lieutenant. The night is dark and will answer our design to a tittle, and we are sure Barker is drunk and most likely will fall asleep in the boat. Therefore our first care must be not to give any suspicion before we are out of sight from the *Athelion*, and not then should he not prove to be asleep. We must have a signal; that must be to heave the bow oar fore and aft over all the rest, and then if he is awake make him fast and tie a handkerchief round his mouth, threatening him at the same time if he make the least noise that moment he shall be hove overboard. This all done then the coxswain take charge of him and the rest of us take our oars and as it is flood tide we will make the best of our way on shore to the Naze, land him there where there is no house near, and he will not be able to give the alarm for some time. At the same time we will pull up Swin to Maldon, there sink the boat, and either go on board a collier or take our land tacks on board in different directions.'

'A most noble plan,' was every man's answer.

May 7, 1803. At this moment a boatswain's mad mate roared out for the *Hussar's* barge to be manned; we quickly were every one in his station, ready to receive our death or liberty as we then termed him. Over the side comes two lanthorns and sides men.

Then bold Barker roars out, 'Are you all in the boat coxswain?'

'Yes,' was the answer, 'Sir.'

Down he crawls as drunk as any porter and was seated, wished a good night and away we rowed for our ship. She have a lanthorn hoist as a mark for us, the ships lay nearly two miles apart and we were at some distance from the *Athelion*, when young Haswell being the bowman (finding by Barkers noise he was awake) hove his oar fore and aft over the top of all the others. That was the critical moment, death or liberty whispered in most of our minds, when the coxswain roars out, 'You bowman, why don't you pull away? What do you mean Sir? Out with your oar this instant; you stop all hands from pulling.'

A dead silence for a moment prevailed and horror seized us all at the same time, we saw the cowardly spirit of the coxswain, betraying us all, when Barker thunders out, 'You damned grass-combers, why don't you pull?'

'It is only the bowman Sir, that is taken short and his oar has confused us for a moment.'

'Damn you all,' says the coxswain. 'That is no excuse. Mind what you do or say. I tell you all to pull away.'

Oh, wretch, what canst thou think thus to betray the undaunted sons of liberty even thine own brother when only an hour hence thou on thy bended knees with the holy Bible in they hands in the name of thy redeemer and in the presence of us all? Wretch thou didst swear to be true in our present adventures, and to stand firm and render every assistance in thy power to gain that sweet liberty, for which we have all left our lives to the mercy of a traitor. As that title is by far too good for thee, thou whose heart is not so large as that of a fly go hide thy face lay down and die. Die. Die. We got all our oars out again and with dreadful apprehensions made the best of our way on board. We wanted to speak to each other but durst not utter a word. What our feelings were at such a disappointment any man of rational reason can plainly understand. However, arrived on board the *Hussar* boat, hoist in, and all quiet. We had an opportunity to speak to each other and that very circumspectively. Having liberty for half an hour's light we drank our grog and turned in. I shall give you all the names of our barge's crew at this time, coxswain Tho. Haswell. after oar John Waddell and next Richard Wilson. Next John Wetherell. James Boatfield Josh Andrews, Ja. Burchel, Richard Lindle Captain top John Patterson Ja. Potter William Smith Robert Sadler Richard Haswell brother to the coxswain bowman. Those are the names of us poor misguided young men that signed the *Athelion* convention.

We were now left to the mercy of this Judas Iscariot as we used afterwards to term him in our discourse, he being a captain of the top and we all stationed in the tops left us under his eyes or ears continually, caused us to be constantly on our guard, and, as the old word goes, we had to take our words and look at them before we spoke. To speak plainly we even were in dread of giving him the smallest offence least he might in his unmanly manner, discover our plot and turn kings evidence. We are now and have to remain in dread of this monster whose sight we dread worse than the sight of Bonaparte the hero of Europe. Our corporal of marines Richard Wright another of Sir Phillips followers had his wife on board, a fine young woman. She took sick and died on board. The boat was ordered to be manned next morning, her body put in a shell made by the ships joiner taken out to sea and sunk, at the same time the ship lay within three miles of Harwich ... inhumane monster to one of the trusty officers.

May 12. This morning several of our married men's wives left the ship and went on board the tender and landed in the evening at Harwich. They would not remain on board where such an unfeeling monster commanded. One morning the little tender came off and the post man with the letters came on board as usual. My name was called. A letter from London. Take the welcome messenger and perused it, found it from Mr. Faith and my brother George, in it I was informed that Governor Nuemburg and my uncle Adams in Stamford had undertaken in behalf of my mother to have me clear by paying for a substitute and informed me my papers were signed by the admiralty and forwarded down to Captain Wilkinson, therefore I might rest happy because my liberty was at hand. This was the greatest blessing, as I considered at this moment, could be bestowed on me. My mind was fixed one minute at home, another at Shields or London, other times anticipating in my simple mind the result of my intended voyage to Jamaica, not dreaming of the numerous changes might take place even at that very moment to rob me of my imaginary happiness. However what leisure time I had was all employed in composing a letter to my sole intended partner in So. Shields. Having at last got a copy to my liking I got paper ink and pens and in a very loving manner, as I thought, revealed the secrets of my throbbing heart, gave every particular of my letter from London and my daily expectations to be discharged. I then wrote to my dear mother informing her of my promising good fortune and my determinations in regard to making the best of my way to London etc.

I then sent my letters on shore by the cutter and on the following day as I sat on my chest forward being the day to wash and holy stone the lower deck I heard Fotheringham the boatswain mate thundering out, 'Pass the word for John Wetherell.'

I ran towards him. 'Sir!' says I.

'Away aft, sir, on the quarter deck (there I suppose I shall have the pleasure of knocking some of the coal dust out of your hide)', says he smiling.

Aft on the quarter deck I went and there stood his worship and his clerk at his elbow, turning towards me with one of his leering grins.

'What is your name? Where does your parents live?'

I told him correctly.

'Have you any relations in town? Their names and occupations?' He then asked me if I would not enter for the *Hussar* etc.

My answer was 'No Sir.'

He then said he had learnt that I had been taking private means to gain my discharge in producing a substitute which my friend in London had in some measure obtained, having got the permission from the admiralty's office to have my discharge by finding an able seaman to serve.

'Ah, ah,' says his worship, 'damn your blood, you son of a whore. In spite of you and all the interest of your damned tribe of grass-combing relations I will let you know you shall remain on board the *Hussar*, and wait my pleasure. That will be at the close of the ensuing campaign. Therefore start off and go to your duty

Sir, make yourself contented, and rest assured your discharge shall be kept safe for you until England no longer wants your service. Therefore take my advice, enter for the ship, and you will enjoy the privileges same as the rest of the crew.'

I made my obedience and retired in a most horrid state of mind being nearly on the brink of leaping overboard to terminate my cruel treatment, at one moment death would have been a welcome visitant; at another I wished to live and see the result of all those trials I was at this time overwhelmed in. However I sat down on my chest and began to reflect in my mind; I am not the only man on board, I have numbers of companions suffering here, suffering the cruel treatment of this tyrannical savage. His feelings are far below the uncivilized race of cannibals on the coast of Malabar; they in their ignorant savage state take delight in massacring a white man for the simple purpose of gaining his shining buttons or any glittering bauble he may have about his person, and afterwards devour his carcase. Those unfortunate beings are ignorant and know not the least sentence of the gospel; therefore we can excuse them owing to want of knowledge, but not this destroyer of man, brought up in an enlightened age surrounded by the laws of Christianity. His laws in their purity are good, founded on the principals of justice, reason, truth, and equity, but under the administration of such arbitrary lawbreakers, who make their own laws and trample down the laws of God and man, and thus it is hard with mankind in general when it is in the power of those arbitrary rulers to say damn such laws and the country governed by them.

May 24. One morning after breakfast a thundering roar came from the quarter deck. 'Send all those fellows aft, those that have not entered for the ship!'

Up we all goes. There stood the terrible ruler and his clerk with the ships books open, our names were called to pass one by one and answer enter or not enter.

'No Sir' was each man's answer.

Sir Philip spoke up. 'My men you had better enter. It will be to your advantage as the ship is ordered round to Portsmouth and will sail shortly. On arriving there you shall enjoy the same liberty on shore as the rest of the crew.'

This to us was all music. Our determinations were never to enter for him but any other of H.M. ships we would enter on board with pleasure, as we were all anxious to defend our country's cause against all those who dare oppose our nation and its righteous laws. Wilkinson finding our determination were not to be persuaded by him turns round.

'Go forward you damn stubborn rascals to your duty, and you shall be sorry for your conduct before many days. Take care of yourselves I shall look out for you.'

May 25, 26, 27. On the 25 of May in the morning orders were to weigh the best bower and ride by a single anchor. At 10 a.m. orders were to weigh anchor and make sail to join the *Antelope*, Sir Sidney the Commodore, in Osley Bay. In a short time our ship was under a crowd of sail accompanied by the *Athelion*. A smart gale at N.W. In a little while we joined the commodore in the bay and made sail to the eastward, passed outside of the sands into the North Sea where we passed away two days exercising. This was exercising—officers, men, ships, sails, guns, yards washing, holy-stoning, small arms, mustering bags. Reefing in two minutes, punishment, up and down hammocks, stow them, scrub hammocks. Up all chests and bags, sprinkle and scrub, serve out pursers slops and tobacco, serve grog, turn all hands up to skylarking, set the watch. All those little changes were transacted in the course of two days cruise in the North Sea.

CHAPTER 2

1803: Sailing Under a Tyrant

May 28, 29, 1803. Returning to our old anchorage in the Swin we anchored, furled sails, took on board beer and water, stores etc., and on the following morning sailed through the Queen's channel bound to Spithead, wind West N.W. At 12 mer. made the North fore-land light, winds inclinable to calm. At 4 pm struck on the Goodwin sands having caught a fresh air of wind from the E.N.E.

'What ho, she comes!—Take in the royals top-gallant sails and all the light-sails. Brace the yards to the wind. Out boats. Fire signal guns for assistance. Be smart my brave fellows, exert yourselves to get the ship afloat. Run away the stream anchor to the S.E. Well done my brave boys. Now man the bars and heave away the capstan. Drummer beat up and fifer play a merry tune to give the men life to heave the ship afloat.'

Such was the language of this terrified tyrant to his men when he thought his honour was in danger, and in one minute after she was afloat.

'Silence, damn you all!' was the first salute of his honour the moment he found the ship was afloat.

May 30. I shall give the credit to three boats from the shore which on seeing our dangerous situation boldly ventured off to us and knowing the channel took an anchor out, weighed the one we already had ran out, and by their directions in a little while our ship was safe in the Downs, came to an anchor and lay till morning, and next day you now have an instance of Wilkinson's generosity. Those men in the Deal boats that were the only means of saving the ship came off to the ship to beg his honour to sign a paper which is customary So that they may deliver it to the custom house and receive a salary allowed them for assisting H.M. ships in distress, this is as an encouragement to those brave fellows for their courage and perseverance. Wilkinson took the captain from each boat and would have kept them had not the admiral ordered them on shore.

The admiral on shore having ordered Wilkinson to grant the boatmen their certificate as their due and then restore every man of them on shore without the least delay as he (the admiral) was commander in the Downs at present and would be obeyed in what was consistent with reason. Wilkinson reluctantly obeyed his orders, and on their landing on the beach our signal was made to weigh and proceed directly for the harbour of Plymouth, the *Athelion* being ordered to Portsmouth in our place. Our boats returned on board, up anchor, made sail and arrived in Plymouth sound on the first of June. Moored ship etc. In the course of an hour the ship was surrounded with shore boats. First the married men had liberty to take their wives on board then the young men had their girls came off and took them on board, a curious sight to see boats crowded with blooming young girls all for sale. Our crew were mostly young men and caused the boatmen to have a quick dispatch or as we usually term it a ready market; this business over, nothing particular occurred that day. Next morning it was found that there was two more women than men on board, a mighty jovial crew 616 souls on board. We took on stores provisions and water, and on the 4th orders were to send all the girls on shore except one woman to each mess and the married women certainly to have the preference. This all settled at 12 mer, fired a salute weighed and made sail; our orders were to join the grand fleet off Ushant. On the 6th in the morning made the fleet, and delivered our dispatches and letters on board the *Ville de Paris*, Admiral Cornwallis. We remained with the fleet two days, then were ordered into Brest Bay as look out ship to watch the motions of the French.

June 12. We remained on this station some time, and used to have pretty rough usage from the batteries on shore when we chanced to be taken in a calm when close under the land. They used to give us pretty heavy doses of both shot and shell; on one of those affairs we were beating close up to the narrows with a smart breeze blowing directly from the land and standing rather too far over to the south shore when we were becalmed and the ship was some time before we could get her head off shore. The land being very high took the wind out of our sails and the French at this time were not idle in the forts; they were not at all sparing of powder shot nor shell before we got our boats out and the ships head towed round off shore.

Johnny Croppoe had measured his distance pretty well for they hove a shell that burst over the ship split the mizzen topsail cut away some of the rigging and a piece of shell weighing eighteen pound fall on the quarter deck and past through close to the foot of Captain Wilkinson, and stuck fast on the gun room table where dinner was ready to sit down. It made itself more free than welcome, breaking dishes and scaring waiters and stewards into the officers cabins. However with the assistance of our boats we got round and caught the breeze just at the moment where another shell fell close under our stern. Had we not caught the light air and got head way the shell was intended to fall on board and then burst, which might have been a serious consequence. Wilkinson was quite offended at the French bombardier for sending such a ragged piece of iron so near him while doing his duty, and we were quite on the contrary—we were angry with the Frenchman that he did not make better use of his shell by sending it in contact with a shell that we dreaded more than that hove by the Frenchman. The *Dragon* 74 being one of the inshore squadron seeing our situation ran close in and sent her boats to our assistance and in a short time we were out of gun shot.

June 17. This day we had a severe conflict. Being close under the land at daylight we chanced to fall in with a number of chasmaries *(chasses-marées)* or market boats from various parts of the coast bound to Brest and we gave chase. They dispersed in confusion; some ran for the shore and escaped and others proceeded towards Brest. We fired amongst them in real earnest. At last we brought one of them along side. She was a large craft laden with wine, fruit and oil.

We took what bold Sir Philip thought he wanted, took the captain and his son prisoners and ordered the rest of the crew to proceed to Brest and inform the French admiral he had taken a taste of Bowideause (Bordeaux) wine in order to drink his health and had taken the captain and his son intending to they shall go to England and taste our beer in return. (How daring a warrior we have to boast of.) A number of such commanders might frighten many of the small coasting vessels.

July 3, 1803. Having cruised some time and nothing particular took place, excepting feeding goats and hops on sandy island, smuggling brandy in the buckets in the place of blackberries etc. We used to run out to the fleet once or twice per week with our tidings, and our sea boats crew being so frequently on board the *Ville de Paris* we got quite familiar and used, sailor-like, to relate many grievances to each other. There was a number of our own cast on board of her, all colliers boys; they used to persuade us to enter for the *Ville*, and finding they had such good usage we began to propose to each other what course would be the most prudent for us to gain that privilege without giving any suspicion to our officers, fearing they might put a stop to our intentions. We had a number of proposals; one thought one thing another thought contrary, generally the case in such proceedings.

At last our resolutions were to leave the whole management entirely under the management of three men, and those three we chose by voices, John Waddell, Captain of the main top and midship man John P.W. second captain and Richard Lindle captain of the forecastle; those three were left to write and do their utmost for the benefit of their fellow sufferers. We at present will leave them to their own judgement and attend to our duty as men. Standing close in to the narrows of Brest we found a corvette of twenty-two guns anchored in Cranmoran Bay under cover of two heavy forts. We had orders to prepare our boats all in readiness to cut this ship from her cables and take her out a prize. That night quite dark about 12 midnight off we goes all volunteers, launch barge and two cutters all resolutely bent. Our oars muffled and the water still we gave no alarm; the men on board the corvette must have all been asleep because we boarded her on both sides and were nearly all on board before we gave any alarm, and this was by disarming the marines sentinels at the cabin door and on the gang ways. We then had a small opposition before we got possession of the quarter deck however this as well as the forecastle was gained without any blood shed. The commander in his cabin was quite loth to give up the command, but however he quickly found Lieutenant Leftwidge our second lieutenant was acting in his place. We carried that vessel cut her cables tow'd her from under the forts and never fired a gun. She was not discovered from the forts until daylight, when she was under sail in company with the *Hussar*, standing out.

July 20. Our prize proved to be the *le Pheasant* of 24 guns from Rochelle to Brest to refit for the Isle of France. She had 187 men on board, mostly cannoneers. After joining our admiral we had orders to man her and send her into Plymouth under the command of Leftwidge our second lieutenant. and forty men. We accompanied them within sight of the Ram Head, then returned to the fleet, remained with the fleet some time cruising round Ushant and at times took a peep into Brest to observe their manoeuvres. Returning from one of our peeping frolics towards the fleet, Wind at S.W., the skies were quickly in confusion, clouds rolling in various directions and thunder rolling nearer, every crash of which pointed out the approaching hurricane. We shortened sail with all speed, and being close in with Ushant and the wind dead upon the land, every moment blowing harder, we on a lee shore were forced to carry sail to avoid the rocks to leeward. The sea rose dreadfully, and it was some time before we could perceive the ship alter the bearing of Ushant light the least imaginable. It was at this perilous moment, we all expecting the ship to dash on the dreadful rocks to leeward, all in a blaze with the foam breaking over them, it was at this dreadful moment our main yard parted by the slings, sprung our foremast main topmast and mizzen mast. By heaven's decree at that moment a sea struck the ship on her starboard bow and wore her round the other way—a happy circumstance for all on board as it was impossible she could clear Ushant on the starboard tacks, and we used every means in our powers to put her head to the Northward and eastward but every effort was vain until the sea managed the affair. We then used our utmost efforts, got what sail we could carry on her, and to our happiness found her clearing the shore fast and by daylight had room to lay to.

July 26. At 8 a.m. more moderate, repaired our damages and that evening made the fleet. Next day were dispatched to Plymouth to repair damages, lay in the Sound, took out our foremast, mizzen mast and main yard, sent them on shore. That night we had a most terrible gale from the S.E. All the small vessels cut or slipped and some got into Cattewater some on the Cobbler and some on Drakes Island. We rode very heavy all night in expectations to see our sheers come tumbling down amongst us. However through good fortune no accident happened and next day was quite moderate. Our she-messmates came off and we lay quite comfortable until the new masts came along side. We took them in and next evening were all ready for sea. On the 29th the women were ordered on shore and on the 30th sailed from Plymouth sound.

August 1, 1803. On the 1st of August joined the fleet, and the first thing we looked out for to send our letter on board the *Ville de Paris*, having during our lay in Plymouth composed three letters or petitions before we could satisfy ourselves. The first was wrote with the three names were chosen to manage the affair signed to it—this would not answer since they were sure to be took for the ringleaders if it should happen that the admiral might present it to Wilkinson. We then made a second attempt, made some alteration in the language and diction and signed with all our names on one side the petition. This would not do; some were of opinion that the first names on the list would be considered as the heads of the plot.

We therefore wrote a third, and placed the names in such a manner that if they should pick out any as delegates it would be an entire lottery whose fate it might prove.

August 2, 1803. As I before observed we took the first opportunity to take the paper on board the *Commodore*, which we found means to effect as all the members of this united society belonged to the barges sea-boats crew. And as it was me that wrote the letter of petition to his excellency it was also me that delivered it into the hands of the admirals secretary on board the *Ville de Paris* and returned on board the *Hussar*, all then waiting in great anxiety to hear the events, watching every signal that was made, expecting our captain to be called for by the admiral.

At last the No 894 was made.

'Now,' says we, 'it will be all decided.'

But not yet; the signal was 894—Make sail to the S.W. in chase of a strange sail reported by the *Dragon* look out ship in the offing. We made all sail and by 8 p.m. were up with a large ship from Baltimore bound to Nantz laden with flour. We took charge of her, sent an officer on board, and sent her into Plymouth; this all done we hauled our wind in order to take our station again. The night was blustery and rainy. Wind freshened, we took in two reefs and by 4 a.m. were hove to under close reef topsails and reef foresail.

August 3. Lay all those 24 hours, blowing very hard and the sea breaking over the ship at a dreadful rate, thunder and lightning was horrid. About 6 p.m. the lightning struck our ship on the head of the mainmast, burnt the eyes of the main rigging, and appeared to burst over the ship, by a horrible report and sulphurous smell. At the same time we were in the act of taking in and furling our foretop sail when another explosion took place; the men on the topsail yard were some of them struck and made a dreadful noise. The men on deck were all laid flat on the deck and the sentinel at the scuttle but was burnt on his shoulder and side. Those who were below in hammocks were all upset and hove on the deck. The fluid then exploded with a report like breaking glass and apparently past out through one of the ports leaving a strong smell of sulphur. This chanced to happen at the time of my look out on the weather gangway from 6 to 8 p.m. The boatswain fell on top of me and we both laid some time in a stupefied state. At last I heard the voice of some man saying:

'What shall I do, my eyesight is gone?'

'So is mine,' says the boatswain.

And at that instant another heavy flash passed over the ship, then after seeing this we were convinced that our eyes were only dazzled by the lightning. We got ourselves all gathered up and the men all safe from aloft without any material injury being done to ship or men. By 12 mer. next day the storm had entirely subsided and the wind shifted round to the northward; we repaired our slight damages and made sail. On the following evening joined the fleet; they made dreadful complaints of their sufferings during the hurricane as they termed it.

We took our station to leeward of the *Admiral* that night and then we began to entertain hopes that Admiral Cornwallis would not pass over our grievances without a farther explanation as we had related every act of cruelty practised on board from our first impressment. Better luck still.

This shows the form of our letter petition and names as sent to the Honourable William Cornwallis Rear Admiral of England, beseeching his fatherly aid and protection requesting his honour to snatch us from the paws of our tyrannical prosecutor. We also beg his honour to accept our volunteer services in his ship or any other of H.M. ships His Honour may please to appoint.

We have inserted our names so that your Honour can demand us at your pleasure. In this act of humanity may heaven add fresh laurels to your honourable brow and crown your days with peaceful blessings, and an eternal crown in the mansions of bliss is and ever will be the sincere prayers of H. Majesties humble subjects and of your Honour's obedient servants British seamen,
Done in Plymouth Sound on board H.B.M. Ship the *Hussar* June 15th 1803, presented to his honour August 2nd 1803 while cruising off Brest on board the *Ville de Paris*.
Commanders
Sir H. B. Neale
Captain Charles Jones

August 4. The admiral (as we afterwards understood by one of his signal men on board) after perusing the letter stood some time with the paper in his hand then turning round to Captain Jones. 'Can it be possible, Jones, that men can suffer this cruel tyranny? Well may our seamen strive to avoid serving their country on board His Majesty's Navy when this is the usage they meet with. Abominable! It is a disgrace to the country they are serving! Such men should not be allowed even to set his foot on board any of H.M. ships, in the capacity of captain of the mast, more so as captain of the vessel. However now I shall not make him acquainted with the affair at this time but will send him out on a cruise; meanwhile we will consider what is best to be done for those brave fellows who crave my protection.' Our signal was made and orders sent on board to cruise between Ushant and Scilly with a letter to take care of his men and treat them well.

August 6. We made sail and left the fleet with a smart breeze from the N.E. and cruised several days. Nothing particular took place; we fell in with all nations on the entrance of the channel. One day a sail was reported; we made sail and with a fresh gale we ran under all we could crowd nearly 12 hours before we got along side. We found her to be the *Swallow* packet from Jamaica to Falmouth—could not trust our private signals and were jealous of us owing to our having tricolour'd vanes at our mast heads. All things being understood we parted the *Swallow* for Falmouth and us on our station. That evening orders were to take in two reefs and that in two and a half minutes.

'All ready! Let go the halyards, trice up and lay out!'

Away we fly, helter skelter. On my passing the top brim I saw the topsail lift jigger was caught under the slide of one of the cannonades (carronades) on the quarter deck, and being in a flusteration, seeing the yard over end, I inadvertently called McAlister the Captain of the after-guard to clear the fall from the slide.

Lord George Gordon was midshipman of the main top and as I spoke he kicked me in the breast with his foot and ordered me to leave that duty to him. I answered that it was too bad to be kicked like a dog when in the act of doing what I thought was right, and made my way out on the yard arm.

'Walk down Sir in a moment, you damned mutinous rascal, and you shall have your desert', says my Lord, and down he goes to the lieutenant on the quarter deck, made his story right on his side.

Down I goes to the tribunal of justice. First salute I met was a blow on my head with a speaking trumpet, then called the master at arms and ordered him to put that damned young rascal in irons. This was readily complied with, so poor Jack was clapped into the brig as we term it. This chanced to fall on the 7th of August. Take notice. Next day chased a Falmouth privateer cutter and took two men out of her with a pretence that had she hove to without us having to chase her we would not have taken any of his men. However we kept them. Next day exercised guns firing at a barrel with a flag on it. Two or three got each four dozen through this day's amusement as Wilkinson calls it.

August 10. Chased a large Swedish ship to the westward. At sunset found out what she was, shortened sail and let her pursue her course. That night blowing fresh took in two reefs and that night the ship rolling heavy by some accident the main top gait stud sail boom rolled out of the iron and went overboard. This chanced to be the boom on the yard arm where I was stationed, and next morning it was missed and reported. All the main topmen were called up and the two captains of the top were called on to strip, John Waddel the first called on.

'Well sir,' says the great Sir Philip, 'don't you think yourselves a set of damned infernal lubbers to loose that boom through neglect? I mean to go through the whole of you; therefore I shall begin with you two first; strip, Sir. The quarter masters seize him up. Boatswain's mate, go on.'

Four dozen was his dowry. Next was Richard Lindle.

'Strip Sir and not a word from you. Go on boatswain's mate, four dozen more there. That may be a warning to you both. As you are captains of the top I thought you merited double allowance.'

John Patterson was next, two dozens. James Potter, two dozen. Ja. Boatfield, do (ditto). Wm. Surtees do. Tho. Fostor do. Tho. Green do. Tho. Thompson do. Wm. Ferguson do.

'Now gentlemen,' says this monster, 'you all deserve the same but time at present will not allow us the pleasure of fulfilling the laws of our country—it is your country and not me that is chastising you. However the first opportunity I shall not forget the rest of you damned rascals. Boatswain, pipe belay; drummer beat the retreat'—after a small morning's distribution of only thirty dozen.

All this time I was listening to hear my name called; as they were paying off their debts I felt very much afraid they were due to me some small accounts. However my expectations were at this moment disappointed; he left me laying in suspense in expectations of being called every time I heard the boat's pipe or the drum.

August 14. This morning we fell in with the *Speedy* brig from the fleet bound into Falmouth. She also had orders for us to proceed immediately towards the fleet; accordingly we directed our course for Ushant and next morning were in the centre of the fleet. We hove too under the *Ville de Paris*' stern and the signal was for our captain. Now methinks I will perhaps be the means of my release one way or another.

After our captain had been on board the admiral some time he returned with dispatches for England. We took the letters of the fleet and directed our course for Plymouth. After all was snug and the fleet dropping astern down came the first lieutenant, into the gun-room.

'Damn me,' says he, 'gentlemen, what do you think of those fellows on board that would not enter for the ship?'

'I don't know,' says one.

'Nor I,' says another.

'Pray Sir what is it?' cries mad Barker.

'Why, they have wrote to the admiral informing him with every thing we do or say on board, and are all going to leave the ship—old Cornwallis is going to take them all out of the ship on our return from Plymouth and Captain Wilkinson has got part of the letter they wrote. Tomorrow we are going to have every man sign his name and by that means find the damned mutinous rascal that wrote such an infernal ditty. By God, Barker, he has wrote a cursed well contrived ditty and a good deal of truth can be found in it, but Sir Philip swears if he can find out who he is God help him for thus exposing him to the commander in chief.'

All the time of this discourse I being in irons close to the gun-room door and the door partly open I had an opportunity to hear every word. Now, thinks I, you are under a great mistake for if you call me to sign I shall write quite another hand. Therefore this gave me no kind of concern as they unknowingly had given me particular notice. This all past on till next day, then all hands were mustered aft and called by the ship's books to sign their names. At last I heard my name called.

'In irons,' says the master-at-arms. 'Go enquire if he can write.'

August 17. The master-at-arms and Mr. Maxfield the captain's secretary did me the honour of a visit. I was in readiness.

'Can you write your name Wetherell?' says old douse-the-glim.

'Yes sir' was my reply, 'but I am left handed.'

'What, do you write with your left hand?' says Maxfield.

'Yes sir.'

'Oh damn your crooked disposition; you are not worth the time it will take to release you out of irons to go and sign your name and afterwards clap you in again. Let him remain where he is, Hill, there is no fear of his destroying the nation with his treacherous writings.'

Away they goes; my trial was over so far. Barney Appleby, a young man entirely void of learning, could not read his own name—in fact he knew not his alphabet. This man being a very ready witted fellow as we usually say made all the watch on deck amusement through the night with his curious stories; he would take a book of any kind and open it, sometimes upside down, and repeat one of the stories of the Arabian Nights, as correct as if he had been reading it out of the book, and continue every night in the same manner with a fresh tale every night. The officers frequently on the first watch would stand all the watch laughing at Barney. And on this same account when he was called to write his name and told them he could not write he was called a liar and they made sure he was the writer of the letter to the admiral and on that account would not own to writing at all. They even accused him of it and told him they knew he wrote it but if he would only tell them for satisfaction he would not have any reflections past on him nor yet come to any trouble. His answer still was:

'No Sir no, I tell you the truth. I neither can read nor write.'

This was all stuff in their opinions. Some of the officers swore he was one of the first readers on board, they had repeatedly heard him reading and he was the very man that wrote to the admiral.

August 18. Therefore no farther enquiry was required; it was concluded that Barney was the man. All hands were dismissed. A strange sail reported to windward; haul our wind and make sail in chase. Found her to be the *Heroe* lugger privateer from Guernsey in company with two brigs she had captured the night before off St. Maloes, and she was conducting them into Guernsey. We bore away for Plymouth and at seven bells all hands for punishment.

'Mr. Hill, the master at arms, bring forth the prisoner.'

Oh my hard fortune, thought I.

However up to the gang way goes poor Jack and above him stood the great distributor of all the tortures hell can produce.

'Oh,' says he, 'this is one of our ring men. Strip, Sir. You are also one of the damned rascally topmen that lost the studding sail boom. Part of your top-mates have already had their pay and the rest of you will not be forgot. Boatswain's mate give him a dozen.'

At this moment I began to inform him that I had been three or four days in irons when the boom was lost.

'Gag the rascal I say, gag him with a pump bolt and stop his damned lip.'

Immediately a pump bolt was introduced into my jaws and tied back of my head. In this manner they gave me four dozen and punished me for a thing that was done three days after I was in irons for what they termed a crime (my speaking to Gordon was never mentioned nor was I allowed to speak one word in my own behalf).

After cutting my flesh in a dreadful manner they cast me loose and poor Barney Appleby was called up and ordered to strip.

'For what Sir?' says Barney.

'There is no occasion to stand spending my breath with this damned fellow. Gag him.'

Those orders were fulfilled and poor fellow had six dozen then was cast loose and him and me both ordered to our duty. Beat to quarter; we were so cut and our backs so stiff and sore we sat still and did not go to our quarter. This was reported and a boatswain mate was sent to start us up with a ropes end, and made us exercise guns nearly two hours in this mangled state. God help sailors.

August 19. At last retreat was beat, and believe me the shirt on my back was like a butchers apron, and so stiff that every time I had to stoop down, it would tear off the bladders of blood and water that were on my poor mangled body, well may tortures like those cause the unfortunate sufferers to cry out for revenge and have it at the risk of his life. His life did I say? His life is only a burden to him and it is the cause of his long suffering which causes him to be careless how he conducts himself when drove to desperation, and tortures has steeled his once feeling heart so that he no longer being able to govern his bleeding heart, in frenzy he rushes forward to crush his oppressor and with vengeance in every nerve looks for revenge or death. This has been the same on board H.M. ship the *Hermione.* and the *Dency*, but we cannot look for much better from Wilkinson. It was the same tyrant that caused so much blood to be shed on board the *Hermione*; it was he that wound the crew up to a state of desperation, and revenge was their whole intention. He smelt something of the approaching tempest (and mark his plan to escape the snare he had caused to be laid and lead his brother blindfold to destruction). At this time the *Success* frigate, Captain Picket (Pigott) was ordered home and the *Hermione* was to remain on the West India station. Captain Picket (Pigott) wishes to remain in the West Indies and Wilkinson through dread and a guilty conscience was afraid to remain on board the *Hermione*. It was therefore agreed that they should change ships, which was done the day previous to the *Success* sailing for England. We must observe that long before this the crew of the *Hermione* had bound themselves under solemn ties to take the ship the first time she left Jamaica and revenge themselves on their oppressors and run the ship down to Laguira and give her up to the Spaniards as a prize, then enter the Spanish service or lay in prison as long as life existed.

August 20. Those unacquainted with the tale of the *Hermione* may refer to the history of England time of the French revolution and they will shudder at the name of such a ship and commander. This unfortunate circumstance will never be forgot by the seamen of England, thus you have the outlines of this unmerciful tyrant's proceedings. We will leave him to the pleasure of the great Sovereign of earth and sea and proceed on our way to Plymouth. That night we made the Eddystone light and having light winds lay nearly becalmed all night. However about 8 am a light breeze sprung up from the S.E. and by 4 p.m. we anchored in the Sound. Moored ship, our boats etc., landed dispatches and land the ruin of the British Navy. We laid in the sound two or three days. Nothing particular except Wm Kippis a young man fell from the fore rigging and broke his thigh. It had to be cut off. He recovered and was sent to the hospital.

CHAPTER 3

1803: The Dutch Indiaman

August 25, 1803. On the 25th in the morning our boats were ordered to attend a sham fight off the Mew Stone by the gunboats from the harbour. All the dockyard and navy boats composed two fleets. Our boats being ordered to join in the fun the sea boats' crews were called and ordered to get ready to go into the boats. They all mustered except poor Jack whose back and heart was too sore to partake of any of what young men in that time called a frolic. My name was called but was sick and in the Doctors list and you may believe me was very desirous to die. I shall mention a circumstance of the good effect a few lessons has on the youth that are sent on board the navy to be instructed and made sometimes the pillars of our country. Those are midship men, and it was one of those tools of Wilkinson's, Hopkinson by name, a thing not higher than a man's knee, going down into the boat and not thinking one of the men paid him due respect by moving his hat, Hopkinson looks at him and in great pomp, says, 'Pray Sir, do you know who I am?'

James Burchel, the man we allude to, looked at him and laughed.

'Yes sir,' says Burchel, 'I believe your name is Pug. Pug I think was what Lieutenant Barker called you that night he had a rope round your neck making you dance on the table in the gun room, when he roared out, "Damn you, Pug, hop round", and then he gave you a slap with the rope's end, made you hop, squall and grin—this, Sir, is all the name I know for you.'

Burchel at this time was set on the after thoft, or seat, and Pug stood on the stern sheets.

'Damn your blood, sir,' says Pug, 'must I take all this from a rascal like you?' and kicked Burchel in the mouth with his foot, made the claret fly.

'What, shall it be said Jim Burchel would suffer this from a brat of a boy? No I will die first! Here we go my boys.'

He sprung up, took the midshipman in his arms, and overboard plunges head foremost, determined to die with him in his arms. One of the men immediately put down the boat hook and caught Burchel by the back of his jacket and thus saved him when nearly both strangled. (Burchel has often said since that had it not been for that damned boat hook he was determined to die with him in his arms, as he would rather die than live the life he had to endure on board that infernal ship.) They were both taken on board very much exhausted, but in a short time hove up the salt water and were ready again for the next attack, that would be with the prince of devils Wilkinson. Burchel was put in irons and threatened to be hung by lieutenants, Midshipmen, and all the combined forces of Sir Philip—he being on shore at this time was not in the tribunal. Several boats were passing the ship at the time the affair took place and one of those being from the admiral's ship, the *San Salvadore,* this news was soon on board the admiral, and he came on board the *Hussar.*

Shortly after the affair the signal was made for Wilkinson. He was on board in a hurry, and meeting the admiral on board, was expecting another of Blackrock affairs was going on. However on meeting Admiral Sir Robert Calder on board he soon found the whole concern, and Sir Robert wished to have Burchel brought into his presence. After hearing the story from the midshipman he then heard Burchel, and turning around to the midshipman.

'You, Sir, that ought to set an example to the men, and placed in this situation by the rulers of your country who trust you to act with good conduct to protect the laws of your nation which you most outrageously have broken, by taking that authority on your self to lift your foot with violence against the face of one of our bravest of men, which he has just proved in being willing to die with you in his arms rather than suffer such cruel imposition.'

Sir Robert turning to Wilkinson addressing his honour, 'Captain Wilkinson Sir, it gives me reason to speak, you may perhaps think unreasonably, but I believe not. This present act of cruelty committed by one of our officers in your ship and under your command will cast a stain on you and your officers for ever. Our laws are good and will give satisfaction to all parties, if put into execution, but, Sir, you well know you are placed here as a lawgiver appointed by your country, and when you thus suffer your midshipmen or children to raise their hand or foot against one of His Majesty's subjects, you set the laws you are entrusted with, or the power you are invested with, to be taken out of your hands, and your officers are ruling according to their own tyrannical disposition and set England and her laws at defiance. And sorry, Sir Philip, I am, but it is my duty to inform you what has been hinted from the Honourable Wm. Cornwallis concerning your ship and crew. This is a strange method you have adapted to be placed in your situation as a father to your men, to encourage them in what is just and right, to see them justified and protected against any false charge brought against them, and on the other hand to teach them their duty with due obedience to their superior officers, to obey every order with due regard, to be sober watchful and diligent. Use them like men and as I have always found they will act like men. However Captain Wilkinson I desire the prisoner to be released and return to his duty and not to be as is customary in the *Hussar* for officers to upbraid a man with every thing he might have done from his first joining the ship. I observe he shall not be abused and upbraided with this circumstance any more and as for that young gentleman the midshipman he may prepare to join the *San Salvadore* tomorrow morning.'

His Honour stepped a little on one side and says to Wilkinson, 'I am sorry to hear that your men are using every means to leave the *Hussar* and join any other of His Majesty's vessels or ships of war and are willing to lay down their lives for their king and country, but it is impossible they can any longer bear with the cruel usage they have on board the *Hussar*. Oh, Wilkinson look back to the unfortunate *Hermione*. You well know my principles Wilkinson. When I commanded a single ship it was my chief delight to have the goodwill of my men, and I can safely assert every man under my orders would freely lay down their life to obey me or my commands, and by such means I made my crew both love and fear me. They loved me for my humanity and feared to cause my displeasure, and this I found the best school for seamen. They will fight for you and if required die for you. I have been advised by the honourable William Cornwallis to have a watchful eye on the *Hussar* while in port. He also informed me of the barbarous methods you practised daily on your crew, and now I am satisfied with the truth of the complaint and will use my interest to put an end to to such base proceedings. Therefore I must wish you a good morning', and down he goes into the boat and returned to the *Salvadore*.

That afternoon our signal was made for the captain and he was not long on shore before on board comes Lieutenant Pridham with an order for Lieutenant Wallis to join the *Salvadore* and Mr. Pridham was appointed first lieutenant of the *Hussar*. Wallis gave Pridham a terrible character of the crew but Pridham answered him:

'Sir, I am already informed by the Honourable Sir Robert Calder what the men are and how they ought to be treated; therefore your recommendations are unnecessary in that or any respect.'

Wallace took his baggage and out of the ship and left us. Thank God one rogue is gone.

August 26. All hands were called and Mr. Pridham was then appointed first lieutenant of the *Hussar*. He then very kindly addressed us.

'My men, I am this day appointed to your ship as first lieutenant. I have been advised how to proceed with my office by the Honourable Robert Calder. Therefore I have only to observe to you that as long as you conduct yourselves as men, I will make it my chief delight to use you as men should be used, and expects to be used.'

We wished to give him three cheers with pleasure.

'My boys,' says he, and off pulls his hat to receive them.

We cheered him and all hands returned to their duty. Everything wore a new face and we were all life thinking we had got rid of one of our greatest prosecutors. Next morning the midshipman left us and went on board the *Admiral*. The first lieutenant gave one quarter watch liberty to go on shore 24 hours, on those terms that should any of them break their liberty not any more liberty should be allowed. However every man returned within the time, and next day another watch went on shore and returned in due time.

August 28. Next morning our signal was made to prepare for sea, and at 2 pm. Captain Wilkinson came off with his orders. In a little while after our signal was made to weigh which was all performed with activity and life; every thing went right and no damning of eyes, nor threatening with starting, stopping grog etc. We made sail and at sunset that evening the Eddystone was astern of us some distance. Our orders were to cruise off Cape Finisterre to look out for French vessels returning home from the West Indies. We had a very pleasant run out to the Cape, where we had the misfortune to loose one of our messenger boys named Tilford. The night being hot he got into the mizzen chains, fell asleep, and rolled overboard; was not heard nor missed until next morning. This happened on the 12th of Sept. 1803.

September 13, 1803. This morning the land dipping stood to the westward at 12 mer. A sail was reported to the N.W. We made sail having a brisk gale from the southward, and that evening overhauled her. She proved to be the *Le Spark* from St. Pierres, Martinique, bound to Havredegrass, a fine vessel richly laden, and a number of passengers returning home to France with their property etc. Sent her into port, and took care to accompany her part of the way into the Channel. Her boatswain, a Dane, Wm. Wilson, entered for our ship to share with the ship's crew in prize money. He informed us there was several more large ships sailed in company with them from St. Pierres. We directed our course to our cruising ground and on the 15th another ship hove in sight. We boarded her, found her the *Le Peace* from Port-au-Prince bound to Dunkerque with a valuable cargo on board, manned her and sent her into port.

September 25 to October 7, 1803. Having remained on our station some time and nothing particular occurred on the 25th of September we fell in with the *Le Flora* from Port Royal Martinique bound to Nantz, another valuable prize, manned her and sent her into Plymouth. We remained on our station until the 29th do., when we fell in with the *Active* cutter with orders from England to the *Hussar* on station off Cape Finisterre.

Our orders were to make the best of our way towards St Helena to detain a large Dutch Indiaman that some of our India ships left laying there repairing her rigging, painting ship etc., having not heard of any war between the two nations. We had every particular description of her, how she was painted with red sides, had her foretop gait mast on deck, had part of her guns in the hold, was weakly manned, her decks all lumbered up, and would be an easy conquest. This was all great news; we were on the road to make our fortunes. All was life and glee, we carried on all sail, got hold of the N.E. trades, ran them down until we began to approach the equator, and it chanced to happen one fine evening all hands had just been turned up to skylark when a sail was reported just under the place where the sun had set. The sky being clear showed her after the sun was down.

October 7. On hearing the report of a sail all was in a state of desire hoping she might prove the ship we desired to fall in with. All sail was quickly crowded on the ship and just by the close of night we were near enough to make out that she was a large ship. We then were all in raptures and made sure of our being rewarded for our long search.

Our officers were in the same state as the men, all making sure she was our chap; but cowardice and tyranny—always united in one body—disappointed all our expectations. That night we had a dead calm and at sun rise next morning we could just make her out to the N.W., quite a small black speck in the horizon; about 9 am. the trade wind sprung up and we made towards our grand point and found by 12 mer. she was a large ship with two tier of guns or ports and had no foretop galt mast up. All right, yet by 2 p.m. made out she had red sides and was jogging on under an easy snug sail Dutch fashion. At 5 p.m. we were within one mile; made signals and showed our colours to him. He then hoist up a large Dutch ensign. This was all we were looking for.

'Now my boys', says Pridham, 'she is our own.'

October 9, 10. 'I think we are a set of lucky fellows,' says Robin Gray. 'What do you think *Van Trump* will share amongst us?' Up comes the Captain Steward.

'Oh men', says he, 'you are taking a wrong idea perhaps; as Captain Wilkinson observed this minute in his cabin she may have all her guns mounted and then should that be the case, the captain says she will blow us out of the water.'

'Go to hell you preaching old bugger,' says Waddell; 'we are able to send her to Davy Jones in five minutes. You are all always pretending you know how many beans make five and after all know nothing at all, I know devilish well she is from Batavia and there I know she would bury half her crew at least, and more than all that she left Amsterdam on the peace establishment and has neither guns nor men to lay five minutes along side of our gallant *Hussar.*'

'That's right Waddell,' says old Pollard; 'let them lay us along side of her and that old Dutch flag will soon come down.'

By this time the breeze fell away with the sun and we were within gunshot quite becalmed.

'Blow up good breeze', says one.

'Why don't they out boats?' says another.

'What a foolish set of fellows you are,' says McAlister; 'as soon as the breeze springs up we can run along side with the ship and take her without firing a gun.'

'She is all our own my boys,' says the French cook.

'Maybe not,' says his mate.

Thus we debated about her. Mr. Pridham came forward.

'Have patience my boys,' says he; 'when the breeze springs up we will soon be along side and by her appearance she will not make any resistance.'

At this moment she caught a light air and we also began to fell the effects of it. He hove his main topsail to the mast and lowered his studding-sails down on the booms and lay waiting for us and seemed eager to hear what news from Europe. They little thought our intentions at the time. As will be seen afterwards the men on board were all busy taking in sail etc.

Captain Wilkinson says to Mr. Pridham:

'She is too heavy for us and is only waiting her opportunity to give us a whole broad side. I can see them at their quarters all ready for us. She has 64 guns. She is a Dutch 64 and most likely mounts 76 and she is full of troops returning home.

'We all know what the Dutch are if they were to subdue us. They are unmerciful enemies; therefore I think it is most prudent to lay with our head to the Eastward all night, keep to our quarters, and be all ready should any thing happen through the night. It is now sunset and little wind so that the ship is not very governable, therefore make no delay but let the ship's head be laid to the eastward.'

'Well Sir, we certainly obey your wise commands with pleasure, but if you will have the goodness to hear my simple opinion and that of all your officers on board it is that she is weakly manned and we cannot make out more than six guns mounted on this side next us and we all are of the opinion that she might be ours without the least resistance.'

'Pho. pho. pho.' says the man hater; 'let my orders be obeyed

Sir, immediately', and very sternly steps up to the rest of the officers. 'Gentlemen, you must allow me to have more knowledge in this undertaking than any of you; therefore obey my command and lay the ship the other way while you have a chance. Perhaps the air of wind may die away and then the enemy might fall on board of us.

'I know the cruelties of the Dutch. Remember the cruel massacre of Amboyna, oh. oh. oh. I know them, I know them,' and down he goes into his cabin.

For a while every one stood in a state of stagnation; the officers shook their heads but said nothing, and as for the sailors that was the time to hear sailors pray in secret for their fatherly humane feeling tender baited courageous commander.

'Damn his massacre of Amboyna.' says one, 'let him look back to the massacre of *Hermioney* and then I think he may keep his cursed mouth shut and hide his Cain like face.'

This was a private prayer, with numbers more on various acts of his most humane and lender hearted performances to his crew.

October 11. During this dramatic romance I must remark one instance of secrecy. We had a midshipman on board named Matthias, a Jew, Wilkinson's tale bearer. He lived in the cabin with him etc. every word that was spoke worthy of notice this young imp was encouraged to carry, and as sure as any person made any remark or let slip an unguarded word it was no sooner utter'd than it was in the cabin. Men used to observe on seeing him stealing round 'a privateer in sight;' this was their watch word to look out for him. Officers and crew all were aware of him. To return and proceed with our duty we put our ships head to the eastward and stood in that direction all night with a light little breeze and all lay by our quarters according to orders. Officers and crew all grieving but could not help it; at sun rise in the morning we could barely make out the *Van Trump* to the westward quite down in the horizon. Mr. Pridham went down to inform our warrior where she was and what was his opinion and his orders etc.

October 12. 'Sir', Says Wilkinson, 'by what passed amongst you and the rest of the gentlemen on the quarter deck and the damned mutinous crew you would soon run His Majesty's ship to destruction. You would sacrifice both yourselves and ship. But, Sir, I let you know I have better knowledge, and finding what a set of unruly officers and mutinous crew I have to deal with I am afraid with such men—I say I am afraid—to bring His Majesty's ship into action, and am determined to make the best of my way to England. Go Sir, make sail on the ship, and—wait a minute' (looking at his chart) 'Steer N1/2E for St. Jago's one of the Cape Verde Islands. At present the ship is in the lat. of 6. 37N and Long. 32 24W. and as you are all great men with your tongues make it appear in your government of the ship', and down he lays his skeleton shape.

Mr. Pridham came on deck shaking his head and gave orders: 'All hands make sail.'

All hands were at hand in a minute expecting it was to go in pursuit of *Van Trump* but soon found the mistake.

October 13. Great murmuring took place amongst us but the watch word of 'Privateer' we had to observe, as the Jew was always on the look out. every one was as much in dread of him as they were of his prompter. We made sail and stood to the northward four days with a smart S.E trade and on the 15th of October made St. Jago's. From the time we made sail until we made the Cape Verde Wilkinson never appeared on deck nor were any of the officers invited to dine with him as usual.

When the land was reported he came on deck and gave orders to continue that course after passing the islands and proceed directly for England. Down he dives like a devil into the lower pits of hell and his heart as full of devils as the whole herd of swine. May the Prince of the infernal lake be his constant companion may he neither eat drink nor sleep without the visitation of Picket (Pigott) and the remorse of a doubled mind. May he be constantly tormented with the ghostly appearance of the numbers of innocent lives he has caused to be taken.

CHAPTER 4

1803: The *Revenge* 64

November 1, 1803. In the course of thirteen days from the Cape Verde islands we made Scilly and on the 1st of November arrived in Plymouth Sound. Wilkinson went on board the *Admiral* and told a long tale of his falling in with a large Dutch two decked ship full of troops and he thought it most prudent to lay by till morning and see how she might act through the night, it being night when we came up to her near enough to make out her force. However in the morning nothing in sight, so returned to England according to orders that he might have made another attempt to overhaul her, but there was something he did not like to trust amongst his officers and crew, therefore for the safety of His Majesty's ship and his own honour he deemed it the most wise plan to proceed directly to England.

'This, your Honour, Sir Robert, is the heads of my cruise.'

We learnt all this afterwards from Sir Robert's coxswain who heard the whole story and as boats crews will talk and repeat over old stories our men told them in Sir Robert's gig all the particulars of the Dutch Indiaman and of his showing too many teeth.

November 2, 1803. This was soon made known to the admiral and caused many a laugh amongst the officers of various ships meeting ours. The word would be 'any countryman's teeth except a Dutchman. He grins so damned able hard as to terrify the hero of the *Hermione*'; they was private jesting when all met passing their jests on each other. This we shall pass at the present moment and return to our duty. We had our orders to refit ship in great haste and on the 4th of Nov. took in provisions and water, stores, etc. On the 5th our orders were to proceed with all haste and join the grand fleet. We sailed and on the 7th fell in with the fleet, delivered our dispatches and letters. We then, members of the ring confederacy, were in hopes to be called on by the *Admiral*. We lay close by the *Ville de Paris* and not having any orders to take our station we made sure something was doing for us. At this instant not being very far off the land we heard the report of guns under the land.

'What can that be?' says one.

'Why', says the midshipman a fine young gentleman, Mr. Smithson 'I rather think by the direction it comes from it must be the French exercising their guns on St. Mathews.'

By and by the signal was made from the inshore ships that the *Defiance* 74 was in pursuit of a large French ship of war and had caused her to seek refuge under the forts of St. Mathews. In the morning the *Defiance* ran down to the *Admiral* and gave the intelligence that the evening before he chased a large ship from the southward bound apparently into Brest. She found the *Defiance* gaining her and she had anchored close under the guns of St. Mathews. He also stated that she was a 64 gun ship and full of troops. The *Thunderer* seventy four was left to prevent her running into Brest.

'Now, boys', says one to another, 'we shall have a scrape with this fellow.'

We had not been long on board the *Hussar* when a signal was made by the *Admiral*. for all captains, and that afternoon the orders were to man a boat from each ship in the fleet with volunteers and the *Hussar* to tow them close up to the French ship.

November 8. 'Now the game begins. Volunteers for the barge' was the word on board our ship, and it is the rule with seamen for the boats crew to be the first volunteers for their own boat and should more be wanting then volunteers. We all got ready our cutlasses, pistols, ammunition and what was requisite for such an undertaking. We were eight men to row the boat, two marines and the first lieutenant eleven in number. Orders were for the boats to assemble and join the *Hussar* at 9 p.m. all in order, to have all their oars muffled arms and ammunition an officer and two marines in each boat and ten ships launches, each sixteen oars, two officers and eight marines. Our expedition when united together along side were as follows—eight launches, twenty-five barges and cutters etc. We mustered 396 men at the commencement, in all thirty-three boats. Being all ready at 9 p.m. made sail stood in shore towards the light house and at nearly half past twelve midnight were close enough to see the ship.

The orders were on seeing the ship—the boats were to form in two lines, one under orders of the lieutenant of the *Ville de Paris* and the second under order of the lieutenant. of the *Royal Sovereign*. Our barge was appointed to cut the cables while the rest boarded on each side. Now begins a horrid slaughter. Away we rows in two lines, one for each side, our oars all muffled, and not the least noise was heard. The sea was smooth as oil. All was still and silent. We approached the ship and each division took his side appointed, larboard and starboard. Up along side we goes; not a word nor any noise was heard by them on board. We supposed their sentinels were taking a small nap. We soon found the reverse. Our commodore lieutenant, of the *Ville de Paris* and the second in command lieutenant. of the *Royal Sovereign* were in the centre of the two lines and not in the list of the thirty-three boats composing the two lines. Each of those launches were armed with a long gun in their bow and full of men, so that our boats all included were thirty-five not including the *Hussar's* barge to cut the cables.

November 10. The two launches were to lay under her stern and make her at the time of boarding, and by this means take part of the enemy's attention from the boarders. When we in the *Hussar's* barge, being the van boat on the starboard side of the ship, passed her side in order as we were stationed to cut her cables, we were struck with astonishment to find her quite ready to oppose us. She was surrounded with boarding nettings which we little suspected, and when we got under her cable and made the first stroke with the hatchet. To our great surprise the cable was wormed with chain from the hawse beneath the water, caused fire to fly from the hatchet with the stroke. The boats were all ready for boarding but dreadful to relate at that moment a cataract of fire burst from the Mouth of Strumbolo could not gush from its confined regions with greater fury than these infernal engines of destruction vomited death from all parts of the ship. She was all flames in one moment as it were so that it was instant death to every man that attempted to mount her side. Those who had gained hold of the nettings were all either shot or run through with pikes or sabres and fell back into the boats or the sea. We never heard of one man that gained her deck. Meeting with such a formidable reception (all hands were in confusion) muskets roaring over our heads, officers ordering us to retreat, wounded men groaning, and others dying, death stared every survivor in the face. We shall refer to our boat where I was one of the unfortunate crew. Directly after striking the cable, we received a volley from her head and bowsprit, which laid seven of our comrades dead in the boat, and horrid to relate we the four survivors were all wounded, and as we were endeavouring to bear our boat astern clear of her head, something come in contact with my head. Putting up my hand I found the muzzle of a Frenchman's musket pushed it on one side just as he fired, saved my own life and nearly shot our first lieutenant near enough to graze his skull by the flash of the gun. I saw the man in the head that fired it and drawing my pistol from my belt gave him the contents through his noodle and laid him in the water under our boat's bow. By this time the boats that were able had got off and gone astern and we being all four wounded were very weak through the loss of blood. Nevertheless we got under her stern and drifted clear of her cursed leaden pills, over our shoes in blood, and in this state as well as possible followed our companions from the slaughter. Richard Pridham our first lieutenant. wounded in the head and right shoulder, John Waddell wounded in his left hip side and right arm, I, Wetherell, left shoulder breast bone broke right thigh and left leg, Edw. Carney Marine (a fine fellow) one ball through his left wrist. We four had to hobble back the boat.

We got under the stern of the ship and by those means were sheltered a little from her constant showers of musket shot. We found our boats were all making their best way towards the *Hussar* but in a very different order to what we were in when we left her; some boats had four oars and some six, nay even some had only two men that were able to pull the boat back to the *Hussar*. The day broke soon after we got from along side, and a most wretched appearance we made, some in one direction and some in another, as for our parts we were ready to give up the ship, being faint and weak through the loss of blood, and our having to exert all our efforts at the oars, in order to regain our ship and having our bleeding wounds dressed by the surgeon. About 8 am. we saw some of the boats gain the *Hussar*, and at 10 am we got along side, and I was at that time as happy to get on board her, as I should have been a few days before to have left her, and never to have seen her again.

Having got along side and waiting at the gangway Wilkinson makes his appearance at the entrance of the gangway and salutes his bleeding partly exhausted first lieutenant in this manner

'Well, Pridham, you have had a fine nights diversion. What the devil were you all about to let the damned Croppoes give you such an infernal drubbing? Why you must have been all asleep along side her.'

'Captain Wilkinson,' answered Mr. Pridham, 'Sir, had you been there perhaps you might have done some great exploit, and as for sleeping we are all convinced you would not have found much opportunity to sleep, there was quite the contrary sort of employment.'

'And, sir,' says the first Lieutenant, of the *Ville de Paris* (having just come up with his launch), 'pray, Captain Wilkinson, what is your meaning by saying all asleep? I wish to inform you, Sir, there were both officers and men in H. M. boats and those who by their merits have gained laurels and honour to their country without ever gaining our experience in the *Hermione*.'

'Sir, we wish you to know that we are all H. B. M. officers, and have never caused a stain in her standard, and again we wish you to remember we are all gentlemen, (and British officers proved).'

Wilkinson left the side and walked aft biting his finger nails, and says to the purser, 'Those young upstarts have a great deal of assurance but I shall have them severely reprimanded for their insolence the moment I meet the admiral.' (We are all gentlemen.) 'What I suppose he means is gentlemen enough to exchange gloves with me. I will convince them of their error and let the damned puppies know I am their superior.' He calls the third Lieutenant. Barker. 'Sir,' says Wilkinson, 'let the officers come on board the *Hussar*, and let the boats be passed astern ready for making sail on the ship. Let our barge be hooked on and hoist up etc. with all speed.'

To his mortification not one of the officers would enter the ship but remained in their boats until they joined their respective ships. Mr. Pridham all this time sitting with us in the boat (what inhumanity).

November 12. Lieutenant Barker obeyed his orders and found the barges crew were not able to hook her on. He ran to the captain with the news. At this his highness struts to the gang way putting his cursed tyrannical head over the side and thus addressed his unfortunate lieutenant. and three wounded men, 'Pridham, what the devil is the reason you don't see the boat hooked on and you come on board?'

'The reason, Sir, is we are unable to do it; therefore we require help to do it.'

'Mr. Pridham, Sir, you are very free with your tongue,' says Wilkinson, 'I have a very great reason, Sir, for my blood and the rest of my surviving crew had been and is at present flowing very free', (a just cause to speak free).

'Well, Sir, please to walk on board and you shall have help to hook on the boat. Why damn my blood, Sir, you have got the barge all shattered to pieces and all over bedaubed with a parcel of stinking blood.'

Mr. Pridham went on board and then we had orders to come on board. Some hands were sent down to manage the boat and we were sent down to the cockpit and patched up by the surgeon.

The ship took us back to the grand fleet; she returned the remaining boats to their respective ships and remained four days in company then took on board a number of wounded men for Plymouth hospital and left the fleet on the 16th of Nov. 1803. Arrived in Plymouth Sound landed our wounded men on the 17th, John Waddell John Wetherell and Edw. Carney were overhauled by the surgeons and thought proper for them to remain on board their ship as they were all recovering fast and they would be fully as well on board On the 18th took in provisions and water, stores, etc., and on the 20th of November sailed with dispatches for the British squadron off Ferroll and Corona blockading the French squadron. Our orders were to Sir Edward Pelew, at that time a commodore with his broad pendant on board the *Malta* 80 gun-ship. This was a great mortification to Sir Philip having to remain under the orders of a commodore.

November 21. This morning fell in with a French brig prize to the *Warrior*. He informed us the ship that we made the attempt to cut out he learnt from the captain of the brig, she being from Brest and gave every particular of our defeat, he informed us she was the *Revenge* of 64 guns from Rochfort to Brest and she had 1500 troops on board for the fleet in Brest. He also informed us that she had twenty-seven killed and forty-nine wounded and on the following morning she weighed and ran into the harbour. Most of her killed and wounded were from our two launches under her stern, as not one of the British ever gained her deck. The weather being quite calm Captain Wilkinson lay by the brig all the evening and the lieutenant of the *Warrior* being the prize master on board was able through the French captain to give us all the particulars. He informed us that they were sure when the British pursued them the day before under the forts of St. Mathews and then left them that they would make some attempt either to set the ship on fire or to cut her out. With those ideas they made ready to receive them on either point of attack. They wormed her cables from the hawse under water with chain. They also got up boarding nettings round the ship and all the troops placed round the inside of the nettings with their muskets loaded, and also a second division to load and the first division to fire. Their orders were not a word to be spoke nor a gun to be fired (Should the British make an attack) until they were close along side and then on the signal being given to fire as quick as possible through the nettings, and the ships crew to make use of cutlasses and pikes at the same time so as to prevent one single souls gaining their deck. This was the account he gave us of that most horrid and bloody massacre.

November 22. Captain Wilkinson having learnt all the particulars of the ship *Revenge* parted company and with a light air we stood at the S.W. I wish to observe that by this time John Waddell, Carney and myself were pretty much recovered of our wounds only I was yet unable to go aloft owing to the ball in my right hip. The first lieutenant. was soon cured of his scalping by the help of a wig etc. Waddell swore he would never die happy until he was revenged of the French for depriving him of his chief delight, that was playing the fiddle. Poor Carney was no longer able to shoulder his musket therefore stood sentinel at the cabin. On the 25th of Nov. we kept up Guy Fawkes day exercising guns and small arms and on the 26th exercising the gratings and boatswain cats. 27th field day, wash all clean. Passed Cape Ortegal with a smart N.E breeze on the 30th made Ferroll.

December 1, 1803. After safe arriving in Ferroll bay, delivering our letters etc., we were stationed off the harbours mouth to break off all communications between Ferroll and Corona. Sir Edward Pellew and the squadron lay up the bay, seven sail of the line British. The French lay in Ferroll harbour nine sail and in Corona one 74 and two frigates. We used to go on shore to market frequently and have fresh beef for all the squadron at a large town at the extremity of the bay. We carried out great rigs amongst the French and Spaniards on shore. We also smuggled tobacco for wine and fruit etc. Got taken with a bag full of tobacco belonging to Sir Philip and had it not been more for fear than love I should have gone to the mines for life. However Sir Edward set me at liberty. On going on board I sat down and wrote verses, mere pastimes.

December 19. We had letters by the *Dragon* for all the squadron, and on the 19th were sent out on a cruise off the cape just to let Wilkinson have his fling for two or three days.

December 21. This day was what we called a grand review. After breakfast the word was passed to muster bags and cloths. The drum beat to muster in divisions, and a long time we had to stand. A great many were short of their complement and were all put in the brig to have pay for what was a missing. Some had sold their shirts, some jackets, stockings, pantaloons, shoes, frocks, handkerchiefs, in fact some had sold all their stock to the Spanish boatmen for aquadent or wine in Ferroll bay. They, poor fellows, only could say they were sold for fruit etc.

Muster over then comes on the dreadful time. All hands to punishment, not one of the Blackrock Convention. His Highness on the quarter deck, his clerk with a large roll of paper—articles of cruelty not of war; those of war are laid on one side, forgot. All the officers planted round him watching even the motion of his eye. Every word he spoke to any of them seemed to have the power of electricity there was such a perpetual bowing, scraping, handling hats and presenting papers that the whole group were in motion.

Mr. Hill was ordered to bring forth the prisoners. This was done.

Next was 'Quarter Masters rig the gratings.'

'Done.'

'Sergeant, are the marines all according to orders? Let them load their muskets before all hands on the gang ways.'

'Done Sir.'

'Mr. Maxwell have the goodness to read the Articles of War, and let the rascals know it is their country and not me punishes them.'

December 22-30. By this time it was near six bells in the afternoon; went to dinner and a poor dinner it was to many, some through pain and others through their feelings at such unheard of cruelties. O, England were only one fiftieth part of the cruel sufferings thy subjects endure known to thee, under those chosen by thee, to act as thy faithful and trusty rulers, when from under thy immediate jurisdiction, I again say did thou but know their cruel treatment to they brave seamen on the ocean, thou wouldst shudder at the very name of it. And almost be persuaded to say this cannot be true. Yes; it can be and will be until that day of revenge put an end to some of the perpetrators of tyranny. In the morning of the 23rd all hands make sail and ran close under Cape Finisterre after a lugger that lay close under the land. Found her to be a Jersey privateer, watching a French brig lay in a small harbour South of the Cape. We then stood out to sea and on Christmas day had a good plum pudding, and a good piece of beef for dinner, but all this was nothing where contentment was fled; however like true old philosophers we bore all as patient as possible and of our bad bargain made the best. On the 27th Dec. saw a brig to the N.E; we soon made her to be the *Ferret* brig from the commodore with orders for us to join the squadron immediately. On the 30th we arrived in the bay and on the 1st of January Sir Edward gave us orders to prepare for England with all speed. He had orders from the admiralty to dispatch the *Hussar* home to England with all haste etc. My friend, Mr. Smithson, heard the orders and told me all the particulars. On Wilkinson reading the orders he looks at Matthias.

'I suppose', says he, 'this is another letter from those damned rascals on board the ship!'

'Ah, you are dark Sir Philip.'

January 1, 1804. Tyranny returns to his study again to consult his infernal adviser which would be the most torturing (and to him give the greatest pleasure) and cruel persecutions to inflict on his cursed crew of low bred rascals. At last His Honour's meditations were interrupted by a notice from the quarter deck to inform him the *Malta* has made a signal for his grace to wait on Sir Edward immediately.

'Damn those upstart half bred gentry, they once get preferred to office, and take the situation out of our hands that we have gained by merit; I say half bred because were they of my brave spirit, they would never wear the broad pendant of their country, and give orders to men they are not worthy to sit in the same cabin with, when His Majesties service can produce such numbers of us brave undaunted bulwarks of our nation, to bear the insulting and austere chastisement from such mean plebians and seven faced commanders of our British navy.'

This was the discourse between Sir Philip and Matthias.

The barge was manned and His Highness was propelled along side the *Malta*, with his chosen pupil Matthias by his side; otherwise he could not have knowledge of half his transactions as he appeared half the time like some person deprived of their rest and terrified out of their life. When alone he was often heard (by the sentinel and by his boy Richard) talking in great agony, groaning and saying cut them up make them fear me; knock them down; run them through; stop their breath; destroy the whole fraternity of rascals; leave none to write nor in any manner disturb my happiness, at times would leap from his bed and run to the cabin door and ask the sentinel who that was in the after cabin groaning and kicking; the sentry replied no living soul had past him, nor yet had he heard any thing excepting His Honour in his dreaming make a great noise, that was all.

'You lie, Sir,' says this bold Lama Moore Lion 'I heard some one in the after cabin and it is some plot to take away my life.'

This lion proved to be a sheep. This man must be a *Hermione* lion.

Sir Edward informed him that all the stores and provisions

could be spared from the *Hussar* must be left with the squadron, nothing left on board, only sufficient for her passage to England, that those were his orders from the commander in chief and were to be put into immediate execution.

How droll, some of us has, and always will have the idea, that Sir Philip on being ordered home, with such strict and immediate dispatch was determined to play them all a trick; and destroy both the ship, crew, and himself, rather than undergo the chastisement his tyrannical behaviour had long ere this deserved, which was fully verified afterwards by the loss of the ship and then by his wicked design nearly destroyed the whole of that noble ship's crew; what he left undone in the ship he nearly accomplished with the boats—had not kind heavens protected us from his horrid design and safely landed us in the midst of our open enemies, as a place of refuge and deliverance from the hands of oppression, and also to let him know that the Almighty would bear no longer with his infernal abominations, but drove him with his boat in a different direction, and drove him from the society of those men's presence he was unworthy ever to command.

January 2, 1804. He returned to the ship and in a few minutes launches were along side to take all our spare stores and provisions, which was soon done. We then took in a little more water and on the following morning January 3rd weighed our best bower and rode by a single anchor. Our appointed hour to sail was 12 mer. so that all the ships might have their letters on board by that time. Our sails loose, boats all on, anchor a peak, and all ready for the word, when as if nature rose to put a stop to Wilkinson's cruel designs. The sky was in one entire sheet of confusion, thunder began to extend his awful grumbling voice; and in the distant S.W. vivid lightning successively followed each awful crash, rain fell in torrents and the wind increased; apparently every peal of thunder brought fresh hands to the bellows, so that by 1 p.m. the gale was tremendous. We furled sails, let our best bower go, and paid out most of the two cables, then the sea ran high. The gale was very heavy all that night, and on the 4th, in the morning more moderate until about 2 p.m. the wind shifted round to the N.E. and blew with great fury. However being off the land the water was smoother than it had been the day and night before. However we rode through all this and on the 5th in the morning quite moderate.

CHAPTER 5

1804: Striking the Saints

January 5-8, 1804. At 8 a.m. Sir Edward made the signal for us to weigh and make sail which was done in a short time as we were all in good spirits at the time hoping on our return to England we should have some overturn in the ship, either in exchange of officers, or men, as we had by this time heard of being recalled home in such haste. However our ship was under sail and left the bay; on passing Corona light house we saluted the squadron and stood to the northward with a fresh breeze from the S.E. all in good spirits. In a short time were round Cape Prior and the wind being off the land, we kept the shore close on board, we fell in with some Spanish fishing boats and got some fish and fruit in exchange for bread, tobacco, etc. On the 7th in the evening past Cape Ortegal chased a schooner under the land. She appeared to be Spanish by her colours etc. We left her and proceeded our course, took our departure from the Cape at 12 midnight with a pleasant gale from the southward all well.

January 8. In the morning spoke the *Philomel* brig on her passage to the coast with dispatches exchanged signals and proceeded. Nothing particular only Wilkinson would not suffer any merriment amongst us while he was on deck. He used to say it hurt his feelings to see a set of damned mutinous rascals take the least sport or enjoyment, therefore after he took his wine and went to sleep it was our time, as the officers used to say:

'Come boys now is your time. The cat is away so now the

mice can fearless play', and generally a bottle of rum from the gun room would open the ball with this precaution, *be moderate, prudent, watchful and wise*, then the officers would rank themselves on the gangway to see our curious diversions and hear our funny tales and droll jests and songs, in this style, playing at tailors, passing through fire and water, hunting the slipper, abel whackets, rule of contrary and all such diversion, then the second part singing all sorts of patriotic songs duets glees etc. but at the same time every man was attentive to his duty such as the look out, helm, tops, on the quarters, gangways, bows, and particularly a bright eye on the cabin door (as we like wild geese took each man his turn).

January 9. In the manner already observed, we generally passed the first watch in moderate weather, unless the young Jew should remain on deck, which he sometimes did on the first watch. When this was the case, everything was quite the reverse. You might walk the deck the whole four hours and not hear a word spoke, by either officers or crew—except as regards the ship's duty, such as relieving the helm etc. and now and then orders to keep a good look out forward, or aft., but that instant the cursed fiend took his flight into the lower infernal regions, to consult his evil genius Lucifer, then all was alive as if some evil spell had been laid on all hands, and on the departure of the necromancer every soul was reanimated to their former state. We must leave them to their tormented conscience and frightful dreams, and proceed towards that fatal bed of danger; which the Prince of Tyranny had chosen, for the execution of his cruel revenge on himself, his country and crew.

January 10. This morning muster bags and cloths, exercise guns, serve out a few dozen at seven bells, with an oath of threatening danger to all. That was 'Damn you all, this is nothing. Before any of you reach England you shall curse the day you first contrived your plot to bring me to disgrace, by your letters and petitions to Admiral Cornwallis, treating of the discipline on board and every trifling chastisement I think proper to inflict on you. But now you shall find the events of your conspiracy. I am your admiral now and shall not forget to let you know it. Boatswain's mates, do your duty or by God I will do mine. If you don't love me I will make you fear me.'

In this manner we passed the fore-part of the day, and in the afternoon having a brisk gale from the S.W. made all sail we possibly could crowd on the ship from 12 mer. to 4 p.m. Steering N.N.E. from eight to ten knots per hour. At 4 p.m. Wilkinson gave orders to steer N E until 12 at night, and then he should give further orders.

Mr. Weymouth the sailing master says to Captain Wilkinson (as the boy Dick said afterwards), 'Pray Sir don't you think we shall be too far to the eastward?'

'That, Sir, is left for me to decide. Go, Sir, and let my orders be obeyed.'

Mr. Weymouth went on the quarter deck to the First Lieutenant Mr. Pridham and related over what had been said in the cabin.

'Why, Weymouth', says Pridham, 'if ever this ship reach Ushant steering N.E. I will eat her,'

'No,' says Mr. Weymouth, 'according to my calculations she can not pass the Isle of Glenan, and we must be very near run the distance from 12 at noon, by observation we were in Lat 46.17.N. and Long. 5..22 West—and not going less than eight or nine knots will nearly bring her the length of the Saints by 9 or 10 ten o'clock this evening.'

'She cannot run till 12,' says Pridham, 'and going at this rate she will go to ribbons in one minute if she strike and all this sail on her.'

'I shall not turn in,' says Pridham.

'Nor I,' says Weymouth.

Barker heard all that. He rises off the slide of a carronade blustering out, 'Why damn me gentlemen, what are you afraid of? You won't go to hell before your time, and my life is as precious as yours is.'

'That is all right Mr. Barker, but we have our ideas. You Sir perhaps have very little regard for yourself and much less for others. With us the case is quite on the reverse. We are studying the benefit and safety of ourselves and the whole crew. At this moment I feel greatly alarmed and cannot rest below.'

At that instant Mr. Pridham goes forward and looks very carefully ahead of the ship; at the same time she was flying through the water at a great rate. He would then walk aft then to the fife rail and every few minutes would repeat the same words:

'Keep a good look out forward there.'

And every few minutes him or the master went forward and took a strict look ahead; at last the quarter master reported ten o'clock, four bells, my look out of the larboard gangway, the helm, and looks out were all relieved. Took in the top-gait. Studding sails running nine knots per log.

'Keep a good look out forward' was all the cry,.

The night was very dark and a little squally. Took in the royals, and were in the act of furling them when Something sounded like the distant roll of a drum.

All hands stood in a state of surprise for a moment and anxiously listened to hear from whence the noise proceeded, when a most dreadful crash ensued which nearly sent the masts over her bows. That was followed by another when she stuck fast. Up comes Wilkinson in pretence to know where they were going with the ship as she had just hove him from his cot and nearly broke his arm.

'Why, Sir', says Pridham, 'she is just where I expected, on the Saints.'

'That be damned Sir, take in sail and heave your ship clear of where-ever she may be. Carpenter sound the pumps.'

All hands in a state of confusion; some let go halyards others let go sheets and braces, in fact all was terror and confusion. By this time the ship was half full of water, the pumps were rattling, Boatswain's mates roaring, ship striking, sails flapping, and officers bawling, which formed a most dismal uproar. At last some person on the forecastle saw a large rock under the bows quite above the water. Got sails furled, sounded, and found nearly as much water in the ships hold as there was along side. Out boats to sound for a channel; all this time the tide was falling. The ship fell over on her starboard beam ends. Then knock off pumping and get topmasts over the side to prevent her falling any farther over. This was a scene of confusion; some were crying out for the lord to help them, others contriving how to raise some grog, some packing up their cloths, others hoping she never would float again; some were desirous to know where the devil she was, others making their calculations how many could get in the boats, etc., etc. We fired minute guns, hove up rockets for help, but all to no purpose, sounded with the boats, and could find one cast of the lead four feet, at the next ten, and sometimes sixteen and twenty feet water. In midst of our confusion a light was seen over the starboard bow and was soon made out to be a man on the shore holding up a lanthorn; this gave us fresh hopes as we saw there was some place of refuge not far distant; however we fired minute guns and rockets until daylight made its welcome appearance and then Oh,—horrid! All round as far as we could see from the deck was sharp ragged black rocks and on our starboard bow was one of those destructive masses of rock, which without either leave or licence very abruptly had made his way through the bows of the ship and was very contentedly placed with part of his black huge body in the fore hold, and was there determined to keep possession and not to give up his hold as long as the ship hung together. Finding such hard hearted feelings from this sea monster our looks were directed towards the shore and there as the daylight approached we beheld a number of men, and one with a flag making signals for us to come on shore. Then arose a story that the island was full of troops and they would either kill or take us all prisoners immediately after landing. Some said one thing and some another.

At last the word was passed for the third division of small arm men and marines to get their arms ammunition and every thing in readiness to land immediately; little doctor Newman to prepare his necessary articles to attend the men on shore under the command of Lieutenant Leftwidge the lieutenant of marines and my friend Smithson. They were all landed, and the men we had seen on the beach ran away and hid themselves. On the other part of the island was the town and harbour of Glenan inhabited entirely by fishermen. Their Governor was himself a fisherman and their only traffic was in carrying fish to Quimper and Le Orient, as we afterwards learned from them.

Our little army marched up to the town in great pomp, the drum and fife leading those daring invaders. Our gallant leaders conducted their forces up to near the town without seeing any living soul and on the entrance of the town was two large rocks where the head gentry had boldly ventured with their Governor in their front to know what might be the wish or request of us, also what was the cause of our firing guns at them all night, but when they saw us advancing in such a hostile manner, they knew not what to make of our manoeuvres, therefore they took shelter behind those two rocks lest we might fire on them before we came to a parley. However by some means doctor Newman saw the heads of some men, as he said, peeping from behind the rocks and he was sure they were waiting a favourable opportunity to let fly amongst us, and there appeared to be a great number of them all armed, and in the position they were posted, they would kill one half our men before they could see them, that he would advise the lieutenants to return back to the ship and get a couple of 18 pounders on shore and more men to work them.

Then they would be forced to lay down their arms and surrender the town etc. Leftwidge burst out on him in great fury.

'Why you are a damned cowardly fellow, Newman. If your country had all such valiant leaders as you what would become of her fleets and armies? I advise you Doctor give your box to Anderson the loblolly boy, and you return to the ship, as it is my determination you shall not proceed one yard farther with us. Why Sir, you would dishearten a whole army with your infernal imaginations. Return, Sir, immediately back.'

About ship goes Newman. Our invading army advanced a little closer to their supposed enemy when Leftwidge advancing in front sword in hand saw some of the enemy peep from their ambush. He had the forces drawn up and load their muskets ready for an attack; the old Governor seeing our men making ready for action took to his heels and ran to the town with his terrified citizens at his heels.

Such an army as Newman had discovered was a great curiosity, to see them retreat from their redoubt, and fly for shelter to their own habitations. A few poor inoffensive innocent half naked ignorant unarmed scared to death Briton's fishermen, wanted to speak but durst not make bold enough to approach our officers. We stood like a set of statutes staring at them, some in frocks, some without shoes or stockings and others without hats, to see them flying from the rocks to seek refuge in their own houses, rare fun for our men, some laughing, some roaring for them to stop, but this was all folly, home was home, with the fishermen. We advanced to the town, and took every particular description of the situation both of town and harbour. There was a quantity of fishing boats in the port but not a single soldier, except the Governor was on the island, nor yet either arms or any ammunition; as Mr. Leftwidge was informed by the Governor. He spoke a little broken English and on our people entering the town our officers were directed to where he dwelt by an old French woman.

Mr. Smithson was the first man to enter the Governor's mansion. He being master of the French language demanded of a young boy where the gentleman was. The boy burst out crying and said:

'You will kill my father and my mother and then take me away to England.'

'No, my good boy,' says Smithson; 'Your father nor yet any soul in the town shall suffer the least harm from any of our shipwrecked officers or men. All we want is to see your father, so that he may instruct us how to act in regard to lodging our men on shore etc.'

At last the boy took Smithson as interpreter and Lieutenant Leftwidge into the next apartment where sat an elderly lady weeping.

'Where is the Governor? says Smithson.

'Under the bed,' says the woman, 'but pray spare his life.'

'My good woman,' says our interpreter, 'we are come here as friends, and crave the advice of your good husband; it is for that we want to see him,'

'Come out my dear,' says madam, 'those English are friends and wish your advice how to prepare for their men.'

The bold commander crept from his concealment by degrees, looking at the officers then at his wife; at last he got untangled from the boats sails where he lay and talked some time. He enquired what brought us there with the ship etc.

We informed him of all our misfortunes. He told us they had thirty boats large and small belonging the island that three of them had gone to Quimper with fish and that was all the particular satisfaction he could give, and as for lodging the people, there was no place but the church and he would consult the father on that point. Therefore if we could save provisions they had plenty of potatoes and might do very well until we had an opportunity to embark for our own country. He also informed us his orders were from his government to report any enemies ships, vessels or boats that might land or attempt to land on the island by dispatching a boat over to Le Orient, but he had not as yet performed that part, therefore to clear the Governor from any neglect of his duty, it was most expedient for Captain Wilkinson to take possession of all the boats in the harbour, for the safety of himself and crew; this would put an end to all further altercations. Our officers made the promise to repair directly on board, acquaint their commander with the proposals made, and let him have an answer in two hours. In the mean time to prevent any mistake regarding boats leaving the port to give any alarm, a guard of marines was left in charge of the sergeant with strict orders not to let any boat whatsoever leave the island. In the course of all those preparations being settled Newman reached the ship with a dreadful account of the town being full of armed men and it was necessary to send a reinforcement of men and ammunition also some cannon with the utmost dispatch as the enemy were in a very strong redoubt when he left the party with the tidings.

Our officers and men left the Governor and returned to the ship at the very time the Doctor had told his dreadful story, which for a moment made all hands on board look round themselves. The moment before every man was preparing to save what few things they possibly could in their bags etc., but at the tidings of Doctor Newman it was considered in vain to save any thing to be taken from us directly we reached the shore. However this story was quickly on the contrary side of the question, Mr. Leftwidge and the rest of his men returned on board, gave Captain Wilkinson every particular, and in less than half an hour the orders were all hands prepare to land immediately, and put all the provisions that can be got into the launch and cutters with all the ammunition that has been saved from being wet.

'Mr. Pridham, Sir, you will please to see those things all landed safe. Also all the crew must land immediately, armed with their cutlass and pistols, full cartouch boxes, and every man prepared to defend himself should we be surprised by the troops from the main. Let not any person fetch any bags or bundles with them, only what they can put on their backs, to be ready at all calls without any encumbrance. Those are my orders, Pridham, and as it requisite for me to go immediately on shore to consult the commandant you make all haste with your landing. Should I wish to let you know any thing particular I shall write you by Mr. Mathias. Barge men away.'

'All ready Sir,' says the coxswain.

Down comes Sir Philip. We landed him, the purser Mr. Irwin, the Doctor, Mr. Lawmount and Mr. Weymouth. The master, Lord Geo. Gordon Mid and several others landed and went to town with Wilkinson. We returned to the ship with the barge and assisted in the landing our shipmates.

January 11, By 4 pm. all hands were safe on shore and every man used his utmost endeavours transporting our stores and provisions on shore; when we left the ship her main deck was in the water as she lay on her starboard beam ends in spite of all the shores we could invent or put over the side. We then took each a load of the stores up to the church, bags of bread, beef, pork, cheese, butter, candles, grog, tea, sugar, in short every thing that was not damaged. A favourite goat and the pig Jack were the first that fell victims to satisfy our craving appetites; they were cooked on the beach and each man had his allowance, with bread etc. Grog was also served us, and after sunset the watch was set, and the church our tent to sleep in by night. However be as it will there was always something to disturb our peace. Being a fine still evening we were all over the place walking round, when our drum beat to arms.

'What can all this mean?' says one to another.

'Why,' says Waddell, 'it is Barkers watch and likely he is drunk as usual and therefore in his crazy moments has set the drummer to beat to arms on purpose to let the old French Governor see us fly to our post.'

We all met at the seat of corrupt and absolute administration. When we entered candles stood lighted on the altar and the distributor of all good things was sat in great pomp, with his officers in order on each side of him. 'Silence!' was the first salute, then the orders were given to fetch forward Joshua Porter and William Wilson.

Porter advanced up to the bar of pollution (although fixed in the house of the Lord).

'Did you call me, sir?' says he. 'Yes sir, you are amongst the number of mutinous rascals. You have struck my clerk and I mean you to feel the effects of it directly. Where is that rascal Wilson?'

'That's me, sir,' says Wilson. 'I understand, Sir, before you left the ship you stove in the bulkhead of my cabin with your feet and this was contempt to me.'

'What do you want with the bulkhead after deserting it, and landing us all in this barren island and an enemy's country where you are in constant expectation to see the French come over from the main and take us all prisoners? So, Sir, you have a notion to have a little of your cruel diversion put in practice in this house of God, but I hope Sir, as we are on French ground God will show himself above the devil and put a stop to your tyrannical proceedings in this I muse.'

'Gag the rascal,' says Sir Philip, 'I say gag him, Hill.'

'Touch not a hair of his head,' says a number of voices; 'Postpone your sham court martial, until a more seasonable opportunity. This won't answer any longer. We are all determined not to suffer any more of your cruelties, neither in this place nor any other, so we think proper to dismiss, and go to rest and not consider any prisoners amongst us.'[1]

So good night, and out we all went, left Wilkinson to his private devotions at the altar. It was a laughable scene to see the officers grin and wink at each other, some hiding their faces a laughing, and Wilkinson, poor man, drove into a state of petrifaction for some time and had not a word to say to any one of his officers present. At last when he saw us all leaving his hideous presence he rose up and vomited forth a volley of dreadful oaths on such an infernal set of mutinous rascals. We left him to sleep by the horns of the altar nearly all alone, only his Jew brother Mathias was with him. We slept that night some in one place, some in another, but kept our regular watch until daylight appeared. We then got what little we had for breakfast and at 8 a.m. the word was past for the barges crew to go on board and set fire to the ship, which was done in a short time; then the barge was ordered round to the cove or harbour to join the fishing boats. Wilkinson swore he would not stay on the island another night with such a gang of villains, so that he was going to leave that place if he went to hell in the attempt, but should he live to arrive in the British dominions he would have full satisfaction for the insults he had bore both from his officers and ship's crew.

Therefore it was his immediate orders to overhaul the houses and get sails for all the boats, also vessels to carry water. According to orders, we ransacked the town, took all the sails we could find, which they mostly used for their beds, and tubs cogs bottles pitchers, or any vessel we thought any use to carry water, and at 4 p.m. went on board the ship renewed the fires as the tide of flood had destroyed those we made in the morning. We cut away

---

1. It is a debated legal point that the loss of the vessel ended the contract between the crew and their employer, *i.e.* the government.

her masts, cut the anchors away, in short we destroyed every thing we thought of any use to the enemy. As for her magazines they were full of water. All the guns were loaded and double shotted on our first leaving Ferrol. We hove all the arms over the side, and finding the fires burning furiously—as a warning to us one of the guns in the cabin went off, the fire began to rage so fast—therefore we all started on shore and went up to the town. On our way we were saluted with a gun from the old ship and the shot made the rocks fly like an old pitcher.

The ship being all in flames, her guns on the side next the town became a little troublesome to the poor fishermen. Being nearly high water the ship was upright and now and then sent an unruly visitor into the town which gave more alarm amongst them than our first visiting them with the forces. Says Wilkinson to the First Lieutenant, Pridham, 'You will please, Sir, to see what bread, salt, pork and water we have equally distributed among the boats, and let each man have a little of the grog we saved. It will not harm them at present. Then let all the sails you have collected be fitted to the different yards and spars you can find and placed in the boats. As for oars or sweeps they are all supplied already, and be sure you have all the water that you can find vessels to put it in equally divided, and then let me know directly.'

We bent all the sails and fitted our little fleet up as well as sails and rigging would afford, and got our tubs and vessels all filled with water, which was unfortunately all rendered unfit to use shortly after we left the island; it not being covered the salt water breaking over the boats entirely destroyed both our bread and water, as will be seen in the following pages. Wilkinson being informed the boats were all as well prepared as time and materials would permit his orders then were for all hands, officers and crew to assemble on the square fronting the church, and there we were stationed to the different boats, according to their size or burthen and formed in two divisions, the first division under Mr. Pridham to hoist a blue flag and the second under Barker a yellow flag and Wilkinson to lead the van with the barge.

CHAPTER 6

1804: The Open Boats

January 11, 1804. At 6 p.m. we all embarked and made sail with a fine breeze from the S.S.W. Our orders were to follow the barge and use every effort to reach Ushant or some of the British ship's cruising off Brest. During the night the barge was to show a light and blue lights at intervals. We were all clear of the island by dark; then we formed our two lines and made all ready for the nights sail. I must not forget one remark we made on our sailing round the point which forms the harbour or rather a cove. We all made a wonder to see more people gathered together on the shore than we had seen before on the island. Some of our men observed they had been hid in some cave or subterraneous vault, being struck with terror on our first approaching their seldom visited barren rock, and those few we had seen before were their chiefest men of valour.

Our small fleet having all passed point look out (as we named it being the point nearest the coast of France) and night fast advancing the orders were to sail in two lines through the night and follow Sir Philip in the barge by his light, which was soon performed, as the *Hussar* through her great affection towards us very friendly afforded us a most brilliant light to arrange our grand Armada. She made a dreadful lamentation when she found us all deserting her and leaving her to the mercy of those uncultivated islanders, which was clearly proved because every minute or two she set up a most thundering roar, as much as to say:

'Stop this night and see the last of me; then you can declare to the world you saw the total destruction of the fatal *Hussar*.' But Wilkinson regardless of forerunners to approaching danger rushed forward and regularly hove up rockets for us to make all speed after him. By this time the sky became quite cloudy and dark.

At 10 p.m. the wind blew a smart breeze at south; we still carried all sail in order to clear Point le Abbe steering west distance fifteen or eighteen miles. At this time we were apprehensive the wind was drawing round to the westward it being very very black and dismal to the S.W. with quick vivid flashes of lightning. At 11 p.m. we considered ourselves to the northward of Point le Abbe, and kept away N.W. for the Isle of Sein (Seins) or Point Croise, distance twenty-seven miles, wind still from the south and westward with squalls of rain and distant thunder continually threatening the approach of boisterous weather. Our commodore still kept in his station. At 4 a.m. being by our account round the Isle of Sein we kept away N.N.W. for Ouessant (Ushant) or St. Michel's distance twenty-four miles. At 6 a.m the wind shifted round to the N.W. followed by a heavy squall of hail and constant lightning followed by dreadful crashes of thunder. The gale kept still increasing, the sea rose in entire confusion through the sudden change of wind, and our sails all blew away.

Our oars or rather sweeps were so large and heavy that we could not make the least use of them in such a heavy sea. As quick as we got one of them over the side the sea either broke it or hove it out of our hands over board, so that all our exertions to use oars were in vain, and another unfortunate affair we had to encounter was all our water and bread entirely destroyed by the sea breaking continually over the boats, sometimes nearly overwhelming them never to rise again. We bailed out the water by turns with our hats etc. and some of our men were in constant exercise keeping the boats free and their blood in circulation, while others laid in the water perishing with cold and thirst for want of exercise and courage. About 12 mer. the squalls of hail and rain were so quick in succession that it appeared we must all perish. We were one minute in total gloomy fog so thick we could not see one of our dispersed fleet, and the next minute wrapped in flames, as it were, by the continual lightening.

We could not hear any thing except the howling tempest and rending cracks of thunder with frequent surges of water rolling over us. In the midst of this disastrous situation being separated from the rest of our unfortunate shipmates and driving before this dreadful hurricane at the mercy of winds and wave.s I somehow had hopes we should reach or drive into some place of refuge knowing the land was not far off, according to the distance we must have drifted from 12 mer. to 4 pm. Therefore I stuck close to the pump and took turns at pumping with two or three others all the time, and by this little exercise we kept in good spirits and hopes. The boat it was my fortune to be placed in was a very large boat and had a small pump fixed in her. This was of infinite service to us in freeing the boat, and also keeping us in motion. We were twenty-five souls on board; Lieutenant Barker was our officer, and was invested with charge of the second division of our flying squadron.

Our foresail, the only sail we had left, was of very much service to us in keeping the boat before the sea and also preventing her from shipping the water she would have shipped by laying in the trough in the sea. We suffered a great deal from the severity of cold more particularly in the snow squalls which followed each other successively. Sometimes we had a glimpse of bright sky for a moment and enjoyed some hopes of seeing some of our dispersed brethren, or land which must be in; very near us to leeward. This small hope was suddenly o'er-thrown by a repetition of either rain hail snow thunder lightning and wind, and within the confines of the bay with a most frightful raging confused sea. However we drifted on between hope and despair before the howling tempest. Sometimes one thought he saw a boat, another would imagine they saw land etc. which is a very common case at sea when approaching land. Imagination can see any expected thing at one hundred miles distance, when the real object is not visible more than ten or twelve in clear daylight. We had a great many false boats, ships, lands etc. reported. They all proved delusions and dark night spread her blackest mantle round us. In this situation our strongest hopes had nearly fled; the only man in our boat who neither had hope nor dread as long as his brandy enlivened his spirits would frequently hollow out: 'Pull away you bug—s, and let us get on board the ship. My guts are burnt out for want of water with my brandy.'

At another time he hollowed out, 'Loose the topgalt sails and let us make sail to clear this damned rocking and jolting; it is impossible to take a drop of brandy without loosing most of it with her damn'd kicking.'

He would snatch the helm from the steersman and say, 'Why don't you steer her steady as I do?'

At the same moment he would heave her broadside to the sea and run a great hazard of both his own, and all our lives. Thus he realized the old story when liquor's in wit's out. Barker would then perhaps have a sea or a spray strike him in the face or break over the boat and half fill her with water, then he would power out a volley of curses on the boat sea wind and weather and very frequently on himself and all on board. Thus we drove at random until about ten at night, when to our great surprise a gun was fired close to us, and looking round we were saluted by a second. The water was smooth all in the same time. We soon perceived a large ship close to us and the weather became clear at the same instant, and we saw the land on each side. By this time we were drove close to the ship. They hailed us in French and French Taylor being in the boat informed Barker they ordered us along side.

'Let them go to hell,' says he; 'I shall go on shore and when the weather abates we can run out to sea again, and not be made cowardly prisoners by them lousy Frenchmen. Let her run my boys out of his sight then we will all land in some cove or bay where we can get some refreshment and a fire to warm us and dry our cloths then we are able to clear our way through all the ships in Brest.'

He had only made a finish of his fantastical proposition when a boat from the guard ship made her appearance rowing towards us full of armed men. They came up along side and ordered us to heave to immediately; if not they would fire on us.

'Prisoners, by God!' says our brandy proof champion. 'Heave our arms all over board so that they may not find us armed. By this means we may fare the better.'

We hove all our muskets, pistols, cutlasses and ammunition over the side and hove the boat round, lowered down our foresail and lay till the guard boat boarded us. They enquired what we were and what was our intentions, where we were from and where bound to, in short every particular was explained to the officer through our interpreter, Taylor. They then took our boat in tow. By this time we had drifted into Brest harbour and were taken first along side the *Le Indian* frigate but could not hold on.

Every person was so wet and benumbed with cold. They hove us a rope from the frigate but the wind sea current and the weight of the boat caused our half frozen hands to refuse their former grasp. We drove clear of her and were again taken in tow by the *Indian*'s boats towards the admiral's ship the *Le Alexander* 80 gun ship. They took us on board and showed us the most tender humane usage could possibly be expected from enemies in a foreign land. We had brandy bread and herrings on first entering the ship, then were placed in the galley over a good fire, and after warming and drying our selves we had a sail prepared for us to lay down. By this time it was twelve at night. The officers got Barker into the gun room and with their cognac soon sent him to sleep. We all laid down and slept until morning, then were roused out to have breakfast, and make up the sail we had to sleep on. Also to make ready for us to be questioned by the admiral.

About 10 a.m. Barker made his appearance on the break of the quarter deck, and as some of the French officers spoke English they gave him to understand that we were going on shore to the hospital where we would be better taken care of than we should be on board, it being the most comfortable asylum for half perished creatures like us. We soon heard Barker on the gangway in his stupefied state of insensibility hollowing out for Graham the boatswain's mate, ordering him to call the *Hussar's* to muster. The French officer of the deck smiling at his ignorance observed to him that he must consider the prisoners were no longer at his command, and when they were required to go on shore they had officers attached to the ship able to give orders when required by the admiral.

At 11 am the first lieutenant, of the *Alexander* came down amongst us. He was a fine old gentleman and spoke good English. He took every particular means to make our situation comfortable. He told us the steward was drawing off some wine and we should have bread and cheese with it as he expected the admiral on board very shortly, to send us on shore as soon as he arrived on board. He also told us to be obedient to the officers into whose charge we might be entrusted and then he knew by long experience a prisoner of war was not the most wretched mortal in existence. He also informed us news had arrived in town from different parts of the coast with information of boats landing full of British mariners. On the shore of St. Mathews two boats landed and their crews were made prisoners until further orders etc. The wine bread and cheese came for us and he returned on deck. The steward gave each man a good cup of wine also some soft bread and cheese, enough and to spare. We all eat what was required and then were called up on the quarter deck; we were placed in a line and the admiral a fine bold looking gentleman stood a little while in front of us then turning round to Lieutenant Barker who stood on the right of us addresses him thus in English.

'Pray Sir,' says the admiral to Barker, 'were all your ships crew such men as those are?'

'Yes, your honour,' says Barker, 'our crew were all young men.'

'Well then, Sir, I am not ashamed to tell you that such men as those are prizable and rare to be had, therefore you ought to have taken more care of both your ship and men. However I know the men were not the cause of their present situation therefore I will use my interest to make them as comfortable as their present situation will allow. I am going to send them on shore to the hospital and there they will be nourished and taken good care of by some of their own country ladies sisters and nuns.'

The boats were ready and we all embarked, being twenty-eight in number. The admiral looked over the side as we left the ship in the two cutters.

'Be of good courage, my men. Your confinement in France will not be long, and as it is the laws of our two nations to hold fast all prisoners at this present time my duty to my nation compels me to transfer you to some place of confinement as prisoners of war. However your treatment shall be as good as we give our own men, and reason will not desire any more. I have sent my recommendations to the hospital with the officer that superintends you at present, so go on shore like men, and you shall fare like men and brothers.'

We parted from the *Alexander* and made the best of our way on shore; we landed close to the back gates of the hospital and were mustered by the matron of the hospital, twenty-eight men; she took us up stairs and placed each man to his cradle or bed. Then she had a number of convicts to attend the hospital and she in one word made them fly in all directions, some of them after sheets, shirts and caps others after water to wash.

January 14, 1804. She also spoke to us in English telling us to be steady and not make any disturbance in the hospital. Only let her know and those poor unfortunate creatures she said (meaning the convicts in red caps frocks and a ball to their leg) what ever you want and they shall fetch you as far as our rules will allow.

'You can have wine or beer but no spirits are allowed within those sacred walls. Another favour my dear young country men I beg you all to be very careful not to swear nor make use of any loose mean or unbecoming language, because that is contrary to our wish, and as we are all Christian sisters under whose care you have had the fortune to be placed, abide by our rules and you will find yourselves comfortable clean and happy. You must take care of those men that have to attend you. They will take any thing from you they can get hold of. Now, men, I have given you our rules therefore you have not the least excuse for breaking them, which I hope you will not. Rest yourselves a little while and you shall have some soup to nourish you and what ever will be of any good to you shall be had.'

We all thanked the lady and prayed God to bless her.

In a short time we were served soup, boiled beef, mutton, veal cutlets, potatoes, bread etc., also every man a pint of beer and before we had one mouthful our good lady gave a blessing in the midst of us, also after eating the same. She told to us all not to think strange of those blessed ceremonies she made use of as it was the duty of every soul in existence to return thanks to the Blessed Father who is the giver of all good things, and without his blessed goodness we could receive nothing at His hands. We thanked her and all sat down on the wooden benches. She then informed us that she was born in Ireland and at the time of the rebellion her father and mother owing to religious principles left Ireland and went to Nantes in Brittany. In a short time her parents were called to mingle with the dead; she was the only child left and was by some Christian friends sent to a convent and through the help of her blessed Saviour was translated to the charitable office we saw her in. Her name was Emma Burke born in the city of Limerick, County of Limerick, Ireland.

By this time it was near sunset, our lady bid us all a very goodnight, and left the ward; we all repaired to the beds allotted to us, and all our discourse was on the humane and heavenly treatment we found in the midst of our most inveterate enemies; although prisoners of war, our foes were our benefactors, and treated us with so much more humanity than we found in the service of our own nation that we could not but observe to each other what a blessed change we had made. No boatswain's mate, master's mate nor yet Wilkinson to curse and abuse us both day and night; no, the lord saw our sufferings were not much longer to be bore, and through his great mercy towards us contrived this, as the means to snatch us from the inhumane bonds of oppression, and to deliver us out of the hands of tyranny. Thus we lay in our beds discoursing until one after the other we all fell fast asleep, and slept till daylight next morning, when we arose quite refreshed and rested. Our red birds, as we termed them, were all ready to make up our beds and sweep the room show us the washhouse etc.

January 15, 1804. About eight o'clock this morning our governess Miss Burke came to visit us; she enquired how we all were, and how we had rested through the night.

'Well, men,' she says, 'I have good tidings to relate to you this morning. After I left you last evening we were informed that a number of boats had landed on various parts of the coast and all their people were on their way towards Brest.'

Those must be the remainder of our shipmates were were all the time enquiring after; therefore we might be contented for they would be in Brest in a day or two. We thanked her for her good news and then were served boiled milk and bread for breakfast etc. In the afternoon one of the red birds came running up into our ward saying:

'Come, come, comrade, come.'

And soon we found the crew of one of our boats had arrived. They, poor fellows, were almost exhausted and wore out. When they saw us and heard how we fared they were twice glad, first to find us alive, as they like us concluded all the other boats were lost, and secondly to find by us they were in the hands of good Christians. They were put in a ward downstairs and had the same tender nourishment we had already experienced. After they had some refreshment, and dry apparel put on we sat down and heard them relate their late sufferings etc. That evening one of our boats crew named William Jones that was in a poor state of health when we left the ship and suffering so much through cold and wet in the boat and was on our landing was put in the sick ward and medical aid was given to him but in vain; the frame was too far exhausted and the Lord took him out of all his troubles to another and a better life. He died on the 15th of January 1804. We all went to our rest again for the night and on the 16th we had a number more of our unfortunate shipmates arrived. They all had the same melancholy tale to relate in regard to sufferings etc. We enquired after the barge but no one heard nor saw any thing after the gale arose.

January 17, 1804. Thus we kept mustering our dispersed crew from all parts of the coast round Brest, and by the crew of the boat in which the carpenter (Mr. Thomas, a fine man) was lost we understood by the men that when the boat struck on the rocks he leapt in the dark, thinking to reach the shore, and was buried beneath the boat; he was the only person lost in all that dreadful disaster. The fact is this: We kept mustering; every hour fresh parties from St. Mathews and distant parts of the coast arrived; and thus we continued until we were all present except the barge's crew, with Captain Wilkinson the purser and master, they were all in the barge and we did not feel in much trouble of mind for the captain and purser, not one of us lost our dinner through grieving for them. but as for the master, Mr. Weymouth, he was lamented by all the ships company. He was a sailor and a sailor's friend. Our lost shipmates being nearly all found we began to think how good the Lord must be to spare so many sinners.

January 25, 1804. Miss Burke gave us a recommendation and a letter to present to any of the Sister's we might fall in with, and on the 25th day of January 1804 we were mustered, served shoes etc., to those who stood need, and in the evening we were served four days bread and seven *sols* per day beef money for four days with orders to be ready to march in the morning. Every thing went well with us in this mansion of happiness, but we had to leave it and travel in search of new adventures. Therefore we shall pursue our journey through France. And as nearly as possible give a hint of our various overturns scenes and curious circumstances that we went through before we reached our destined prison.

CHAPTER 7

1804: Prisoners of War

January 26, 1804. On the 26th of January we left Brest under a guard of steel jacket horse soldiers and the good wishes of all round Brest hospital. We had a cart allowed for our baggage etc. It rained all day but we got through the days march very well and at Landernau were put in an old castle and had straw etc. The town's people flocked round us with soup, fried liver etc. to sell, and several with a drop of what most sailors are fond of to warm the cockles of their hearts.

January 27th, 1804. We marched to Landivisian, twelve miles, lodged in a jail, and on the 28th went to Morlaix, fourteen miles. There we were put in the city prison, had soup, beef and potatoes served to us, and could buy a red herring for two *sols*. The prison was the first place we saw the miseries of a French Conscript in Prison, and there was a great number of poor unfortunate souls, lousy, dirty, hungry, and naked, all confined in cells under ground, some singing, others cursing, some begging at the grates, some fiddling, some dancing, others lousing themselves and on the other side card playing, dice etc., dram smuggling from the gaoler.

January 29, 1804. This was the first introduction we had into a city prison or cashot (*cachot*). We were very glad when morning came for us to start from this scene of misery and woe.

Jan. 30th. We left Morlaix for Belle Isle, twenty-two miles. There we found humanity had for some time left that place. We were wet and cold and drove into an old ruinous church with a guard of gendarmes round us. They treated us very uncivil. The least thing they did not like the flat of their sword was used very readily. An old lady of humane feelings sent her servant with Some bread and cheese for us; the gendarmes beat the man and hove his basket with its contents over the bridge and would not suffer any person to give or sell us any thing, but we got along with all those little things pretty well when we consider the different dispositions there always exists amongst 307 men in our situation; we had some that made two or three attempts to persuade others to join them and do great things by force, but we had good informed men amongst us that used by fair reason always to persuade them to consider the place of a prisoner of war, even in England and they would have but little to say, and in this manner we passed over numbers of little obstacles that befell us on our march.

January 31. We left four of our men in the hospital sick in Belle Isle and of the rest of us started for Guimgamp, fifteen miles. Snow fell all the day and our guard could not bear the severity of the cold and heavy roads any better than us; they were the guard of the town we left and had to conduct us to the next town to deliver us up to the mayor etc. They are the same as militia in our country, a composition of all sorts. In this place we had another misfortune befell us that was nearly costing numbers of lives, entirely through neglect and carelessness; when we arrived in this village of Guimgamp we left many of our guard on the way and what we had with us were glad to deliver us up to the mayor so that the towns guard might take charge of us and they take shelter from the severity of the weather. They put us in a large shed, their market house, and the people and children brought us fire wood in abundance. We made a large fire in the place to warm and dry us and our clothing, we being all wet entirely through.

So far all was well; our next difficulty was we wanted some victuals and saw no signs of any preparation for any. However this was soon found accomplished. In the vicinity of the village lived a rich old English gentleman; he had been many years residing in the castle and was a father and friend to all the neighbouring poor people. He kept a number of them constantly in employ on his vast domains and in short he was beloved by all around him. This gentleman heard there was prisoners of war arrived in the village and sent his valet to know what we were and how we came into France. We told him all particulars; he told us we should soon have some nourishment from the castle, and accordingly in a little time a cart came with raw mutton, beef, and pork, bread, potatoes, cabbage, beer and a pail of milk, and wood to make fire to cook with; this was a heavenly gift to us which was on the point to cost a great many lives, as will appear in the sequel. Some of the people in the village furnished us with large cooking pots and in quick time we showed every prospect of killing that that would kill us . . . hunger.

I cannot refrain mentioning this dreadful accident that was making its ravages round us, when fortunately we discovered the rafters of the market house, our prison, all on fire; an outcry was made, and in a few minutes all the whole village was in an uproar; the mayor gave strict orders to the guard that surrounded us to run every man through that offered to rush from the prison, as they had set it on fire says the commandant every prisoner shall perish in the ruins or in their attempt to fly from the flames; this was told us by the interpreter. This was the time to see us poor, unfortunate creatures run round the place, in horror and confusion, nearly suffocated with smoke, and chilled with the barbarous consequences of our commandants orders. We saw nothing but death before us, the fire on one side and the sword on the other; however we were roused from our dreadful apprehensions by a lucky turn of providence. Some of the rafters after the fire took hold of them fell, and the roof being an old rotten concern that part most on fire fell on the floor, which we quickly smothered, and put out all the fire, and the roof being wet assisted us greatly, and through the exertions and activity of some of our men climbing up inside the roof and knocking down the parts on fire, and with the humane manly aid of Sir Charles and his followers on the outside we entirely extinguished the fire. Then you could each face resume a contrary appearance.

We were as we considered ourselves like brands that were snatched from the fire; when all the confusion was over and all things in their usual order we had a visit made us by the commandant and Sir Charles White. We told them every particular, how the fire made its way to the rafters etc. Sir Charles observed to the commandant that it was no wonder, as there was no fireplace, chimney, nor any place for us to cook our victuals, only on the middle of the floor; and poor unfortunate creatures like us almost perished with cold and wet hungry and fatigued were much to be pitied and not to be blamed for what had already happened. He made intercession with the commandant to let us cook outside the house and he himself would be answerable for any thing that might take place time we lay in the place; and he was ready to answer for any one of us that might desert whilst we lay under the charge of the commandant.

At those words the guard was dismissed, and we had our orders to behave like men and show by our actions what we were and to what nation we belonged. Sir Charles smiling says to us in English:

'My brave countrymen, I have done all for you that delicacy according to my present situation will permit, I have humbled myself to the laws of France, and at this moment the state of things are very ticklesome, and we know not our friend from our foe. As we say to ourselves we want no bodyguard for one neighbour is a strict watch over the other; this is the present system of affairs in this country; however I have reason to believe there is not an individual in this quarter that would hurt a dog of mine, from the commandant down to the meanest peasant, and this comfort is all my pride. I have no apprehensions of thieves, murderers, nor that of a bad name; therefore as my word is taken as security for you take care and give no cause of complaint. Let those people see that you are men of principle and scorn the idea of anything unbecoming the character of Britons and men.'

At those last words we gave him three cheers and also our words that we would rather suffer death than bring any trouble on him or his connections. We thanked him gratefully for his good will shown to us, and thus he took his leave and left us all cooking.

Some of the women in the village assisted in cooking, furnished us with dishes, spoons etc., and thank heaven we sat down to a good plentiful meal such as we were much in need of after our evil and good fortune in that place. We had a plentiful supper and plenty left for next day, and after supper we had each man a pint of beer. Mr. White also sent us a wagon load of straw to make us a comfortable bed to rest our wearied limbs.

February 1, 1804. We went to rest early that evening and in the morning were rose by the villagers, some with coffee, others with milk, and some with a little drop of what sailors mostly enquire after when on shore. We had good and hearty food for breakfast and made ready to leave this place that made us twice glad and twice sorry. We were glad on our arrival hearing of Sir Charles's generosity, and glad when the fire was extinguished and Sir Charles was our security, we were sorry when the sentence was pronounced that we should perish either by fire or sword; and sorry when we left this asylum of charity humanity and love. Sir Charles visited us in the morning when we started and gave twenty-five pair of shoes to those most in want; he then took his leave, recommended us to the officer of the guard, and left us. February 1st 1804 we left Guimgamp for Chatelaudren fifteen miles. There we were lodged in a church, had soup and bread served us, with each man a dram of brandy, and plenty of straw at night to sleep in; thus we past the first of February; on the morning we arose early.

February 2. Mustered and marched away for St. Brieuse (St. Brieuc), nineteen miles. There we were lodged in the city prison, there we had salt beef and bread served us with two large buckets of salt beef soup, pretty good. When hunger hovers round he often makes salt, fresh, and bitter or sour, sweet. We left seven of our people sick in the hospital and in the morning we had to encounter a severe snow storm. We also had a fresh guard of foot soldiers and two carts for our baggage. They served us three days bread and seven *sols* per day for beef etc. Then we started again for Lambale (Lamballe), twenty-five miles. There we lodged in the town's hall or the *minsipalitie* as they term it. The mayor ordered the inhabitants of the town to prepare us soup and bread, also to prepare for each man a sheaf of straw etc., with wood to make fire and dry our cloths. This was the good will of the mayor and citizens, for which no doubt but they will have their reward, as not a single charitable deed is left unrewarded by the giver of all good things.

February 4. The next day the 4th we again began our journey and to our disadvantage had to travel twenty-seven miles in rain and a very heavy road, and our guard was not composed of the most humane men in France. They took a dislike to us through some of our men being unable to walk fast enough through the middle of the heavy road; indeed the sergeant of the guard (a Dutchman) said if we did not go faster along he would break his sword cross some of our backs. He also made us keep the middle of the road, and when occasions required any of us to step towards one side without leave he was sure to have a blow from one of their muskets or a sabre across his back. Our officers were with us this day: before this they were always two or three days march before us. However we came up with them this day at the half way house, a village where travellers stop to take refreshment, and the gendarmes exchange their prisoners etc.

Mr. Pridham our first lieutenant, seeing a man named Robert Devine very foot sore and barefoot, Pridham being on horse back dismounted and made Devine mount and ride the rest of the days journey; he himself took willingly to his legs on the rough and heavy road. He said to Lieutenant Leftwidge publicly that he took more pleasure in walking and seeing that poor lame man ride, than he would to ride in a carriage and if it was in his power, there were more men that he saw on the road stood need of a lift. In the whole Pridham gave the officers all a very great hint to follow his example (they being all mounted) but they could not take an English hint (they were in France). However thank the Lord we got through this days trouble as well as many others, and reached Jugon, where we were put in cells under the city prison. Oh, this was a horrid place; the roof and sides of those cells, or caverns, was all dropping from white parts of the rock like salt, and we being all wet and much fatigued, laid down on the few rotten blades of straw that was strewed in the corner. In a little time the gaoler brought us down two vessels full of soup and some black bread but this went down very good. It was warm and we were quite the contrary. We saw no more of any living mortal that night, our iron doors were bolted on us and we were there to fare the best we could. We laid us down like a flock of sheep to keep each other warm and first thing that we heard in the morning was the creaking of the bolts and the rusty hinges that secured our dismal bed room. We had not one glimpse of light could approach us only what was brought by the gaoler; when he came we got a candle and eat our remaining morsel and then a brigadier of the gendarmes came and ordered us all up to muster. We obeyed; if we were wet and cold on entering this place of horror it was the reverse on leaving it for then we were wet and smoking hot, and so weak that we scarcely could walk up the stairs of the prison. However we partly got over this when we had been a little while in the air. We left three men in the hospital, had our rations of bread, and began another days journey towards Broons, twenty-one miles. We got through this days work quite charmingly. The ground being froze and dry made the roads quite good. Our guards were the corresponding gendarmes. They treated us very well and gave us plenty of rest on the road. We saw nothing of our officers this day. They took a different route and went two stages in one day; thus we for the present lost them. We got to Broons and there were put in a large old castle with plenty of clean straw, wood to make fire, and the inhabitants brought us plenty of victuals; God bless them. We were as happy as kings and laid us down quite warm and comfortable. In the morning we had warm soup and bread for breakfast, were counted over by the mayor, had our orders and off we went, fine hard weather best for us to Becherel thirty-two miles. We made this days journey in as good spirits as if it had been only ten miles; we had fine weather, and a good officer and men had the charge of us. They had three wagons that they made keep all the day up with us, and if the captain of the guard saw any man that was any way fatigued he made him mount one of the wagons and ride. Thus we past this days journey, and at night slept in a large barn, with plenty of straw etc. The place being only a village the villagers brought us boiled milk, soup, bread, bacon, and plenty of potatoes for supper; so much for a good officer.

February 6. In the morning we had a plentiful breakfast of boiled milk and bread, with a good share of cold bacon and bread to carry with us and the same good officer and guard had to conduct us to Rennes. We started in good spirits and with four carts we commenced our days work from Becherel towards Montflort (Montfort-sur-Meu), twenty-eight miles. The weather being fine we past through our days journey with pleasure. We halted at the half way village during the celebration of mass and stop in church until divine service was over. Eat a bite had a drink of cider and away we trudged. We reached the town in good time and for the first time were billeted on the inhabitants like soldiers with orders from the mayor to be nourished and lodged, which we really were.

February 7. We rose in the morning like young farmers and with our same guard started for the city of Rennes in Brittany; the weather was a little severe on our first starting but as the sun rose we had more moderate times. This day we had our baggage wagons and every thing in its former order. We past a regiment of horse soldiers on their march towards Brest etc. When we got into the city we had orders to march up to the grand place, or the town's hall. There we were ranked up nearly an hour to be reviewed by the general and commandant, In the interval great numbers of the inhabitants flocked round to see us wild English sailors, and as we stood we took particular notice of two young ladies passing up and down the front of our ranks, looking at us and laughing every few paces they went.

Tho. Steward was in front of me and when those ladies stood looking at us, he says to me, 'Wetherell, if I had that girl in the red dress for what I am suffering as a prisoner I would bear it all and ten times as much for her sake. I think she is the greatest beauty I ever saw.'

He speaking in English had no idea she could understand him; but to both our astonishment she turned round to Steward and smiling says in English, 'Young man, you may wish a good while before you wish to yourself any harm; however I thank you, Sir, for the honour you have done me, and were I left to my own choice you would not be the last of my choice, but my situation is so that I am sent to this place to pass my days in a doleful convent.'

At those words the commandant made his appearance. She bowed her head and mixed in with the crowd; we were left in entire darkness and could not conjecture what she meant nor what nation she was from; Steward said he thought she was Irish and my opinion was that she was the daughter of some English family sent over to France to be confined in a nunnery etc. Thus we formed different ideas of this mysterious stranger. Our former officer and guard left us, and we were put into the city prison amongst every class of people to be found, murderers, thieves, pickpockets, forgers, traitors, deserters, spies, incendiaries, lawyers and tailors composed this lousy herd.

February 8. In this prison we were attacked by their committee in order to make us pay the prison fee, as their custom is to make all prisoners when they first enter pay their entrance to the Captain of the prison as they term the chief of their gang. He is generally the oldest prisoner, if not he is elected by the majority, and all the prisoners are under his control. He makes certain laws and rules which all have to obey. He is very often an eye servant for the gaoler, and it has been common for those sort of characters to remain in large city prisons on their own choice for many years and accumulate large sums of money in this miserable manner. However they demanded our fee and some of our rusty lads told them they would give them their fee over the face and eyes. This being interpreted to their captain he ordered them to retire and not interfere with prisoners of war. We had our soup, beef and bread served out and a bundle of straw for four men. Thus we finished this days adventures. In the morning we had a guard of cuirassiers to take charge of us and started with fine weather for the grand place of city hall and there we stood nearly four hours with our guard around us waiting for the commissary of war and the general of marines, to review us. About 11 o'clock they mustered us, gave orders for our men that were sick or lame to be left in the hospital of Rennes, and to give shoes to those that wanted them. The commissary spoke middling good English; he asked us how we fared on the road and we told him only very indifferently most of the time, and at present we had been standing in the square all the morning and never broke our fast; he said as for the time past there had been no arrangements made for prisoners of war; but this was his present business to see regular allowance and good usage given to all such people; therefore for the future we would be better taken care of; he also said he would give orders for us to halt five days in Rennes until his affairs were settled in regard to our daily routes etc. We also were to have seven *sols* per day paid every morning, a pound and half of bread and soup beef etc. after our day's stage was completed. We also should have a halting day every fifth day and he had given orders for us to be lodged in the *citadella* in barracks so that we might be rested and gain a little strength; for in our situation he thought we wanted some care and nourishment which was already provided for us;

therefore we were going now to the barracks where arrangements were made for us. He then left us and we went down to the *citadella*; were put in good warm rooms, twelve in each room; there was a stove, bedsteads, table and benches, with wooden dishes, a cooking pot and water pail for each room served us by the barrack master; we were also served wood beef potatoes and salt for soup, half a pound of white bread and a pound of brown each man. We went to work first thing to cooking and some to cleaning the room utensils etc. One man from each room was called for blankets and straw. Thus we passed the 9th of February. On the 10th we arose quite like other men, passed this day in the greatest comfort could be. We took five of our shipmates to the hospital sick through fatigue. One of them, Charles Jones, died the third day in the hospital. On the 12th the general visited us in our rooms and said we looked quite comfortable to what we looked the other day.

February 13. On the 13th in the morning we all assembled in the square and had our rations of bread, marching money etc., served us out and an officer of Horse took the command of us; we marched that days journey twenty-three miles to Vitre with the greatest ease, and there we were lodged in soldiers' barracks, treated well, and went to rest quite happy; full bellies and warm beds. On the 14th we made sail for Laval, twenty-five miles; halted at the half way house, went to church, took a relish of bread and cheese with the peasants, washed it down with a good drink of cider, and then completed our days work. In the town of Laval we were lodged in the gaol but had the liberty to go out for any thing we wanted; our regular rations were given us, and straw to sleep on; we all went to our nests and forgot all care, until roused in the morning to pursue our journey, which we did with great spirits.

February 15 We tripped away for the village of Mayenne, nineteen miles. It being a cross country road made it worse to get along; however with the help of a light frost and two wagons, we made our way through like brave old soldiers.

February 16. Arrived at Mayenne, the mayor lodged us in an old church. We had our rations and clean straw, all things were good. Made sail in the morning of the 16th towards the village of Preenpail (Pré-en-Pail), twenty-three miles. The roads were soft and heavy but our kind officer gave us our choice of the best of it and we drove through like lions. Our baggage wagons did not get in till late, being drawn by oxen they travailed slow. In this place we had a larger farmers barn for our dwelling. He being the mayor we lived like little kings on the fat of the land. The large farm kitchen was our sitting and eating room and the barn our sleeping room. We had plenty to eat and drink of the best any man need, with a good fire to sit by and take comfort. In the morning milk and bread for breakfast and away we tramped across the fields to fall into the main road. February 17th we arrived at Alencon (Alençon), distance sixteen miles, about noon, there we were put in the skeleton of an ancient monastery greatly reduced by time and age. However, we like monks and friars took possession.

February 17. Nothing but naked walls with some few traces of former grandeur and magnificence. We traversed its vast winding passages, and galleries and down into the lower cells and caves of this large former Bastille, as it appeared more like a prison than a dwelling for saints, after all our observations regarding the manners of monks and friars with the innocent charge that was placed under their jurisdiction, and such tales as we had heard concerning this class of Christians. Our drum beat to muster and away we all scampered to the gate, were mustered by the Mayor *Comissarie de Marine, General du depot* and *Commandant de Gendarmes, au la ville de Alencon.* We had shoes ordered for those in need of them and a good many got shirts and some jackets and pantaloons. Thus we fared. Here we had our orders to dismiss and go to our dinner. They left us and we took our dinner in comfort, good soup beef and potatoes, looked round a little while then went to rest in a large room half full of clean straw. Thus we past our day and night in the convent of Alencon.

February 18. Next day the 18th we had a great field day or washing day etc., some of us looking at the curiosities of our dwelling and the extensive gardens that surrounded it with a wall twelve or fifteen feet heigh and a deep moat that enclosed the whole structure. The only entrance was by a large gate and draw bridge; however we were made very comfortable. Those of our party inclined to visit the town had liberty to take one of the National Guard and go take a walk where curiosity led them; our rations were very good and plenty of them, brandy, sneak (liquor like whiskey) and beer were to be had for a trifle, but that trifle was very thinly spread; we had to send three of our brave comrades to the hospital. The stoutest and most robust of our men were the first that felt the effects of fatigue and hardships by travelling. We got our things all dry and made ready to start again. Went to our roost at night and rose all ready for action; February 19th we started, with two wagons to carry our lame and baggage. The morning was very severe. Snow fell very heavy and the wind blew keen and strong; however the storm was partly on our backs.

February 19. This day our officer and his men appeared to suffer more from the severity of the storm than we did, as they stopped at every little place of shelter house or barn and took a moments comfort. We overcame this trial and in Sees (Sées) were put in the school house and had our days provisions served us with clean straw and a warm room to rest in; we had the liberty of the village but preferred a warm fire to that pleasure of wandering round a village in the snow. On the following morning we were happy to see fine clear weather; our officer said we had best rest until ten o'clock and by that time the paths would be better for travelling and lighter for us and them: at 10 we started, February 20th from Sees for Verneuse twenty-seven miles, and this day's journey was nothing in our way; the paths were hard and made us trip along like young hunters. We got to Verneuse in good time and lodged in the gaol being the only place in the village convenient to contain us and make us comfortable; we had good hot soup beef and bread and each man a gill of sneak, a good fire and good lodgings all night. We could hire a good bed of the gaoler for three *sols* per night each man. Some of us did and some had not the possibles, nevertheless they had plenty of straw.

February 21. On the 21st in the morn, clear and cold; we left Verneuse and took our rout for Bernay, only seventeen miles; this we completed quite early in the day and got to our destination by 11 a.m. We had billets served by the mayor, a kind old gentleman, and were two or three in each house. The peasants gave us good entertainment and on the following morn, we had good warm milk, soup or whatever was in the house. Waddell Blacklock and me were at the house of the mayor and we lived like horses and drank like mayors. All the disadvantages attended us was that we could not converse with the old mayor, but we made out to get along. Waddell wanted the old man to give him his daughter which made the whole house echo with the roars of the old man, his lady and daughter, and we all laughed seconds. This overture brought another large brown pitcher of the mayor's Rouen beer and with the help of some bread and cheese we saw the bottom of the pitcher and all went to bed pretty well satisfied. We wanted no rocking to sleep. In the morning we arose, took a good breakfast with our host, shook hands with all the family, and met the rest of our comrades in the square.

February 22. On the 22nd we left Bernay for the town Brionne, only twelve miles, but the weather was unpleasant; small rain and sleet fell all the day and made the roads very heavy. We got in by 12 mer. but our baggage never got up until after dark. We were again billeted on the inhabitants and well used. My lot fell in a tavern where our officer of the Guard put up, and there my treatment was very kind. I had plenty to eat of the best and as much as I wanted and more to drink; had a good shirt, waistcoat, pantaloons, shoes and stockings given me and a good bed to sleep on. They took away my wet dirty cloths as I supposed to dry them for me in the morning, but to my astonishment in the morning the servant brought all the old things dry and tied up in a handkerchief and made me understand that I must keep them for a change when I got wet again; that the gentleman of the house gave me the cloths I put on to change with yesterday and as he had not yet rose he left the servant to tell me, and to give me my breakfast and something good to drink before I started from the house, which She really did and gave me a large slice of ham and bread to eat on the journey.

February 23. We all mustered and after fixing our two baggage carts and some of our men comfortable in them that were unable to march we started them off and then we took our leave of this little hospitable place where charity and humanity were their chief rulers and directors; bid them all farewell and left them and on the 23rd we reached another village called Elbeu (Elbeuf), fifteen miles; there we lodged in an old church very comfortable and warm. The peasants soon had plenty for us to eat and drink etc. In the morning they gave us our breakfast and we all started again, this day being the 24th of February, and we reached the famous city of Rouen, fourteen miles. Here we crossed the great floating bridge of Rouen, and passed through the gates and entrenchments that surround this large city. We saw several small sea going vessels laying at the quays on the outside of the walls etc. We were mustered in the grand place and then conducted to the city prison. We were placed in a part of the prison free from any of their own prisoners; and had very good rations served us, considering that a prison is not like being billeted in a small village. We always found large cities the worst for us.

February 24, 25, and 26. On the following day, the 25th, we halted and had a general review by the officers of the War Department, also the Commissary of Marines. They gave shoes and shirts to some of our men, and the military physician gave orders for each man to have a pint of wine allowed per day to strengthen them and give them courage to proceed on their wearisome journey; this was all quite acceptable to us. We were sent to our room again and in a short time had our wine and some good veal soup etc., plenty of good meat and vegetables, white bread etc., served us. We sent three men to the hospital; and during our stay here several gentlemen came to visit us, all people that had correspondence in England or had lived there. They all spoke English and some of them most likely were English. They gave us two *louis d'ors* to drink their healths and also informed us that our officers had left Rouen that morning we arrived. Their orders were for Virdun (Verdun) and ours were for Givet. They told us to be of good courage and maintain the character we already bore and we would be well used in France, and our confinement would not be long for they expected daily to hear of the two nations coming to an agreement and settle all their disputes. Then blessed peace will restore you all to your homes and commerce flourish between the two contending powers. Then all the powers of Europe may sheath their swords and rest in peace free from the alarms of war.

They took leave of us and bid us all good night. We all gave them our sincere thanks, made our obedience, and parted. At the close of the evening we were mustered by a fresh officer of the guard; they were Foot soldiers the 50th regiment, mostly Dutch, and ugly tempered serpents they proved to us before we got clear of them in Amiens.

We left on the 26th and took our rout from Rouen to Cailly, fifteen miles, fine hard frosty weather. Our Dutch guard was no ways bashful to make use of their sabre or the butt of their musket when any of us gave them the least cause of offence, and the first day we could not leave the middle of the road without leave from the sergeant etc. Lucky for us we had several of our crew that spoke Dutch, and some few spoke French and when we arrived in Cailly we told our officer that the *commissarie de marine* in Rouen informed us that we should be treated well during our march; and not be beat and kicked about in the manner his men had used us that day, beating us with the swords and muskets for the least offence and that we had orders from his Excellence the Commissary that if we had any cause of complaint we were instantly to let him know and he would see us justified and treated like men; he also gave us his address how to write to him in Rouen etc. This was all past in the presence of the Mayor of Cailly. We were then put in the gaol, had our days provisions served and a good fire to sit by; in the evening our officer and the mayor paid us a visit; they looked at our bread and then at the place we had to sleep in. They ordered us some more clean straw and plenty of wood to keep a good fire etc. The mayor asked for some one that spoke French, and Robert Taylor a Guernsey man came to him. The two officers told Taylor that they had given strict orders to the guard not to ill use any of us again; if they did by complaining to the commanding officer we should have redress. We thanked them and told them (by our interpreter) we only wanted to be used as men and prisoners of war by distress, not by any battle or capture, but by shipwreck. We were cast on the coast of France and sought shelter and refuge in Brest, producing Mrs. Burke's letter:

'This, gentlemen, will inform you all particulars.'

They took the letter, looked it over, then stepping a little aside they spoke to each other, looked at the paper, and again had some private discourse etc., then turning round to Taylor the lieutenant of the guard says to him:

'Pray inform your fellow prisoners that they shall enjoy all the comfort that my authority can grant to you all. I give my word that not a soldier under my present command shall give any of you the least cause to complain, and any other favour in my power to grant in reason shall be allowed you while under my direction. You are poor unfortunate men and ought to be treated well; therefore I make you this promise in presence of this gentleman the mayor of the town.'

We thanked him and the mayor and him bid him goodnight and departed. We all sat talking over the whole affair some time and after several old stories washed down with a glass of whiskey we all retired to our rest and passed the night in comfort. On the next morning we had two carts for our baggage and sick but we had no sick just then, and so the officer made the carts go along with us so that if any man pleased he could have a lift on the road.

February 27, 28. We left Cailly on the 27th and marched to Neufchatel, eighteen miles. There we were billeted by the good will of our lieutenant and the commandant of Neufchatel. The city is a complete little place, not much larger than the citadel of Valenciennes, but in this days march and this usage after our journey we felt quite elevated. The inhabitants treated us very kindly, gave us plenty of meat and drink and good beds at night; next morning we had good warm breakfast and then mustered in the square; all present and on the 28th of February we set out for Aumale, seventeen miles. We had heavy rain all the forenoon and quite bad roads being only a cross country road from Neufchatel to Aumale; but like other stormy days we at last got through; came into the village and were distributed amongst the peasants; this was our wish. We soon were placed round good fires had plenty to eat and drink and at night good comfortable lodgings; in this day's march I began to be troubled with a ball that had been lodged in my hip from the time we attempted to cut out the *Revenge* 64 off Brest on the 10th of November 1803. This ball through my continual marching had worked down into my thigh and was becoming daily more troublesome and more so when I got wet, but this day it was worse than before and felt as though a needle was at times running into the flesh; however as our old saying goes, I had to grin and bear it.

March 1. On the following morning, March 1st, after a good night's rest my thigh was far better. We assembled and all present, one sick. We took our wagons along with us; it being only a bad country road and our baggage drawn by oxen they travailed too slow for us and we left them behind waddling along. We soon arrived in Poix, a large country town, and there the court house was our castle. The mayor was very good to us; he sent a drum round informing the inhabitants they must bring in victuals and drink the same as French soldiers on march, which they did and that in abundance; also the farmers brought plenty of straw and blankets. This is the old rules of this town. We had liberty to walk round the town and view the great castles and seats all round the shrubby hills that surround this garden of Amiens as they term it, and so they may for it is a real Eden, and the abode of Christianity.

March 2 and 3. In this garden we were used like their own people; they gave us whatever we desired both to eat and drink, and plenty of covering when we went to rest. Our lieutenant said he was glad to see us so well treated under his command, but in Amiens he was apprehensive that we would not fare so well; however he would use his utmost efforts in our favour with the commandant and general of the city. He also told us he would return from Amiens and another officer take charge of us but he would speak to him in our behalf and do us all the good in his power, which he really did; he wished us all good night and we went to rest. On the morning of the 2nd of March we had breakfast and then fixed our two carts with baggage and four sick men, the weather quite hazy and cold. Away we started helter skelter through thick and thin on the beautiful road to Amiens, distance eighteen miles. On each side of the road was country seats, châteaus, gardens, parks and castles so that this day's march was in the midst of magnificence luxury and splendour; after a little while the sun burst through the haze and made our days journey a real day of recreation as we found something strange every way we turned our eyes. At last we saw the huge steeples and lofty spires of Amiens on the road before us like a forest of trees.

March 3. The close of the evening we found ourselves in the city and the *citadella* was prepared already for us. We were put twelve men in each room and had good barrack fare the same as their own troops, and we could desire no better. We were warm and comfortable, went to rest, and in the other end of the barracks was a regiment of Horse Artillery. They had a guard and answered each other through the night. This was a new thing to us and for some time kept us awake; however we afterwards became familiar with *que vive*. In the morning we arose with the sound of the soldiers trumpets, saw them all ride their horses to water etc. This day the 3rd we were mustered by the Commissary of War and had some shoes, shirts etc. served us, and sorry I am to have to say we sent nine of our men to the hospital, all sick through fatigue and bad usage on the first of our march. This is thirty-six we have left on the road in different hospitals, but we have the hopes to have the most of them join us again on our arrival at our appointed depot; we past the remainder of the day looking at a horrible sight.

In one of the large rooms of the *citadella* this awful torture was that day put in force and to be continued until death put an end to the performance. This was a young man aged twenty-one of a respectable family in the vicinity of Amiens. This unfortunate young man was deeply engaged with a young women in the city and it was his intention to make her his bride; they kept company some length of time and were remarked by many what a sweet loving couple they were; and so it appeared they happened to be at a ball during the carnival and by some means he took a disgust to her. They left the ball and he went to see her home as usual to her father's house; he upbraided her before she parted from some of her female acquaintance, and with inconstancy she made a jest of it and smiling told him not to be jealous. They parted from their companions to go home and on the way he took a knife and ripped her bowels entirely open so that she fell that moment lifeless on the ground with a loud groan, which brought the gendarmes on patrol to the horrid place before he made any offer to shun the police. He then started but was taken and brought to justice, where he confessed the whole horrid transaction. He was tried and sentenced to the inhumane torture we were there the witnesses to behold; as a warning to all young people he was exposed in this public hall.

This young man was laid spread flat on his back on a large table or scaffold with his legs and arms drawn over to the four corners and there secured. Above his breast was a machine like a fork or spear; it had three small sharp prongs and went with a spring. Near his mouth hung a loaf of bread and when hunger compelled him to snatch at the loaf this infernal engine went with springs and would dart deep into his breast; or if he fell into a slumber the watching executioner had to touch a spring that drove the instrument deep again into his breast; and in this manner he suffered five days without eating drinking or sleep; and the severe wounds inflicted in his breast by the spring spear his sufferings were most dreadful. It was on the third day of his torture we saw him and his cries and lamentations were enough to melt the stoutest heart; he prayed them to put an end to his life and not to keep him any longer in torment, but this could not be granted for he was sentenced to die in this horrid manner.

March 4. We shall leave this horrid scene and return to our narrative. We went to our rooms, eat our suppers, and went to bed; all our talk was about the poor man his sweetheart etc., until sleep sent us all to silence. We arose in the morning, eat our mouthful and prepared for our journey; our baggage wagons came, and our new officer and his guard of four men. He was an old gentleman, spoke middling English, had in his younger days been a prisoner in England; he used us very fatherly and his men were all quite familiar with us; they were part of the city guard, all men of families. We took our leave of Amiens, and marched towards Corbre (Corbie), thirteen miles; we soon got through this days journey, were billeted in the village, used well, and on the 5th in the morning, all well, we started again for Albert, distance twelve miles. We were put in a church and had our victuals brought by the inhabitants. We slept well and comfortable and on the 6th in the morning we started for Baumpame (Bapaume), fourteen miles. In this town we were quartered on the gaoler and he wanted to be a little extortionate; he wanted to sell us bread and herrings etc., at his own price but we soon let him know quite the reverse.

March 7. Our officer came in and gave him orders to let any of us into the town to purchase what they might want and also to give us our full allowance of rations and good straw to sleep on; those orders given he left us and we soon had our dinner etc., went to rest, arose in the morning, and after all was ready off we started towards the city of Cambray (Cambrai), twenty miles. A rainy day and the roads very heavy cut us up greatly; some of our men had to stop on the way for the baggage wagon to help them along. We got into the city and were ordered to the *citadella* where we were lodged in the depot of prisoners. We were put twelve men in each room; the barrack master served us provisions and means for cooking them, plenty of firing etc., to dry our wet cloths; good bedding and clean. We were quite comfortable and our wagon came up with the sick and our baggage so that we dried all our wet things. Of the sick five of them went to the hospital; the others came along with us and we nourished them up as well as we were able, put them to bed and in the morning they arose with the rest of us quite smart.

March 9, 10, 11, 12, and *13.* We halted this day and got rested etc., refreshed greatly; next morning the 9th of March we had a fresh guard of the *gendarmes*, a brigadier[3] and six men; we were mustered by the general, commandant, and commissary, of the depot, had shoes given to those that were barefoot etc., we had a cart and being all in readiness, the weather quite fine and dry under foot, off we started for the town of Landrecy, twenty-four miles, which we got through in good time and this evening March the 9th we fared well and we got all safe arrived and billeted by sunset. In Landrecy we fared well and on the following morning marched away for Capelle, twenty-five miles. March 10th all arrived, lodged in a tavern, well used, one man sick, and next morning March 11th we took our rout for Vervins, only fourteen miles, were quartered on the rich farmers round the village, well used and nursed like their own children; we left two on the road sick to wait for the wagon which we generally left

---

3. 'Brigadier' equivalent to a corporal in the British army

in the rear. March the 12th we marched to Marle, thirteen miles, were lodged in a large barn belonging to the mayor, had plenty to eat and drink and clean straw to sleep on. In the morning we had our wagon as usual, put four men in and our little baggage, and on the 13th of March we marched to Roxoy (Rozoy-sur-Serre) twenty-three miles.

March 13. In Roxoy we were all billeted on the farmers, and had plenty of milk, bacon and country fare; we were taken good care of by the old women and as we had some rain through the day they dried our clothes and made us quite comfortable. We had good lodgings and in the morning we had a good breakfast and our officer and his men being ready we put our sick in the wagon and all started again across the country for Rumigny, fourteen miles, fine frosty weather. We soon passed our wagon and left them to follow. On the 14th at 1 o'clock we were in the town, mustered by the mayor in the town gaol by 2 o'clock, had our prison soup and bread not made by the peasants but made of pease etc. Slept in one of the cells of the gaol or as they term it cashot *(cachot)*. So much for the Mayor of Rumigny. Our sick were kept up stairs all night; in the morning we gladly left the mayor and on the 15th of March travelled to Maubert, fifteen miles; we had fine weather, got in early, and were quartered on the inhabitants. They gave us share of such as they had and good warm lodgings at night; they were all very poor.

March 19. On the 16th we went to Rocroy, twelve miles, were put in the gaols of the city, and served gaol allowance. Our wagon came up with our sick etc., and we took care of them that night, and on the 17th we halted and sent seven of our men to the hospital. We were mustered by the commandant and he gave orders if any of us wanted any thing in the town we must apply to the brigadier and he would send a *gendarme* with us. This was something new; however this was all well; we knew they would be more strict as we drew near our respective depot. On the 18th we went to Fumay, fourteen miles, lodged in gaol and on that evil day as I may say the 19th of March we arrived at the last halting place for the greatest part of our young and brave ship's crew, when we came in sight of Charlemont, Mount d'Or and Givet prison; our hearts rejoiced to think we had at last through fatigue and many curious turns, arrived at our place of destination; our guard told us which was to be our habitation on the borders of the river.

As we drew near the gates we saw the river that passes the walls of the prison: the River Meuse; we also saw the two towns of Givet on each side of the river and the strong walls, draw bridges etc., that surround this place of captivity situated in the valley of death. In time we came to the gates of the prison and were placed sixteen in a room and when we got inside that was like a new life to us to see so many of our countrymen flocking round us; the day had been rainy and we were wet and cold but our countrymen soon found means to change our cloths and make us quite comfortable. Some brought us soup, some beef, some bread, and others brought a little drop of kill grief to drown all sorrow; and what was singular we nearly all found some old acquaintance neighbour or relation; after we had been in the place a little while the word was past to fetch our straw, bedsteads, and blankets, bread, beef, and wood, in short for all that was required in each room; which the old prisoners readily brought in for us. They fixed our rooms and we all went to rest.

Chapter 8
1804-9: Prisoner of the French

March 20, 1804. At daylight we were roused by the gendarmes to empty our tubs, sweep the stairs, and then all hands to muster in the yard, which was done three times a day, morn, noon, and night, by a brigadier and one *gendarme* to each passage which contained eight rooms, and each room sixteen men, so that each brigadier had 128 men in his department. The sick were reported at muster in the morning so that they could be sent to the hospital directly after muster. Bread and rice or beans was served every fourth day: 3 lb. of bread for four days. We also had salt at the same time. Every five days we had wood and one and half *sols* per day each man but we were generally under stoppages for windows, chimney sweeping, or some repairs to the prison; we also had to pay for our bedsteads and blankets cooking pots etc., all out of our *sol* and half per day, that is about three quarters of a cent per day, but we never received the whole, having always half a *sol* and sometimes more stopped daily, so that of our five days pay which amounted to the enormous sum of three pence halfpenny we never received more than two pence halfpenny. We had beef every two days; our rations were half a pound per day, but heads, shins, livers and lights were beef.

March 21-25. We had everything in due season. In the spring we had what we called staggering bob, which might be sucked through a quill; this was served us for beef, and they called it veal. And in the autumn they gave us mutton, but it had the misfortune to die without the knife of the contractor or butcher and was taken off with the rot. Then it fell luckily to our lot to have a whole quarter of mutton sometimes to each mess and sometimes the sheep were like the bullocks, for we have positively known a bullock to be killed for the prisoners that has had four heads and sixteen legs or shin's and half a dozen livers and sometimes more lights and this was all served as beef. If we made any complaint to the commandant concerning our beef he would thrash away amongst us with his cane and tell us he would make us glad to eat our own d——. Thus the commandant butcher and baker were all in partnerships with their yearly contracts for supplying the prison with provisions. However, some of us made a struggle through all the various overturns we were compelled to endure, confined in a prison like us ten year and four months.

However, as we had got something over the fatigue of our winter's march and become habituated to the rules of the prison we became lost for want of some exercise or for something that might employ part of our solitary time and keep us from repining at our unfortunate fate. I therefore on the 26th of March 1804 got some paper pens and ink and sat down on the foot of my bed with an intention to write something on our travails through France and our long captivity, our release from prison etc.

January 1805. This year we live in hopes of some means being taken by our country to either make peace or an exchange of prisoners. The past year has proved a fatal one to numbers of our brave comrades. Out of our ships crew we have buried fifty-seven men from the 19th of March to the last of December 1804, and other ships have suffered in proportion, so that the number of deaths in the prison last year altogether were eight hundred and thirteen souls, of the prison putrid fever; this malignant disease was considered to arise from cold, and wet sleeping by night, want and ill usage then all at once arriving at the depot, their daily exercise ceasing, they remain inactive with little or no good nourishment, lay a great part of the time in bed in order to shun the severity of the cold weather and drive away hunger and melancholy thoughts with sleep, and so quickly after long marches the most of our young robust men were the first that fell victims to the prevailing disease. When first attacked they were taken with pain in their back, head and side, then a numbness all through their limbs; from that to chills and fever which deprived them of their intellects and hurried them off instantly. Givet hospital being the military hospital for the depot on the frontiers of France and the Netherlands, we had a great many French troops in the hospital amongst our people and they suffered more than our people for all those who had any wounds or sores were sure to putrefy and hurry them off immediately after the mortification set in; this was instant death. The infection was attended with a nauseous smell from the wounds even while living, which in spite of all the means used by the most able physicians in France, such as fumigation etc., burning juniper berries and all kinds of strong ingredients, appeared entirely impossible to keep away the bad and infectious smell that was all through this extensive building. The General doctor from Paris gave orders to have an air hole cut through the wall under each bed to try if the fresh air would be any service, but it appeared that every endeavour was fruitless until about the 15th of January 1805, a heavy frost set in and the cold and keenness of the frost gained the upper hand of the disease and every day the cases were less, and the deaths decreased rapidly; so that in the course of about twenty days the sickness had quite abated, and we all that were spared began to have quite a different appearance. That doleful melancholy low spirited countenance, that doleful momently expected theirs would be the next call began to leave our habitations, and hope, the prisoners only comfort, again returned and animated our drooping hearts, with healing balm. In the month of February our prison was quite free from the disease and we began to take more exercise in the yard etc. In fine we became habituated to the indolent life of a prisoner of war; the frost continued until the month of March. We daily had fresh crews from the various parts of the coast where they had been drove through severe gales in January last so that the depot was kept always nearly two thousand or twenty three hundred strong. So many fresh men joining us caused a great deal of sickness but this was nothing to compare with the putrid fever.

January 1, 1806. This being the first day of the new year we had our flour and mutton served us quite early and the steward, a very good man, Mr. Hewlet, paid us privately twenty-four *sols* each man. This he contrived unknown to any of the French by going into each room privately and paying them, having strict orders not to pay any more money from England to the prisoners; nevertheless he ran the risk. We past a quite comfortable day; I dined with two of my old acquaintance, Leonard Knags of Whitby, and Robson Crosby of Robin hood's bay. We had a pleasant day and at night we had plenty of hot beer and brandy, songs etc.

This month we had some few prisoners arrived from the coast who had been captured by privateers on the Yorkshire coast. They gave all the particulars of Trafalgar, Nelson's death, burial etc. This kept us some time in discourse; we then undertook learning and some of our men that were capable commenced school. They taught navigation arithmetic etc., and what still diverted us on the other hand one of the men lately arrived, James Ruffhead, or Jemmey the fiddler, brought his fiddle with him and undertook to teach us this instrument at three *sols* per week two lessons per day etc. He was a complete hand at his work and fit for the undertaking.

As for my part I devoted part of my time in studying navigation in which I took great delight; and for a change bought a violin for six *francs* and undertook this part of music with old Jemmey; this was all grand employment and made the time pass away unperceived.

By the end of this year the prison was one continual buzzing like a swarm of bees; in every room through the whole prison was from six to ten or twelve scraping cat gut. Every person was inclined to some sort of employment, some making ships for sale; others got work from the people in town, shoe makers, tailors, button makers, and chair bottomers; we also had wooden shoe sole and heel makers, barbers, Jews selling old clothes, watches, books, fiddles etc., and numbers making straw hats; in fact the prison became one entire house of industry. It was a perfect medley for a stranger to behold. You would see a man quite busy at his occupation jump up, take his fiddle, scrape away for some time, then down with it and to work at his book half an hour, then take a walk round the yard, back again, eat a mouthful if he has any left, and down again to his employment. Then he could hammer or stitch away and settle all the affairs of the two contending nations. In this manner we diverted away the time. Health strength and fresh life seemed daily attending us. There was nothing wanting but liberty. We had letters daily from England and sent letters home, after the interpreter reading them to the commandant; they were then sealed and sent to Paris and from thence to the Carteel (Cartel ship) in Morlaix and she ran between that port and Plymouth once per week etc. In the midst of all this learning and bustle I still continued my journal; and devoted two hours every morning in writing.

December 1806. The close of the year drew on us apace. We were all life and spirit, as the negotiations for an exchange of prisoners was in a fair way to be signed between the two countries, The Reverend R. B. Wolfe made sure that he would not be in France six months, nor yet one of us that were prisoners of war. This and what we heard by our letters from England, all gave us fresh hopes of a speedy release. Mr. Mackenzie, the English Minister in Morlaix, wrote to the different prisons informing the whole of us that Morlaix was the port appointed for the Carteels, and we might hold our selves in readiness for marching etc. Such good news as this made us pass a merry Christmas and a happy New Year's day. We bid *adieu* to 1806 and greet the happy approach of the then unknown year 1807.

Mr. Wolfe had made contracts for bread, beef and vegetables which was served us every two days, and the French allowance was stopped as the two ministers had decided that each nation for the future should find their own subjects; that was for England to find us, and France to find her subjects in England. This was a grand change to us, but proved only of a very short duration, as will be shortly related. Every thing was promising our immediate freedom; we made knapsacks, gaiters etc., for the march. Our prison being a barracks built by the Spanish when in possession of the Netherlands was a very extensive building, and on the east end of the building laid the 33rd Regiment of Foot, mostly all Dutch and best part of them conscripts, or as we say young gulpins, and our provisions had to pass their barracks as it came to us. The Dutchmen rose in a mob and said they were determined not any longer to suffer prisoners of war to have the best provisions in the town and leave them all the refuse and that they would not suffer any more to pass their part of the barracks. When the officers of the 33rd informed the general the cause of the men's refusing to do any duty, unless the prisoners lived on the same sort of provisions they did, the general informed them that the British provided for their own subjects; they then made answer that France should find as good rations for her soldiers as England could find in France for her subjects in prison, and they were all of one mind, that they would not mount guard any more around the prison unless they had better provisions or we had the same as them. This news struck the commandant with astonishment. The general gave orders that our provisions must be stopped for a couple of days until he had advice from the Commissary of War in Paris. This was a severe stroke to us after our contracts were all regularity settled and we had become habited to the fresh diet and plenty of it, from our former miserable morsel of the worst that the baker or butcher could contrive which merely kept the vital spark in motion. On the third day the general had his orders from Paris to stop all the arrangements made by the British agent and to serve the prisoners of war their rations as formerly allowed by the French Government until further orders. Mr. Wolfe also had advice from Mr. McKenzie not to serve us any more rations in the name of the British as he had his orders from Paris to leave France in 48 hours or consider himself a prisoner of war; he also said the French would not listen to any reasonable terms; therefore he was sorry to inform his unfortunate countrymen that after trying every way in his power to make some arrangements for an exchange the French were so unreasonable that he could not make any kind of arrangements and therefore he was ordered to leave the country with all speed; his advice to us was nearly as follows.

> Morlaix March 18th 1807
> Enclosed to the Rev. R. B. Wolfe
> *My Dear Countrymen*
> It is with the utmost disappointment that I have to address you in a quite contrary style to what fully had determined last week at this time. However this I can say, that I have made free with all the power put into my charge by our just and wise ministers to settle almost on any terms, with the government of this country for an exchange of prisoners, but all my exertions have prove ineffectual; for instance: the articles we agree on one day, are to be quite contrary the next, so that I am convinced they are determined not to come on any terms of exchange whatever; therefore my advice to you is this, bear your misfortunes a little while longer and no doubt but our wise ministers will work a way for your release. My countrymen, I know your sufferings, and feel for you and give you my word that on my return to the British court I will unfold at large your sufferings, and all treatment, from your tyrannical commandant, and his blood thirsty Dutch guard.
> I am your friend and well wisher
> *Alexander McKenzie Esq*
> Commissary to the British prisoners of war
> detained in France
> N.B. I am to sail in the morning for England on board the brig *Brutus* from Morlaix to Plymouth.
> P.S. keep up your hearts and remain to act as true Britons, *adieu*.

Now, my friend, whoever you are, I shall make free to ask you to stop a moment and reflect: supposing yourself in my place at this moment when Mr. McKenzie's letter was read and the same day our rations were stopped I want to know how you would feel. However I can tell you that for my part I was drove almost to distraction and the truth is this although our French allowance was both small and mean I was several days and did not eat half of my daily pittance, and some took the disappointment to heart so much they were taken sick, went to the hospital and died, such effect had these sad misfortunes on us after all our preparations for returning to our homes. At last hunger compelled us like the dog to return to our old vomit and in a little while we began to do as we did before on the same diet. Mr. Wolfe used his utmost efforts to make us as happy as circumstances would admit. He sent us in our pay privately, and sometimes got liberty from the commandant to send us in flour, which we fried in pancakes, made stir about etc., as bread was prohibited. We began toward the close of the year to renew our old customs of learning music, navigation and various employment.

January 1, 1808. In September the city of Copenhagen was taken by the British and in the fall several vessels that were captured in Copenhagen on their passage to England were drove on the Holland's coast by severity of weather; what was saved of their crews were sent up to Givet. Amongst the prisoners was the much lamented H. Haywood Esq., which we shall give an account of in the following pages. They kept us in motion some daily arriving to join us, so that we daily had some fresh news which kept us busy settling the affairs of the nation, and daily making an exchange. At last Christmas stepped in amongst us and finished 1807.

We had nothing worth notice the fore part of this year. Our agent Mr. Wolfe helped us along; he was much respected by the general and commandant, and any thing he wanted in reason to do for us was done without being noticed by them. He employed our shoemakers that were amongst us to mend and make shoes for all that were in want of them; he made interest with them to gain permission for one man from each room to go to market in town once per week, and also for the *gendarmes* to take liberty men out on their own risk, that was if any deserted from the gendarmes while under his charge the *gendarmes* must be responsible for them and the rest of the prisoners liberty be stopped. This was a trust of honour which amongst us was held sacred and was never once violated, as the liberty of us all depended on it. The aged and cripples had their permission to walk around the ramparts of the two towns, Mount d'Or., etc. Those indulgences with what little help we received weekly through the various stratagems of Mr. Wolfe and his clerk William Mortleman made our time, even on the pitiful morsel allowed by the French for our bare existence, as lightsome and as cheerful as if we had never known what it was to see better days, Thus our time slid away in our various branches of learning and employments. Harvest took its round in our neighbourhood and we being situated in the very midst of the *department des Ardennes* became almost farmers.

I have mentioned before concerning our market every morning at the gates of our prison; this market was mostly kept by the country people. We made use of a great many potatoes apples pears etc., which they furnished us with very low. We could purchase a panier of good potatoes containing a bushel for fifteen *sols* and sometimes less, that is from seven to eight cents per bushel; this was our staff of life. Amongst the peasantry that attended our market were several blooming girls and they were very free with us. They took delight in learning words in English, and in fact several became constant companions, and in the whole I may say lovers. Amongst those young women was a farmers daughter named Rose, a blooming girl, and on her Mr. H. Haywood Esquire, Master's Mate of H.B.M. ship *Alfred* 74, turned his eye (he having the command of one of the Danish ships captured at Copenhagen, on his passage from thence to England in the fall of last year 1807 had the misfortune with numbers more to be drove on the Holland's coast and there made prisoner was sent to Givet, which proved an unfortunate land fall to him and Mr. Gale). Mr. Haywood spoke the French tolerable well and was young. Mr. Gale was a midshipman young like himself. Those two young officers had the liberty to go out under the care of a *gendarme* to take their recreation round Mount d'Or, the ramparts, towns, etc. However in the morning previous to their going on liberty their girls informed them that they were to have a great harvest supper and ball in their little village of Ransend and they were desirous to have the two young men amongst them. On those words Haywood made answer to Gale that if he was alive he would visit Ransend that evening and told his Rose at parting that she might look for him that evening if he had life etc. Accordingly after dinner the two unfortunates went to the town attended by their *gendarme*, took him to a tavern where they played a game at billiards, then all sat down to a bottle of wine as was customary. The two lovers told their guard to call for what he pleased and with his leave they would take an hour's cruise amongst the girls in Petit Givet, this being a general rule to leave the gendarmes in a tavern and take a turn around the town then return at the appointed time and join the *gendarmes* and return to the prison. The *gendarme* gave them his leave to go and return in time to answer muster. Off they went like other lovers eager to gain the desired haven. They came to the gate called Port Ransend, passed the keeper by leaving a crown or six *francs* in his possession, and then bent their course for Ransend, distance three small miles. I have already mentioned that the aged and cripples had their liberty to walk out of the prison every day and take the fresh air on the ramparts etc. It happened unfortunately for those two unfortunate men that as they crossed the bridge that crosses the river Meuse and divides the two towns of Givet they met with a monster partly in humane shape and part of him made by the hands of man like the Gods of Nebuchadnezzar of wood and iron: and this brute more to his disgrace was the one selected out by them as their cook and housekeeper; his name was Wilson, a marine formerly of the *La Minerva* Frigate, captured near Cherburg, where he lost his leg, and a pity it was that it had not been his head. However through compassion the officers made him their house servant and steward; kept him well and clothed him and gave him plenty of money. In the whole he was in a grand and a plentiful situation; all they required of him was to clean their boots and shoes, make up their beds, sweep the room and sometimes cook their dinner and his own. He had all the officers' cast off clothes etc., sold his prison rations, and had five *francs* per month from each officer, and there was eight in the room he was entrusted with. Haywood and young Gale meeting Wilson as they passed over the bridge full of mischief and wanting to have some fun with their brother officers, Haywood says to Wilson:

'Peg-leg when you return into the prison inform our messmates that we are going to Ransend to have a night's cruise with our girls and the country people all met in the village to dance.'

'Yes, Sir,' says Wilson, and off they scampered towards the Ransend Gate. Wilson stood looking after them when the *gendarme* that they had left, having some business across the river, came past. He, knowing Wilson, says to him:

'Have you seen your Master?'

'Yes Sir,' says Wilson, 'him and Mr. Gale have gone to the dance in the village. They are now outside of the gate.'

'Then,' says la Marque, the *Gendarme,* 'I will spoil their sport or my sword shall fail.'

He immediately pursued them. He came to the gate or Port Ransend. Old Monsieur la Clare the gate keeper told him they had gone to the village for an hour to see the fair and then would return as they had often done before, so that he might rest contented and they would be back at the time.

'Yes,' says the bloodthirsty savage, 'I will spoil their dancing,' and after them he went.

It happened that our two adventurers a little way outside the gates stopped to look at some men quarrying stone on the side of the hill they intended to pass. La Marque saw them and he made towards them, full of envy and murder in his heart. They no sooner saw him than they ran to meet him, thinking he was going to the village also and they would go all together. Haywood was the first that approached him and in his merry way of talking says to la Marque, 'Come and let us go together and have a little amusement in the village.'

La Marque drew his sword, Haywood made a halt and was in the act of lifting his arm in self defence when La Marque made a desperate stroke at his head with all his might and split his head entirely in two so that he laid dead at his feet, Gale seeing him strike Haywood was in the greatest amazement and ran to the *gendarme* begging for mercy when the bloodthirsty rascal up sword and cut Gale down the right side of his head face and breast. He fell near his partner. The stone cutters from the quarry saw the whole horrid transaction and ran intending to save life if possible, but alas poor Haywood was gone and Gale had some signs of life left yet. The crowd that by this time began to gather took la Marque, disarmed him, and took him a prisoner before the general. They also took Gale and carried him to the hospital where he expired that night, and the dead body of Haywood was conveyed to the dead house and both were buried in one grave on the following morning. Thus fell two as fine promising officers as ever graced the quarter deck of any ship. The murderous villain La Marque was confined some few days, had his sham trial, was acquitted and sent to some other station; thus finished the tragedy of Haywood and Gale. On the following day the news spread round that Peg-leg informed the *gendarme* they were gone to Ransend. We made search for him immediately, all resolutely bent to make an example of him as an informer. But perhaps it happened all for the best. He was gone to town, where the commandant soon heard we wanted the informer Wilson. The commandant sent Wilson up to Charlemont where he was secure from our threatening of vengeance which he most deservedly merited; he was sent to some distant depot where (as we were informed) he died on the road. Thus we were released from this snake in the grass or in other words a serpent that those unfortunate men had taken and nourished in their bosoms until he rose and treacherously took both their lives. This horrid murderous affair cast a melancholy gloom on all around. The country people all cried shame and the towns people made a great murmuring and told the *gendarmes* they were an inhumane set of brutes. The prisoners all prayed they might live to revenge the murder of their two countrymen then they would be satisfied. Sometime near the close of this year 1808 we were reinforced, as we used to say, by a party of our country men prisoners from Arras prison. They brought us the glad tidings that the murderer la Marque when he left Givet went to Arras and by some means his reason for leaving Givet was made known in Arras. This villain during the time of carnival or masquerade was run through the heart by some one in the character of a French drummer. Thus ended this year of trouble.

January 1, 1809. We welcome the new year in a number of different ways. The greatest part rises in the morning and makes the new year welcome with a bumper of brandy and beer made hot, which they have been gathering perhaps two months back. Every spare *sol* they had was put in the Christmas bag, and that bag could not be drawn upon even on the greatest necessity but was in the charge of the chosen captain or president of the room, and he was to expend it to the best advantage in victuals and drink to be used by all the room mates at Christmas and New Years. And sometimes our bag was so strong we could have two or three friends to dine and pass Christmas or New Years in love and unity. Some again took quite another method. They spent all their spare *sols* in brandy and depended on the old word or as some say the old proverb that was to let tomorrow provide for itself, but when tomorrow came and our bag brought forth its contents I have seen Mr. Tomorrow very glad to sit down and take a taste of the gatherings which the bag had plentifully furnished our table with. Others devoted most part of the day to their various religious duties. We had church twice a day and an able minister to perform divine service.

Our agent was very diligent and used every means to make us comfortable in regard to what was under his jurisdiction, that is to say what was allowed us by our own nation. This month was very severe and we kept close to our rooms so that there was little or no political business transacted amongst us. Music or learning was the chief employment in cold weather.

In the month of February we had another draught of prisoners from Arras to fill up our prison again, and those poor creatures suffered greatly on their march by cold and stormy weather which caused a great deal of sickness amongst us after they joined the depot; the most part of them were taken down by the fever and ague. At this time I had the good fortune to fall in with Andrew Smith, afterwards my son, brother, and companion. It was a cold rainy day and we had the news of a draft of prisoners being down at the gate. As was natural for us to wish to see them we flocked down to the gate. The rain was pouring down and they poor fellows were turned in amongst us to wait until the rain was done, and then the commandant would place them in the vacant berths amongst us.

February 25, 1809. On their entering the prison yard some found a neighbour or an old shipmate; others found relations and many found townsmen etc. In short they were soon dispersed round the prison to take some refreshment. Some of them were left without any one to take them to their rooms, and amongst them I remarked a little boy appeared quite dejected and trembling with cold; no person took any notice of him. Poor little fellow; I felt for him and went to him, took his little bag and desired him to follow me up to my room. I made him strip and put on some of my dry cloths until his own were dried by the fire. We then gave him some hot soup bread meat etc. After he was a little refreshed I enquired where he belonged and what was his name, what ship etc. He answered me that his name was Andrew Smith of Sunderland taken in the brig *Friends* from Sunderland bound to London. I then enquired his father's name and found him to be the son of George Smith my former benefactor when I was a boy prisoner of war in Valenciennes where he took care of me the same as his own son, George. After the little fellow had related his tale to me my heart was overjoyed to think that I had an opportunity to return the part of a friend and benefactor to the child of him who formerly was to me a father and instructor. Andrew informed me that his father was master of the brig *Friends* and took him along with him with an intent to let him stop a little while with his relations in London; that William Rutherford was married to his sister and was mate of the brig, and on their passage to London they had the misfortune to be taken by a privateer and carried into Boulogne and from there they were sent up to Arras prison. Three weeks after their arrival in Arras his father was taken sick and died and left him with his brother-in-law Rutherford. It happened shortly after, there was an order for volunteers to put down their names for Givet. Andrew having heard that his brother Robert was taken and in Givet, went immediately to the bureau and had his name enrolled for Givet; this was his motive, to meet his brother. Having heard the whole of his story and he being quite comfortable my first care was to find out his brother. I knew we had several Smiths in the depot and in a short time I found his brother Robert. This Robert Smith was an interpreter and was a writer in the bureau. This young man considered himself far above any of us; in fact he was a great dandy, and when he heard of his little brother's arrival in Givet it gave him no small mortification. However he came to see him and after hearing the youngster relate his tale, the reason for his coming thus to Givet, the death of his father etc., he turns round to me and asked me if I would take charge of his brother. I then answered him that it was my duty to do all in my power for him, and related to him what his father had done for me etc. 'Well,' says he, 'take care of him and I will put him in your room as you have one vacant berth. You will see that he wants nothing and I will take care you shall lose nothing by him. In my present situation it is not in my power to do for him as you can, therefore I wish you a good night.'

February 26. Employed my time in altering cloths that I could spare for the boy. Robert was very good; he gave the boy his rations along with our allowance of bread, beef etc., and our beef he took care was the best the butcher had in his shop. This was in his power as he had to see the rations served out to the prison and give an account every morning; the number of sick, how many in each room, and how many in Charlemont, in the Cashot etc. March the 1st I put Andrew to school. We had good schools and able teachers in the prison supported by our own country, conducted under the patronage of the Reverend R. B. Wolfe. On the 5th day of April Robert obtained passports for his brother and me to go to town every day, walk the ramparts on Mount d'or, and take the air; only we must attend all musters at the prison. If we did not attend muster we forfeited our liberty.

In the month of May I sent home a will and power to my mother enabling her to draw on the Navy Board for part of my wages, and for her to remit part of the money to me through the hands of Couts and Co. bankers in London and their connexions in Paris, Peregause and Co. This was the channel at that time by which we had a regular correspondence between the two nations. We had daily draughts of money for the prisoners through the same channel, both kings men and merchant men. Such indulgences as those soon made an overturn through-out the whole prison that long lost cheerful countenance began to make its appearance on every side. Plenty and good fortune seemed combined together with full intent to overthrow that tyrant want and reinstate plenty in the midst of us. Mr. Wolfe received a quantity of books from England which were lodged in the schools for the use of the prisoners, so that Givet prison became Givet University. We had letters daily from England, sometimes eighty or ninety; in short our prison was more like some exchange or place of great business than a depot of prisoners of war. Every mail brought some fresh tidings so that we were diverted from day to day with something new.

June 4, 1809. This was a great day amongst us, it was King George's birthday. Old George was very much honoured by our loyal sons of Bacchus calling his name in question with every glass, and that was not a few.

July. We had great rejoicings amongst the French owing to a victory gained over the Austrians at Wagram. What cared we for that?

September. The French squadron returned from the North Sea after destroying the British whale ships; they sent us a fresh supply of prisoners.

October. Robert Smith was detected in his elopement with Madam Gammant, the second commandant's lady, through a letter she sent him from the environs of Antwerp. He was sent in irons to Charlemont and from thence to Bitche, there to lay in cells under ground on bread and water. So much for loving another man's wife; a snake in the grass. Madam Gammant had eloped from her husband in Givet and went down to Antwerp where, as they had planned the trick, Robert was to wait until she had found some means of conveying them to England; then she was to write young R Smith to make the best of his way to her where she lay concealed in the house of a boatman in the neighbourhood of Antwerp, all ready to make sail. The letter she sent was directed to a young apothecary which had been entrusted with their whole contrivance and he was to assist Smith in effecting his escape from the prison and finding him a private conveyance down to Antwerp, where the witch of Endor lay concealed. Madam Gammant was missing; no one had seen her and her husband was almost distracted. He searched every way but all in vain. Several days passed without any tidings of her. Gammant had nearly given her up for lost; sometimes he thought she had drowned herself in the river, at others that she was murdered. In this manner he passed ten or twelve days, while Bob and the Doctor were laughing in their sleeve at him and watching the post for a letter from Madam Gammant. During the interval I was much astonished at Bob. He gave me the most of his cloths saying they would alter for Andrew and he would buy himself some new.

October 25, 1809. It happened this morning as Gammant was turning over the letters in the post office (as was his usual custom selecting out the letters for the prison), he turned over a letter and snatching it up, says, 'This is my wife's hand writing, and if it was not addressed to the Doctor I would swear to it.'

'Well,' says the post master, 'let me open the letter,' which he did and found out the clue to the whole affair.

Gammant stood a little while like a statue and then exclaimed, 'Was there ever such a fiend of hell as this woman, and such an ungrateful monster as this boy that I have been lulling in my bosom until he has stung me to the heart? Oh, cruel young man! Now shall my vengeance fall on both their heads.'

He flew to the bureau. Bob was not there and well it was for him as Gammant was determined to lodge his sword in his bosom. Bob was in town and Mr. Peytavin the first Commandant sent a guard in search of him with order to take him directly up to Charlemount, and keep him from the sight of Gammant. Those orders were obeyed and Gammant was informed where the destroyer of his future happiness was lodged. He made Bob secure and Gammant being somewhat (overwrought) Mr. Peytavin dispatched a brigadier of *gendarmes* with all speed down to Antwerp to (find) my lady and bring her back to Cambray where (she could) be in confinement and clear of Gammant. (Accordingly she was taken brought part of the way and lodged in the *citadella* of Cambray, not to have any liberty from the *citadella* whatsoever and not to have the liberty of writing nor receiving any letters, or having any correspondence by any means. Madam being secured the Doctor was sent to the military depot at Liege to join the army, and poor Bob was condemned to Bitche; a horrid place. On the 1st of November 1809 Robert Smith was marched from Givet in irons. His brother Andrew and me went to see him before he started and as soon as he saw us he burst into a fit of laughter.

'Wetherell,' says Bob, 'you see what a load of trouble that infernal woman has brought on me and herself, but I don't care. When I get to Bitche I will write to the minister of war, and I know he will be my friend and restore me once more to my former station.'

November 1, 1809. Andrew and me took leave of poor Bob. He parted in good spirits; his last request was that for the sake of his poor father I would take care of his brother, which I promised to perform as far as lay in my power.

'Andrew,' says Bob, 'there is no fear of me; my tongue will always stand my best friend. I will write as soon as I reach Bitche. Goodbye. Here we go,' and off he started, poor boy.

The Reverend R. B. Wolfe used every possible means to have him stop in Givet but the commandant and general said it was not prudent as he would only hurt the feelings of Mr. Gammant and some evil consequences might arise through it. Therefore it was right for him to leave Givet. Robert Smith was a favourite of both the general and commandant also of Mr. and Mrs. Wolfe. The general said it was a pity such a smart young lad should be led astray by that wicked deluding monster, but he hoped this would be a warning to him and all other young men never to be led astray by the flattering tongue of woman. Mr. Peytavin the Commandant sent for me and young Andrew. He told Andrew that he would always respect him on account of his brother and any favour that he craved in reason should be granted. He recommended him to Mr. Wolfe and advised him to pay every attention to learning the same as Robert had done, that being the first step towards promotion. Mr. Wolfe being present said he made no doubt that Roberts misfortune would be a caution to him and all young men in the prison never to stray beyond the limits of reason, nor like the snake in the fable rise and sting their best friend and benefactor in the heart. They also said to me they hoped I would take care of the young boy and instruct him in the paths of virtue etc. Mr. Peytavin told us we should continue our liberty the same as when Robert was with us and as for me they frequently needed my assistance in the bureau and he would speak to Mr. Gammant so that I might attend the bureau.

CHAPTER 9

1810: Napoleon Passes By

With the assistance of feast days rejoicings carnivals and such like pastimes we found Christmas calling out for us to prepare for the approach of another year, which according to the predictions of the learned philosophers in France, is to be a year of great overturns in Europe. And My prayers were that the greatest overturn we experience might be to turn from France over to England.

This year commences rather, rather gloomy. Our first salute was the death of General Moore and the whole account of his retreat down to Corunna. This we learnt by letters from British State prisoners in Verdun, etc. We also learnt by the bulletin the surrender of Seville in Spain to the arms of France. As we have past so many years in this great university and been constantly in the practice of study, we have become great politicians and pay great attention to the Various revolutions and overturns in Europe. We are like some of the old barbers or tavern keepers in England that can give all the particulars of two contending armies or fleets with more punctuality than those who had been eye witness to the very subject of the present discourse, which every one may readily prove while waiting his turn on a barber's shop. We were as most men that have that patriotic spirit kindled in their heart would be; and as all men ought to be, sorry to hear any tidings that were contrary to our wishes, particularly any thing in favour of France; but on the reverse then we were somewhat elevated, although we had to keep our ideas confined within our own district or our own class of people that could think much and say but little.

January 12, 1810. Peter Borden or Pierre Badeau, formerly a clerk to Pereguan, banker in Paris, having by some means offended some of Clarke's[1] tools in Paris, was arrested and hurried off to the depot of prisoners of war as a state prisoner. After laying amongst us a little while he made friends with the minister of police to recommend him to the commandant and general in Givet, where he soon was made an interpreter to the depot in the place of Robert Smith. He was then appointed to the interpreters room, which made up our former complement of four. That was William Aplen interpreter, Pierre Badeau interpreter, Andrew Smith and John P. Wetherell interpreter and nurse in the hospital as I afterwards was made

In February I went by the request of the *Commissarie* General Purnier (Fournier) a *Provender Pour 1. Armie du Nord*. He lived in town and I only had one horse to take care of and attend the distributions of grain, hay, straw etc., to the horse soldiers. My pay was twenty-five *francs* per month and twenty-five *francs* for my prison rations which made me quite rich. In this month we had the account of Rome being annexed to France.

In March that dreadful malady the putrid fever made its appearance again in the Hospital, it being at this time full of wounded soldiers from the armies in Germany and Spain; made it very alarming. Richard Baker nurse in the hospital broke his leg and near all the French nurses died of the prevailing disorder.

In April the two Irish recruiting captains made their visit to our depot. Captain Devrause (Devereux) and Captain Mackay, to enter volunteers from the prison in order to form two battalions or brigades; the prison gates were hove open and a great number enlisted under their banners. Every one was taken that said he was an Irishman, Dutchman, Swede, Dane, Prussian or any nation, only not to say openly they were English.

In May Sergeant Hatton committed his treacherous information. This inhumane monster was formerly a sergeant in the 13th British Light Dragoons and on General Moore's retreat through Spain this fellow being an out picket, deserted his post,

---

1. The Duke of Feltre, Napoleon's Minister of War.

and like a traitor to his country went over and delivered himself, horse, arms and accoutrement up to the French advance guard. He was taken to the French general and desired to give his reason for deserting his colours. His answer was that his desire was to serve under the banners of Napoleon, and this was his plan to effect his long intended design. Hatton having revealed his mind to the French general was disarmed and that night kept in confinement. On the following day my brave Hatton was conducted to the general's tent where he received twenty-five crowns, the price of his horse and accoutrements, and this unexpected news was related to him by the interpreter, that he was to consider himself a prisoner of war, oh, shocking, since he as an officer on the British Army had betrayed the trust he was in charge of and would not stand true to one nation. No man of any understanding would ever trust such a false traitor to be enrolled amongst his brave country men and the safest place for such cowardly traitors was to be kept safe confined in a strong prison where he could not betray his trust again, as he had done, nor deceive any more his companions in war. He was delivered over to a guard of *gendarmes* and marched with other prisoners through Spain into France, and on his march he being a good scholar gained considerable hold of the French language and when he arrived in Givet he passed for a sergeant of the 13th that had been taken on the retreat to Corunna, and he drew the Lloyd's money and every other advantage as an honourable loyal British subject. What a hoax.

As such he passed amongst us and by his false tongue made himself a great many friends in the prison; by this time he was master of the French language. He made interest with the commandant and had in a short time liberty to go out to town every morning to mass etc. He got liberty to keep a canteen in the prison in company with the much to be lamented John Mclagan. He in fact made himself acquainted with every person both in town and the prison, and being a clean, smart soldier in his uniforms the commandant was quite partial to him and granted him many favours. Thus we nourished this snake amongst us.

June. Bonaparte's marriage was celebrated in Paris. On the 8th of June Mr. Peytavin the Commandant and Mr. Wolfe the British Agent sent for me and they requested me to leave the commissary and go to the hospital in order to assist Tho. Stevens attending on the sick. Several of the French and English nurses were dead and the sickness spread such terror through the town and prison that every person was afraid to undertake the unwelcome office of nurse and interpreter. I obeyed the call went and rendered all the assistance in my power.

July. I had a bill from England paid me in Givet of fifteen pound sent by my mother from England and in August another of £30 by Peregause & Co.

September. The sickness was very severe and proved fatal to nearly all the wounded men. Their sores would mortify and hurry them into eternity in four hours. One curious circumstance I wish to mention that took place one night on my middle watch from 12 to 4, as I sat nodding on my seat near the stove in the centre of the ward; my patients at the time were all quite silent, the lamp burning quite dim and every thing was silence when to my astonishment a heavy stroke on my shoulder made me start with a terrific surprise, and looking behind me there stood a huge tall skeleton of a Horse Grenadier.

'Come,' says he to me, 'make no delay but carry me immediately to Paris. I am ordered to bear those private letters to the Emperor.'

With that he tore me from my seat, leapt on my back, hove his long arms round my neck, and with his heels he kicked my shins, hollowing and driving me up to the door of the ward (which we made a practice to lock every night and hide the key). When he got to the door my jockey dismounted and very sternly demanded the key in all haste I then answered him that the key was under my pillow and he must let me go after it. He then quit his hold of my jacket and made me promise to make all possible haste back with the door key. After being released from the ponderous weight and the rough feet and hands of my rider I made no delay in making my escape from his unmerciful grasp. All the while he was bellowing out for me to make haste with the key, or he would be too late to reach Paris that day. I kept answering the fellow all the while that I was coming which he soon found out. I went to the bed where Tho. Stevens and me laid in turns. I shook Tom and told him to look at my jockey standing by the door and he would shortly see some sport; I then went to the fireplace at the upper end of the ward and got my broom which had a brave long stout handle and with this weapon I made bold to advance my horrible ghastly impatient trooper swearing he was out of all patience waiting for the key. He was reaching his hand for the key when I gave him a bounder across the shoulders with my broom stick and made him set up such a dreadful roar that he rose nearly every person in the ward. I followed my blows with all my strength so that my trooper took to his own legs in the place of using mine and made his way back to his bed, and I followed close at his heels dealing out my broom physic in unwelcome portions to the flying horseman roaring out for quarter as he retreated towards his bed; the rest of the patients all rose up in their beds and those that were able came to the scene of action. Tho. Stevens all the while roaring out to the horseman for him to turn round and mount me in all haste and he would help him to mount his horse but my medicine had such effect on the patient that he sought shelter beneath his blankets and hid his face from the naked group of both his own and other nations. Some of his own regiment laughing and shaking him, asking if he wanted another ride to Paris. Thus was finished this secret expedition and all hands returned to their tents to take their repose the remainder of the night. Nothing more was worthy of notice until 9 in the morning when the Doctor came to pass the morning visit; Stevens and me went round with the Doctors as was usual; we passed round until we came to my bold grenadier. 'Well my man,' says the Doctor, 'how do you do this morning?' No answer. A number of patients were all listening to hear the soldiers tale, but he said nothing. 'What is the matter?' says the Doctor, at the same time taking hold of the bed cloths that covered his face, in order to look at him, but the soldier kept them fast over him. At this Stevens and all the spectators burst into laughing. The old doctor looked at me smiling. 'What does all this mean, John, that he is ashamed to show his face?' Stevens in his lively way says, 'Why, Doctor, you must know that the poor man is quite wore out with riding; he had been to Paris last night on express and on his way his unruly horse hove him, and has kicked and bruised him most horribly, so that he was glad to seek refuge under cover in order to save his life, and now he trembles as you see him lest his horse should again repeat his unpleasant dose of broom essence.' The Doctor smiling desired Stevens to unravel this mystery; Stevens then related the whole farce, made the Doctors and all the spectators laugh at the joke; the Doctor then desired us to uncover him, which was no sooner done, than the doctor pronounced him cured. The fever was turned and he was quite feeble, poor fellow, and looked very pitiful; however he recovered hourly after this, and the Doctor used to tell him, that the balsam of broom saved his life. He daily gained strength and when I came to his bed side he would kiss my hand would smile at me and say, 'Oh my good nurse it is to you that I may always pay every respect as a friend and brother; you and you only were the cause of my being as I am at this moment.' In five or six weeks he recovered so fast that he was able to walk on the ramparts and in a short time he left the hospital and went to barracks quite hearty. Whenever he chanced to meet me in Givet we must be sure to have a glass before we parted. In a little while he left Givet to join his regiment in Germany. At parting he gave me a razor and pen knife to keep in memory of him. Poor young man.

October 4, 1810. A day never to be forgot by those who had the hard fate to fall under the horrid feelings we had the misfortune to suffer that day. It had been long in preparation to undermine the prison yard from a stable that was constantly shut up. You must understand that the prison was first built by the Spaniards (at the time they had possession of the Netherlands) for a horse barracks, so that the under storey of the whole building was stables, many of which we converted into canteens and dancing rooms. This stable, where the mouth of our subterraneous passage was, laid under a room we used to call itchy bay and was always kept for the purpose of a room for those who had that filthy disorder to rub in and keep them from the rest of the prison. It was in this room that all those concerned in the plot used to meet; they had a private passage from the chimney down to the stable where they took their regular turns digging in the secret mine and piling their earth all around the stable; this was a laborious task and attended with great risk and secrecy. Those who went down used to strip in the room above, put on an old shirt to work in, and on their signal being given by one always to watch (whilst they were at work) they would instantly repair up to the room, wash and dress, then all disperse. Their work was on the point of finishing; they were through under the yard and had the stones loose that formed the foundation of the wall and faced the bank of the river Meuse; every thing was ready, the night appointed for this intended escape, which was to take place the first night of the new moon: this was also their pass word.

Sergeant Hatton all this time had been listening to their various proposals and intentions. His canteen being close to the secret mine they used to go in there and take a glass or drink of beer and often times meet there to consult each other with their private business etc. This audacious monster on that very day that they had proposed to start at night, and at the very moment they were some of them in the passage moving the last stone, he starts to the commandant and revealed the whole mystery. Mr. Peytavin the Commandant could not believe him but smiling shook his head at Hatton and said this was all pastime etc. Hatton swore it was so. Peytavin went into the prison yard as he was used to do every day and look at the boys dancing and fiddling etc. He walked round and took no notice. When at the fatal spot he stopped short, looked in the window, and there to his astonishment he saw the stable piled nearly full of fresh earth, he walked away, took no notice, but went to the guard house and sent all the guard to the fatal stable. They had just got out of the mine and were putting on their cloths when the *gendarmes* burst in upon them, took fifteen of them to the cashot, and then drove every man to his room to muster. Afterwards locked all the doors until the mine was filled up and made secure. Then the doors were opened and things went on as usual. Two or three days passed over when the fifteen men were sent to Charlemount.

It happened a few days after this some of the men were out on liberty with their brigadier (a fine young man had been prisoner in England and with several more escaped from Plymouth with a beer lighter). The Brigadier, Monsieur la Garde, spoke some English and being in Madam Berrie's *Auberge* drinking with some of his liberty men he chanced to say, when he was in English prison, should any of his prison mates discover his means of escape, the same as that blood thirsty Hatton had done, they would not have let them live to see the light of another day. William Shead was the man in discourse with him and answered him thus, 'Sir, if our people in the prison knew positively that he was the informer, no men in the universe would be more ready to seek revenge on such a vile Monster.'

'Well,' says la Garde, 'let my name never brought in question in Givet on your word and honour.'

'No Sir. May I never see God if I do,' says Bill Shead.

'Then,' says La Garde, 'the truth is that infernal Sergeant Hatton relates every particular circumstance that takes place in the prison daily to the commandant, so I give you timely notice to be ware of him as he is far worse than an assassin that lurketh in the dark and stabs his adversary to the heart when he is least prepared for him. Now, William, I shall feel content since I have warned you all to be ware of that viper. I consider it my duty between God and man to reveal his cursed designs to you, and my advice to you is to put a stop to his career as soon as possible. He is a pest to us as well as to you. If we chance to take a glass with any of you in the prison we are sure to hear of it from the commandant and all through the treachery of that audacious bloody villain. Mind your promise of Secrecy and punish infamy.'

Thus they returned after their afternoons recreation back to the prison in time to answer evenings muster. Shead did not reveal his secret to any of his companions that were in town with him, nor yet to any of his room mates that night, but next day was the day of retribution. This was the 4th day of October 1810. William Shead stood down by the gate with many others looking at the French girls selling their market stuff. In came Sergeant Hatton.

'Well, Sergeant, says Shead, 'have you had any tidings to the commandant this morning?'

'What is that to you?' says the villain.

'Yes, you damn'd informing rascal,' says Bill, 'Look at the poor men on the Mount'.

'I will take care of you when I go out again,' says Hatton. At those words the fire began to kindle.

'What was that you said?' says one.

'He is going to take care of Shead when he goes out,' says another.

'He proves himself an informer,' cries out two or three more.

'Let us pin him and make an example of him' was the general cry through the whole prison. He went to his canteen in haste. This infernal cannibal was no sooner in his cave than the cry of revenge flew through every room in the prison.

This was the alarming moment when uproar rose its horrid head. This monster stood in conscious dread his looks his fears confessed. His partner Mclagan enquired what was the cause of such an uproar round the door for at this time a great multitude had assembled with full determination to have revenge.

'Drag him out' was the cry from every side.

Mclagan went to the door to hear the meaning of this strange mystery where he soon learnt the cause of Hatton's paralytic fit.

'Take him out of this quickly, the infamous bloodthirsty savage. He shall not remain in the same room where I am.'

At the same time Mclagan turned him out to the mercy of a set of men in full determination to have revenge and make an example of him for the first; I must say it was something rather awful to behold. He was no sooner in the yard than Jack shut the door and he was laid prostrate on the ground by a blow from a large stick. Hatton roared out for the guard but this noise was quickly put a stop to with the toe of a man's shoe. Some danced on him, some kicked him, some beat his head with sticks, and some ran knives in him, while another party were busily engaged fixing a rope to the lobby of the passage in order to hang him up, where they dragged him to the place of the intended execution.

All this time the sentinels round the prison turned their backs and smiled at the fun, he being an enemy to them as well as us. Having got him to the scaffold and the rope adjusting to his neck, a Dutch brigadier chanced to come down the yard. He saw the mob and ran to see the cause. At that moment the rope was hauling him off his legs. The old brigadier drew his sword and rushed through the crowd, cut several that did not quickly give him way with his sword, and cut down the informer and hollowed for the guard, who had to obey his orders. They rushed in amongst them sword in hand, rescued the sergeant sore against their own will, drove the men all to their rooms, locked up all the passage doors, and took the mangled body of Hatton to the hospital. Stevens and me were both very glad that he was not put in our Ward No. 3. He was put in No. 1, the only French ward in the hospital; all the other were French and English intermixed. He was entirely covered with blood and wounds and by his dismal groans was not expected to live through the night (which numbers hoped might be the case). The prisoners on liberty were all sent to the prison to wait further orders. The commandant gave orders for Tho. Stevens and John P. Wetherell to remain in the hospital as usual but all others must go to the prison until he wrote to Paris.

On the 5th in the morning we were sorry to hear first thing in the cook house that the informer was not hurt anything like what he appeared to be when first brought to the hospital. After he was washed and changed, he certainly had several cuts and bruises on his head and body, but none of them any ways dangerous. He recovered every day, and on the ninth day of his being in the ward he was able to walk round the hospital yard.

All this time the prison gates were closed, no liberty nor any privilege to buy any thing at the prison gate. The old general of the town was greatly enraged at the prisoners for attempting to chastise such a useful tool as the sergeant had been to him. The commandant was quite the reverse; he was a gentleman of great honour and disdained the man that was guilty of any thing beneath honour. It was on the 20th of October 1810 in the morning we had orders to be in the prison to answer muster at ten in the forenoon. We also learnt that the 33rd regiment had orders to mount guard round the prison and that the *commissarie de marine* was to pass a review of the prisoners. Also the sergeant was to pass through the ranks with a strong guard and point out those he had seen in the fray of the 4th. Tho. Stevens and me went in according to our orders at ten to muster etc. We stood some time in our ranks when the whole regiment of soldiers marched in front of us; all the *gendarmes*, both Horse and Foot, were under arms, four pieces of cannon were planted at the prison gates, and then in came the general, the *commissarie*, commandant, and several officers of distinction, followed by the infernal sergeant and a strong guard of Horse *Gendarmes*, a very grand review. The soldiers were formed in a line fronting us, where they loaded their pieces with ball cartridge, and then the brigadiers called all our names. This done, then began a scene made our blood run chill. That fiend of hell was sent loose and ran the gauntlets through our ranks as he passed up and down the ranks. Every person that he had any kind of dislike to he made a motion to the guard and they were dragged that moment to the cashot. When he came to William Shead he had him taken away. At the same time we all knew Shead never lifted his hand to him. Another young man that he had a dispute with a month before this affair, named Ja. Boatfield, who at the time of the plot being discovered was laid drunk in his room, was taken, and in the whole of the twenty-seven that were dragged away there was only nine that were leaders of the advance line of correction.

After this lottery, as we termed it, was done drawing we were all drove again into our rooms and locked up as before, and in the evening Stevens and me, Mr. Wolfe's servant and Smith the

Jew, with two or three more, had our liberty to return to town and resume our former stations; the hell hound of a sergeant was sent to the hospital on Charlemont to be out of the way of any further danger. The twenty-seven men were sent to the cells on the Mount and on the second day afterwards they held what they called a tribunal, but we called it a court martial. It was a meeting of officers composed of generals, *commissaries*, commandants, and officers of the 33rd and 34th Regiments. This court was called to pass sentence on our poor fellows in confinement—in all forty-two men. They sentenced the fifteen taken in the secret mine to the bullet at Liege during the war and the twenty-seven drawn men to Bitche the same term. When that happy day came, out of the fifteen in slavery at the public works at Liege ony three lived to see the restoration of their liberty; the other twelve all died of grief want and fatigue, and those sent to Bitche fared much the same as in Givet. Hatton was sent away privately to the South of France where he changed his name and passed for some other nation. This we were told afterwards by the *gendarmes* and many times afterwards I have heard the young *gendarmes* say if ever they chanced to meet that notorious rascal he should never make any more mischief either for them or us. Thus we leave Hatton and give a small hint of our noble Irish Brigades as Clarke the *Ministerre de Guerre* used to address them. Their depot was in Landeau (Landau) near the Rhine and being disciplined and formed into two battalions, each fifteen hundred strong, the Emperor was desirous to let them try their courage. The first battalion was sent down to Flushing where they got such kindness shown from their countrymen then landed in the Island that they killed them with their kindness and very few returned back to Landeau to give an account of the kind reception they met with from their countrymen at Flushing. This great disappointment put Clark to his trumps; finding the British had no mercy on his countrymen in Holland he was determined to have satisfaction and prompt them up to take satisfaction of the British in Spain for all their ill treatment in Flushing. Accordingly he joined the remains of the first to the second battalion and called them the battalion of Royal Foreign brigades. They were upwards of two thousand strong, a great number of them English sailors. They were sent to Spain and joined the army under General Messina (Masséna) and at the Battle of Burgos they proved their gallant courage. Those brigades were placed in the centre of the French Army and at the time the two armies met on the field in battle array (those brigades had so contrived their plan that should they have any chance at all they would fly to the British colours, arms and all their whole baggage accoutrements etc., and give themselves up to the mercy of Wellington) the battle began and was for some time disputed by both sides. However the French general thought he saw an opportunity to charge the centre of the British, it appearing to be their weakest point. The orders were given for the French centre to advance, which was composed mostly of Germans, Swiss, Italians and the brigades. They advanced a few paces; the orders were to halt and engage but the brigades in the lieu of halting quickened their steps, left the wings behind and made right up to the British Army. Wellington saw the movement and caused the British to open right and left. In this manner the brigades passed through the centre of Wellington's army, laid down their arms, colours, etc. The centre closed, broke in upon the French broken lines and in this manner gained a complete Victory over the French near the walls of Burgos. At the same time the staff of brigades had recruited a great number more Irish from the different depots of prisoners of war, in Givet, Cambray, Valenciennes, Arras, Longwhy (Longwy), Besancon, Briancon, Bitche, and other small places of confinement, nearly eight hundred strong; numbers of those poor fellows fell into this cursed snare through a desire for their liberty and to follow their brothers, shipmates, townsmen, or their companions that entered on the first enlistment with Deveraus and Captain McKay, two roaring Vinegar hill croppies. After the Battle of Burgos the tidings soon reached Paris and the treacherous conduct of the brigades made their countryman Clarke stamp and curse their treachery. Bonaparte gave orders to break up the brigades and never let the name be found amongst his brave troops to lead them to death and dishonour. Accordingly orders were sent to Landeau to disarm the brigades, take away their uniforms, and leave them only their foraging cap and barrack dress and then disperse them through the different depots of prisoners of war. One draught nearly three hundred were sent to our depot and intermixed amongst the old prisoners which was very near causing very serious consequences. The old prisoners that had remained true to their colours through all our sufferings and hard trials could not bear the sight of men that had taken up arms to fight against their own country, their fathers, brothers, and friends. To be intermixed with treacherous rebels caused constant fighting and disturbance; the chief commandant seeing the cause of such constant uproar amongst the prisoners wrote to the Minister of Marine in Paris concerning them, and in a short time the whole of the brigades from the various depots were all sent to the *citadella* of Cambray and thus we once more regained our old rules and customs, and Givet prison was once more transferred from a place of execution for information; and a nursery for brigades into its old occupation, that of a university of the fine arts, mathematical arts and sciences, modern languages etc. The liberty of the ramparts for the aged and infirm was again renewed, the various sorts of mechanics were again at their work in town. The Reverend R. B. Wolfe paid us Lloyd's money and kings pay as before and we wanted nothing but our liberty to return home to complete our happiness.

On the 1st day of November 1810 as the porter was opening the hospital gate we had the pleasure to see our old friend John Smith the Jew with an invitation for Tho. Stevens and John P Wetherell to attend his christening at 8 that morn. We gloried in the sport, went and had a jovial day at Madam Debausc's tavern; we had Smith baptised, married, and turned from a Jew to a Catholic by ten that morning. He married a fine girl, servant to the Mayor of Givet and a curious christening and wedding this really was.

November 10, 1810. On the tenth of November a messenger passed through Givet and brought information that the Emperor, Maria Louisa, and all their train would sleep in Givet that night, as the Emperor was on express to Paris and left Namur that day at 12 o'clock and would reach Givet by 8 p.m. This unexpected news made Givet all in a bustle preparing the town hall for the unexpected visitors. The prisoners, every soul, were sent immediately to the prison excepting Mr. Wolfe and his family. We all slept that night well guarded from robbers. The cannon on Charlemount were all blown off, the soldiers and *gendarmes* were all under arms, the city guard were all dressed in their best bib and tucker—all the town was in as great a bustle, as they were afterwards in 1814, when the advance guard of Cossacks entered the gates of Petit Givet. Towards evening all was in readiness and under arms waiting to hear the guns at Dinant which were to fire on their passing through Dinant; all this time the rain fell in torrents and had done so several days successively which caused the river to swell very high and run with great violence against the light moored bridge of boats where the royal visitors were intended to pass. At 6 the guns at Namur or rather Dinant were heard and at 8 Charlemount made our castle all tremble and thus continued till nearly nine o'clock when they ceased and we all went to our beds. Next morning we were mustered in our rooms and then all locked up again so to remain until the Emperor had passed the prison at 8 am. The guns on the Mount began again to roar and we kept looking through the windows to see them pass but looked in vain. By and by the packet was that Daniel Owlet the first interpreter with two or three *gendarmes* and the second commandant were running towards the prison. This was true; they came into the yard and called the liberty men, nurses and mechanics. Stevens and me were the first two, then Mark Taylor and several carpenters, William Crown, Samuel Clark, and a number of active young men, Edward Cardiff, Walsh etc., in all we were thirty three. 'That will be enough,' said the commandant. We were mustered and away we went and where we were going no one of us could think. And it would be impossible to relate the different conjectures of those left in the prison; however we soon found what we were wanted for. When we got to the bridge to our astonishment the bridge of boats were all gone and the current ran with such force that the French people could not cross the stream with a boat by any means whatever. They had been striving all the morning in vain, and only one boat had been able to gain Grand Givet; the others were drove some distance down the river before the foaming current. In the boat that got across was one of the imperial officers with a message to the general and commandant requesting them to send to the prison and fetch some English seamen and they would find a way to cross the river in a short time, and that he was not in the least afraid to trust his life in the hands of British mariners. This was related to us by the commandant and to work we went; got two of their largest flat boats; in one we coiled nearly three hundred fathoms of small line, and four men to assist with rakes; in the second boat we put eight men with rakes and two to steer or attend the boat. We then made the boat with the lines in her fast to the stern of the other boat, towed them up the side of the river some distance, then let them make the best of their way across. This was the time that those large wooden rakes were dragged through the water of the Meuse and over they went nearly at the landing of little Givet bridge where lay all ready a large hawser kept on the purpose of crossing the river in the time of ice. This they made fast to the small rope, the end of which was made fast to a tree in Grand Givet. They made the other end of the large cable fast to the capstan in Petit Givet, then took the most of the hawser or cable in the two boats, hauled on the small line, and when nearly on the other side made the end of the cable fast to the line and let the people on the shore haul the end on shore and make it fast to a tree and heave it tight with the capstan in little Givet. Thus in fifty minutes we effected the means of a safe conveyance across a stream 327 yards wide running from eight to ten miles per hour. When our cable was hove tight by the capstan in Petit Givet and found all secure our next care was to prepare a vessel to convey the carriages, horses, and all the imperial train across the river. When the bridge gave way on the night before some of the large flat bottom boats drove on the shore on each side of the river. They were very large and the very vessel we wanted. We took one of those boats (they being square) and we got a large block and made fast to one corner of the boat, then placed the cable in the block and by using a little exertion the boat crossed the stream and gained the opposite shore amidst the shouts and acclamations of the numerous beholders. We then transported two heavy carriages and eight horses also a number of soldiers across without any trouble, landed them in Grand Givet with another cheering match. Our next freight was the Emperor, wife, and all the nobility, which we transported across in a short time all safe. Our next voyage was the heaviest cargo that was the imperial travelling carriage where they slept and eat their victuals.

After we got over to Grand Givet we had a misfortune happened. One of our men, Edward Cardiff Walsh, in landing the Emperor's carriage, had his arm through the wheel lifting it on the side of the boat when the crowd on shore dragged the carriage with such force that the wheel broke his arm. He was sent to the hospital with all speed and orders from the Emperor not to let him want any thing. We transported the whole train across the Meuse by noon that day to the satisfaction of all beholders. We were then all called to give in our names to the Prince de Neuf Château (Neuchâtel) which we did. The Emperor then told us that we should all be sent home to our native country after he arrived in Paris and could make proper arrangements; we should have clothing and other presents to make us comfortable on the road; he also recommended us to the general and commandant. His carriage being ready he went to Colonel Flayel's house, stood godfather to his son, and then took his leave of all the officers and quality, entered his carriage amidst the shouts of the spectators and the constant roar of cannon, music, bells etc., and off they scampered helter skelter for Paris. As they passed the prison the prisoners made their obedience to him. He took his hat under his arm, bowed his head to them, wove his hand and disappeared. I shall leave them on the road to Paris and return to our own affairs. We all stopped at Monsieur Barrett's to wash down our future prospects of liberty and our return home with a drop of Cognac brandy. I shall now take time to relate a little singular joke that took place in the boat at the time we were transporting the Emperor across the river.

We all had been a little free with the bottle that passed round plentifully. The Emperor and Prince of New Castle (Neuchâtel) were laughing at the droll expressions some of our men made use of. Some wanted to know which was Boney, others said his wife was a fine lady etc. A young man named Tho. Thompson seeing the Emperor present his snuff box to some of the nobles that were in discourse with him.

'Damn me,' says Thompson, 'but I should like to have a pinch out of the Emperor's box.'

Bonaparte smiling said, 'Yes my man, you shall with pleasure.'

He then presented the box to Thompson. The youth seemed dashed when he found the Emperor understood what he said.

'Come my man you need not be the least alarmed. Perhaps you may never have another opportunity to do the like again.'

The Emperor then presented his box to Thompson; he took a pinch made his obedience and went towards the rest of his countrymen.

'Give me a grain,' says one.

'Let me have a snuff,' says another.

'Here,' says the Emperor. 'Take each of you a snuff.'

We then each man took a dust of his mill, made our obedience and to our duty, greatly elevated at the honour conferred on us, to take a pinch of snuff from the hand of an Emperor. My God, this will carry us all safe to heaven; we shall be no longer in need of any support. Such nonsense passed amongst us afterwards when we met over the social bowl, or amongst any of the French people in town. After a few days carousing in town and in the prison we began to think about the promise made us by the Emperor, that in a few days we should have an answer from Paris.

Cardiff Walsh was recovering quite fast in the hospital.

November 20, 1810. Day by day passed away and brought us no tidings from Paris. Many of our men had gone so far as to sell their cooking utensils and every thing they had to spare and bought shoes, gaiters, knapsacks, and other thing necessary for a march, being confident that they were going directly home to England. Many of our townsmen had wrote letters for us to take home to their friends. Yet no answer whatever. We consulted the commandant what was the best means for us to take. He wished to see the general and Mr. Wolfe before he could give us any advice. We also enquired of Colonel Flayel what he thought was the reason we heard nothing from Paris: he said he could allude to nothing only that some very important business must have taken the Emperor's time entirely in attending his private counsellors.

On the 20th November, the commandant informed us we must write a handsome petition to the Emperor, and the general, him, and Colonel Flayel would sign it and forward it to his Excellency *le Duc de Feltre Ministerre de guerre*, and he would lay it before the Emperor and by that means we would have an answer. We had a petition wrote in a very submissive humble manner and it was signed as proposed and sent to Paris and time passed away in expectation of an answer. At last the day came that put an end to our expectations. The general had a letter from the minister of war which was to this effect; he had received the general's letter and our petition which he laid before the Emperor and had for answer that the Emperor had considered it would be a very unwise action to send us to England as it would cause great murmuring amongst our countrymen left in France. It would also cause great discontentment in the prisons in England when the Frenchmen there confined heard the news that thirty British prisoners had been released from prison by the Emperor. He therefore had considered that could not be done but every liberty and favour that could be given to us in France should be granted. We also were to draw a *louis d'or* each man and suit of cloths of a superior quality etc. This was our answer; and this our long looked passport that was to take us down to the water side to embark.

'Oh, oh. Now what must we think of the word of an Emperor? A mere puff of wind!'

I think this was the greatest disappointment I ever met. All the men in the universe could not have made me believe that an Emperor would act so mean, as run back from his word and honour, with as little concern as a tinker, or even, as they say in France, a Savoy, and that thinks no more of his word than the bark of a dog. But when we come to reflect, and consider what man it was that we were placing our confidence in, then we might have looked back a few years to the revolution where he as well as many others swore to do away all crown heads and royalty and make him consul for life. This he grew too large for; his consul robes all grew too small for him, he could not wear them any longer, but it happened that they found a suit of King's robes that just suited Nappey; they put them on him, and he felt quite comfortable, therefore the people said he should wear that suit and still be their ruler until they could muster money enough in Germany and Holland to purchase him a more costly suit for any Emperor. This suit was made and put on him. He liked it well but poor old Josephine could not help him on with his imperial robes; therefore she was discharged with this fault, that she was too far in years and not able to do up his imperial linen. He then went to Vienna in Germany where they heard of a famous laundry maid, named Maria Louisa. He knocked at the Emperor of Germany's door; when the porter asked his business, he said he heard there was a girl within named Maria Louisa, and he wanted to engage her to do up his linen. The old porter told him to wait, and he would inform his master what business he came about. 'Well, be quick, says Nappy. The porter not returning in time, my noble fortune hunter followed him in to the old Germans house, took the laundry maid by force and hurried out of the country destroying all the toll gates that offered to oppose him, making all the stage-coach offices furnish him with coaches free of charge—if not he took them at his will and pleasure. This is the man we were placing confidence in.

Well we are disappointed and must do the best we can to get over it. Numbers were worse situated than me, or even my young messmate Andrew Smith. I had plenty of clothing, books, music, etc. I left the hospital and came back to the bureau where Andrew had been improving his time during my time in the hospital. We began again to live as formerly and devote part of our time to political affairs etc.

Chapter 10

1810-13: The Allies Invade France

December 1810. My inclination led to drawing and music, to which I devoted the greatest part of my time all this winter, by the side of a good stove, which we supported by keeping a canteen in our room, called the interpreters hotel; it being the room where we that were interpreters all lived together. We were six messmates, and a young man named George Critchlow was bar keeper; we got our liquor at the lowest rate, had permission to have our beer from the brewer by the barrel, and we used frequently to share from four to five crowns each man, weekly clear of all our expenses.

January 1811. Very severe frost, the river all frozen over. very little alterations took place amongst us until the middle of March, when Lloyd's coffee house in London contrived the means of assisting the merchant men's crews that were in France by the means of the tonnage money etc., which was all sent over for the prisoners of war in France, and we that belonged to the navy had three *sols* per day from our British wages, paid every ten days; we therefore gave our part of Lloyd's money to the merchant men; and that made them nearly equal to us; this made us all quite comfortable. On the 20th of March 1811, a great day in France, Bonaparte's son was born; Charlemount made the prison all dance with its peals of thunder from its three hundred guns. In April we had the news that all the old men and crippled were to be returned to England by the way of Morlaix; May, the old men and cripples were all granted permission to walk out of the prison round the ramparts etc. Letters and money were daily arriving from England. We devoted great part of our time to music. A number of us formed a society, and bought instruments in order to form a band amongst our selves; we had several of the first performers on different instruments that had been captured in Spain and sent to our depot. The commandant was so good as to give us a large officers' room to practise in. We bought instruments for the musicians from Spain; they took delight in giving us every instruction in their power, so that in a short time we mustered a complete band of twenty-four in number; we made such progress in this delightful amusement that in the course of a few months we could perform some very grand pieces. We made exchange with the French band for their different pieces, we gave them ours, and in the course of a short time could surpass them in their own music. This simple amusement put away many solitary hours throughout the whole prison. We were frequently visited by numbers of the French officers and musicians from different regiments, passing through Givet. Another beautiful manner of employing our time to advantage was sacred music in the church, which was brought to great perfection amongst us; we had an elegant choir of singers, and the Reverend R. B. Wolfe took pleasure in providing the works of several authors such as *Rippon's Collection of Sacred Music*, so that Givet prison was called by the French a repository of arts and sciences.

In this manner the time crept away and in rapid strides this year passed away. We began to think that it was mere folly to think of ever being released; therefore we might make ourselves as happy as our situation would allow, and thus we brought Christmas close to hand before we thought of it. However, we made timely preparations for our yearly feast of hams, brandy, and strong beer; thus we pass our time in captivity, from year to year. We also had some Maltese, and Italians, taken in the English employ up the Mediterranean. Those men performed operas, and plays, for amusement; we also had Free Mason's lodges, Odd Fellow's societies, Orange Clubs, and a number of free and easy meetings; Methodist, and other professors of religion, also had their meetings. The canteens had their days appointed, for singing and music, where we were generally visitors with our band, which caused them to sell great quantities of the liquor. On those days we were frequently visited by the commandant, general, *gendarmes*, and inhabitants of the town, on which days we performed a number of select pieces, such as the battles of Egypt, Prague, Agencourt, a great many choice marches, rondeaus, and waltzes etc., both French, German, English, Prussian, etc. Our depot at last was entirely the chosen place of the gentry from the town when they wanted to take a pleasant afternoon's excursion with visitors from other parts of the country, so that Givet College was no longer a prison but a repository of arts and sciences.

Midst all those various ways we had to kill time, as we used to say. Time was not laying idle; he found means to be killing some of us day by day; Mr. Joseph Williams, a fine young man, one of our ablest scholars in the depot, was called to his silent tomb in the midst of health, and promising abilities. He being a Free Mason, the commandant and officers in town requested him to be buried with all the honour due to Masonry. All the Masons in the prison were present. All the French officers, and townspeople, were also there, and our band led the procession through the town to the hurrying ground, playing the dead march in '*Saul.*' This was what had not been seen before in Givet, but was frequently made use of afterwards both over the French and English Free Masons.

This being the 24th of December, we then returned to the depot and began to look forward to tomorrow (Christmas day). We past our holidays as usual, and welcome the New Year.

January 1812. Principal remarks in Givet depot this year promises us many flattering prospects which all proved only false delusive stories; nevertheless we drove Jack Frost as far from our presence as possible; and in our various amusements, over a good warm stove, past away January, February, and March.

April 1. The boys in the depot were all mustered by Mr. Wolfe, and Jack Jones appointed as boatswain over them: to instruct them in their duty on board of ship. They had three masts, all rigged with yards, and rigging, complete, in the depot, where he taught the boys to strip her, rig her, send yards up and down, bend sails and unbend them. He also taught them how to splice, heave the lead, etc. The masts and rigging were large enough for boys twelve years of age to pass up and down the rattlings, to send the yards up and down. It was large enough for a vessel fifty or sixty tons. This was fine amusement for the boys every Saturday.

April 5. The commandant had orders from Paris to give all the Americans in the depot liberty to enter for the American brig *True Blooded Yankee* laying in Brest. We had a number of Americans that sent their protections to Paris and were released immediately, to join the brig. We also heard of the invasion of Canada by General Hull of Wellington's taking Ciudad Rodrigo (Ciudad Rodrigo) in Spain. On the 13th, 14th, and 15th of April the armies of France passed our depot by forced marches on their march towards Russia. Such a sight as we had never seen before. All the wagons, carts, etc., through all the country they had to pass, were ordered to meet the commissaries at certain appointed stations, in order to transport the troops through the country, without the least delay, and this was the means they took to transport the army to the frontiers in such a short space of time. When a soldier was fatigued, or foot sore, he was put into a carriage and rode; provisions was ready for them at every town, when they arrived, one division in one town, and another division eating in the next; and so they kept on continually marching, day and night. They slept in carriages, taking their regular turns to ride and sleep, eat, and march, by day and night. Such regular order was kept through the whole army.

Our depot being situated on the *grand route de Paris* on the main road from Paris through the Netherlands, to Mayence, where the bridge crosses the Rhine, gave us a fair opportunity to see all the army that passed by day, and hear those that passed by night. On the third day of their passing Mr. Peytavin the Commandant came to the prison with several of the officers and desired us to turn out with our band, and salute the army as they passed, which request we willingly complied with instantly. We assembled at the gates where they passed, and struck up *Bonaparte's March* and made the yard and Charlemount echo with the sound. The French music ceased playing, and we played different national airs, until all the main body of the army was past, and then we gave them the Austrians retreat, and dismissed. Mr. Peytavin and the rest of the officers were very much gratified with our conduct, and performance; and gave five crowns to drink. One of the colonels gave Leversage, the bass drummer, a crown to buy him a set of heads for his drum, and said as he passed out of the gate that he never was more astonished in his life than at that time, to have the pleasure of hearing so many of his own country's favourite airs performed in such grand order and so very correct as had been done by the British seamen that day in his presence. The commandant laughing replied, 'Ah, Monsieur, those are my children.'

We will now leave the army to their commanders and look a while at our own affairs. I shall mention a singular circumstance that took place at our depot. It is already observed that the aged and cripples had liberty to walk out of the prison. One of those cripples named Edward Bonner, a very sober religious little fellow, and a townsman of my own, had unfortunately lost his arm on Board H.B.M Frigate *la Minerva* at the time she was captured under the forts of Cherbourg in 1803. This Bonner was the man, the very little fellow, that deceived all who knew him, having, as was customary, taken a walk to town in the afternoon, and passed the gates that lead to Dinant with an intent (as the gate keeper thought) to take his daily country walk. But Bonner was bent on trying a longer walk than usual. He forgot to return that evening, but bent his course down to Ostend. When the evening muster was called, Bonner was absent. At this time there had been a very heavy spell of rain for some time, so that the river Meuse had rose to a great height, and the current ran with great fury. When Bonner was missing the *gendarmes* said he was drowned in the river; otherwise he would not absent himself from the depot, they were certain. Next day no Bonner; even his bedfellow could not form any idea what was become of him. Bonner was a good Free Mason; he kept his own counsel, and even his most intimate acquaintance were all kept blind in regard to his intentions. Well, days, weeks, and months passed over and not the least tidings of him. In fine, the commandant, general, and Mr. Wolfe all concluded Bonner was drowned, poor little fellow. In a short time we were all the same opinion, and were sure, poor fellow, he was gone—yes, gone.

'What a pity,' says one. 'He was such a clever little fellow.'

'Yes, and such a sober steady man,' says another.

'Ah,' says old Dick Hornsby, I always thought something would happen him. He was so sad and could scarcely smile at any thing he saw or heard; this was a certain forerunner of his death.'

'Well,' says Robin Gray, 'he has gone to heaven by water, and will not be able to ferry himself across the river Styx: only having one arm, so that he will wait there until some of us meet him and help him across the river.'

At last Bonner was forgot: he was drowned and no more thought about. But only listen a while, and you will laugh at the jest. Bonner got into the woods first night he left the depot, and the following day laid in the wood until night, then made the best of his way towards Ostend. He continued this mode of travelling for nine successive nights, and only called at small cottages where he was very singularity directed to the sea coast, close to Ostend. On the tenth day he ventured into Ostend, went down to the port, where he heard some men in a boat speaking English. He watched their motions, and followed them up to a tavern which proved to be kept by a man from Dover.

'Old fellow,' says the landlord (to Bonner), 'where the devil have you sprung from with your one flipper, eh?'

'Well Sir,' Says old Ned, 'I have sprung from Antwerp where we have sold our boat, and I am going over to Deal to buy another, to come over again after the rest of our men, and a large quantity of lace we have bought with the price of our old boat; we sold the old boat to a French merchant that is fitting out a large lugger as a privateer, and wants our boat as a galley, to board vessels and if required to row away.'

This discourse brought the rest of the English men round so that according to Bonner's wishes, they all sat down and joined in company. The bowl passed round and Bonner was soon convinced that he was in the midst of a set of Deal smugglers, and they were to sail at ten the next evening if the coast was clear (that was clear of English cruisers). They offered Bonner a passage over to Deal; this was just the thing his heart was wishing, only he was afraid to ask for his passage, lest they might suspect him to be a prisoner or some imposter: he very humbly thanked them for their kind offer, and called for a bottle.

They passed that night quite jovial, and at an early hour in the morning went to rest; he got a bed in the same house, and next day kept very close quarters; the rest of the smugglers were all employed, settling their various accounts.

Next evening the signal was made that the coast was clear; they settled their accounts with old Walter Jones, the host, embarked, and sailed along the shore; the wind being light they lay under the land all day near Dunkerque; and next night with a smart breeze they all landed safe in St. Margaret's Bay, close to Deal, landed their goods, and made all safe. They all went to Deal, where they had another day's carouse. Bonner then took his leave of them all, returned his sincere thanks for their generous treatment, and parted. Bonner made the best of his way to London, went to Somerset house; in short, he drew his pension, wages, and some prize money. With this he took his seat in the coach for Stamford the place of his birth, where he meant to pass the remainder of his days in comfort. But Bonner, like other birds that have made their escape from a cage, and being overjoyed at his good fortune, and happy release from prison, made a little free with the long wished for Lincolnshire Ale.

He arrived in Stamford, in the middle of the day quite happy; and as he passed my mother's door the old woman was looking out and saw him looking round like a stranger. She says to Julia my sister, 'There is a poor sailor looking for some person. Go and enquire what he wants.'

She went and found he wanted his brother John Bonner; but alas, John was dead, some years before. Mother called him to her, asked him where he came from, he said from French prison.

'Come in,' says the old woman; in he went, and she soon found by his discourse that he was from Givet and was particularity acquainted with me.

He informed her that he left me in good health. Mother then took him to the house formerly occupied by his brother John. It was then a boarding house kept by a Widow Toulson, a particular acquaintance of my mother's; with this woman Bonner took up his quarters, and lived there until I returned from France and met him in Stamford after the overthrow of Bonaparte, and the restoration of the Bourbons, Louis 18th, to the Crown of France. However, in the interval Bonner was not idle; he made love to the widow his landlady, and so far gained her consent to marry, that she would have him, if she could get a line from me, to prove his character in France, and that he was not married in Givet, as She understood numbers were. However, this line they never got, until I was the bearer of it. Nevertheless, they remained faithful to their words, and two days after my return to Stamford, which was the 7th of June 1814, Edward Bonner and Jane Toulson were married, in the Church of All Saints in the Parish of St John, Stamford, Lincolnshire. I gave her to Bonner for better or worse, but she was good.

I shall now leave Bonner alive and happy in England and return back to Givet, where his unfortunate body by this time must be nearly destroyed by fish; he is drowned, gone, and almost quite forgot. In the month of June the orders came to Colonel Flayel the chief engineer, and the general of the town and garrison, to commence the necessary preparations for building a bridge of stone, across the river Meuse at Givet. Those orders were immediately put into operation. The wood for Spiles to lay the foundation of the pillars on was soon conveyed by water down the river from the forest of Ardennes. Stages were made and the machines all made ready for commencement then; the prisoners were called to put down their names to work at the bridge; the rules were to have one shilling per day, and one shilling per night, to work, watch and watch, day and night; this was a real treat to the prisoners. Numbers of them had never before been out on liberty, and this to them was welcome amusement; they were one hundred working men that had not before had liberty, and fifty that had passports; those were interpreters and leaders of the work. There was a number of mechanics employed, besides the labouring men: such as carpenters, masons, blacksmiths, etc. this made entirely a turn over through the whole town and prison. Numbers that had suffered extreme want at different times in the prison felt the good effects of this daily employment, owing to the commandant granting liberty for the men to change with each other daily if they thought fit, only to keep up the complement of 150 constantly at work day and night. The work went on with great success all the remainder of this year. When the winter set in and ice began to make in the river, they had to leave off their works until next Spring. In the papers we have daily bulletins from the Grand Army; in November we heard of the burning of Moscow on the 14th of September, and the close of the year brought daily fresh losses from the army, their sufferings by the severity of the winter, want of provisions, want of rest and nourishment, and worse than all the unmerciful sword and lance of the savage Cossack that harassed their rear, both night and day, sparing none that fell in their way. This was the news, at the close of the year 1812, which we, to speak the truth, were glad in our hearts to hear anything that had the smallest signs of overthrowing Bonaparte, and his numerous army. We said nothing but thought the more. We were all fully convinced that nothing but the overthrow of Bonaparte could ever restore us to our friends and country, once more to enjoy the blessings of sweet liberty, and we again began to enjoy some small hopes that that happy day was not far distant when we should burst the chains of tyranny, and trample his cruel orders under our feet, and he, seeing his bloodthirsty eagle lay gasping, beneath the outstretched paw of the lion, should burst his heart with panting for revenge and leave Europe to enjoy that blessed peace she has been many years longing to enjoy. Thus we passed away our Christmas and New Years, eating, drinking, and wishing the lord to strengthen the arms of bold Alexander.

January 1813. Commenced with a violent snow storm which continued four days. The mails bring the bulletins from the Grand Army, with most dreadful and destructive accounts of their deplorable situation and daily losses by the Cossacks that are constantly harassing the rear and wings of the army. They frequently cut off some hundreds of men and take great part of their baggage and at times both artillery, ammunition, arms, colours, and what was worse of all very often cut off their supplies of provisions. Even the horse soldiers had to march on foot, their horses either dead or unable to proceed any further entirely through want of forage. They eat the bark from the trees when they found any uncovered with snow, but this was nothing amongst Such a numerous train of cavalry, flying artillery, cannon, ammunition wagons, commissary stores and baggage wagons, the greatest part of which fell a prey to the pursuing enemy or died through fatigue and want. And as for the poor men, alas, their situation was too dreadful to be described. They were harassed day and night through deserts, overwhelmed in snow, no shelter to take a small repose; only the canopy of heaven for their covering and a snowy rock to lay their wearied heads, even that was rare to be found. We used to murmur at our hard fate, but how happy and comfortable we were situated to what those unfortunate men were that some few months ago past Givet, in great pomp being fully persuaded they would make an easy conquest of all the Empire of Russia.

Those daily tidings made us often reflect and say to each other how happy would those poor fellows be if they were in our situation or even in the cells of Charlemont. Those reflections caused us to make ourselves quite content and say it was all working for our good, and was the only means by which Bonaparte could be subdued and we all be restored to our Native land. We all were convinced that nothing but the overthrow of the French Army or the destruction of Bonaparte could release us from our threatened imprisonment for life. On the 24th of January we had the account of Bonaparte at the bridge of Vesselovo on the 27th of Nov. 1812. This was another article in our approaching treaty of release. Everything seemed to be in our favour; the British Army were triumphant in Spain and the Prussians under General York deserted Bonaparte and fled to the standard of Alexander. All in our favour. Thus we passed January and February debating on the politics of Europe.

March. We had a letter from Robert Smith directed to me and his brother Andrew in which he informed us that after he had been in Bitche some time he gained the good will of the commandant, the commander of the fortress, so far that he was made the commandant's clerk and in a little while after that he made intercession with the commander, to use his interest with the minister of war so far to as to grant him liberty to marry Madam Gammant; she, through her intended elopement with Robert, having been divorced from Mr. Gammant, was single and at liberty to marry at her own pleasure. The minister of war gained him the grant to marry her and he sent to Cambray for her. She went to Bitche and they were lawfully married. This was the subject of our letter which caused many a laugh both in town and the depot.

March 12. The bridge commenced again with all speed. The prisoners went to work at it the same as the last year; 150 of the prisoners and as many French were employed day and night to complete this great undertaking. William Carter and William Applen returned to Givet again after being two sergeant majors in the brigades. Our depot was kept full with prisoners taken in Spain. Small parties frequently joined us from hospitals and various prisons between the depot and the frontiers of Spain.

William Carter was married to Janet Rankey and young Andrew continued in the bureau and as for my part I worked by turns at the bridge, fine exercise every two days to have a good day's exercise and the same every other night. We were laying up money for a rainy day, or for a hasty turn out of our present habitation. We daily hear of great works going on to the eastward all in our favour. Wellington causes a great deal of whispering, wry faces, thumping tables, and stamping on poor inoffensive boards, accompanied with many a sacred oath, or curse, on the English. Bavaria and several other Austrian kingdoms or princedoms had rebelled against France. Indeed it is plainly seen that enemies are on all sides of France and they are determined to work out our long treated for in vain release from prison.

August 27, 1813. We got the intelligence by some men that had the misfortune to be taken in the same affair regarding the great Battle of Pampelona (Pamplona) in the Pyrenees. It is in this manner we have to keep up our doubting hearts, being fully convinced that nothing but the fall of ambition was of the least benefit to us, and by what we can learn that day is not far distant. Therefore we content ourselves with hearing, seeing, and saying nothing.

In the middle of September we had a very remarkable night while working at the bridge. In the middle of the night we were all covered with a cloud of locusts that fell two inches thick on the stages and all round the bridge. The place where they fell was only four or five hundred yards across, and outside of that bounds they had very few. We found afterwards that they drew towards the lights that we wrought by, as was evidently the case because on the following night the inhabitants made large fires on different parts of the ramparts and they were entirely surrounded with those aerial visitors, which expired the instant they reached the earth. The old people in Givet were of opinion that those strange clouds of aeriel visitors must be the forerunners of some strange armies crossing the river at the same place where they first fell.

October 4, 1813. The news of this day caused great alarm amongst the inhabitants of the town. The orders were for every man from sixteen to sixty that was able to take the field in defence of his own and his country's cause must turn out immediately and march to assist in protecting the frontiers of the Netherlands against the numerous armies of Russia that spread death and desolation as they passed through the different countries where e'er they came and at the present moment were advanced to the banks of the Rhine near Mayence. This was the time to see confusion all through the town. The people were running backward and forward wringing their hands and lamenting at the approaching desolation that was hovering over France. Wives lamenting the loss of their dear husbands, mothers must part with their son's brothers, and every male that was able to carry arms was called to join the *levée* in mass and march with all speed to stop the advance of their invading victorious foes. Ah, what must be our opinions of the state of France at this present moment! Well I will tell you we were all of the opinion that our welcome day of liberty that we had been so many years looking for with the greatest anxiety was very rapidly advancing triumphant.

October 12. All the men that were able to carry arms marched from Givet towards Liege and left the town in a lamentable state. Nothing but a few *gendarmes* and invalids were left in the garrison. On the 1st of November we heard it whispered round in the town that the Russian Army were part of them crossed the Rhine and the French Army was making their retreat into the borders of France as quick as possible where they intended to make a most vigorous resistance and in one grand attack put a stop to the advance clouds of Cossacks that spread horror and desolation where e'er they came. Now, says we, it has many years ago been the word amongst the French to say to us. 'Ah, John, me today, and you tomorrow,' which has every appearance to be very shortly verified, as our tomorrow is on his way from Mayence as fast as he can get his horses to draw his sleigh through rough rugged hills and vallies covered with snow. Towards the middle of November we had more news in our favour: the Confederation of the Rhine were all marching into France, Wellington was on the way to Bayonne, the Austrians were marching towards Strasbourg with all speed. We hear that their advance guard have already entered France by the ways of Strasbourg, Bale and we shall certainly have to desert our dwelling and leave our university where we have devoted many years to study, particularity politics. Something like the nuns in France that kept in continual religious ceremonies much against their own inclination, and like us cut off from all intercourse with the world in general.

I shall give a proof of our expected release shortly which was as follows. We met every afternoon with all our band for the sole purpose of rehearsing and selecting out tunes such as we intended to make use of as we marched through the country, which was afterwards the case, as will be seen in the following pages. Our men that were employed at the bridge had orders to leave off the stone work, and leave the wooden stages to pass and repass the river, or take them away if it was required to destroy the passage of the river.

December 5, 1813. The bulletin of the army was not any longer permitted to be circulated through the country as it only confused and terrified the whole population at large.

December 19. Ah, what a joyful day to us! Daniel Howlett the steward of the depot brought us the glad tidings that we daily were looking for, orders from the *Comissarie de guerre* in Paris, to the general and commandant of the depot, to have all the British prisoners of war in readiness to march in an hour's warning and to divide them into eight divisions one party to march each day and also each man to have a shirt, shoes, and stockings that was some time due them and laid in the magazine. Glorious glorious news! Now, my boys, all hands to work, some making gaiters, bags or knapsacks, some taking their kitchen ware down to the gate to sell or partly give away for a try to buy a little brandy to drink for joy at such good news. Thus all hands were in some way of preparation for marching. All the men that lived in town returned to the depot to be in readiness when the happy tidings reached Givet. We were all mustered in our divisions and numbered as first, second, third, fourth, to the eighth division, and the commandant also made the arrangement so that the officers, such as master's mates, midshipmen, gunners, boatswains, in fine, all the officers and the band, were attached to the last division which consisted of nearly three hundred men. The commandant's reason for this was that he might have the music to play each division through the gates of Givet when they marched away. This we all were quite happy to perform, and so it was afterwards there was no more regular rules observed amongst us. All was bustle and confusion, watching every motion of the *gendarmes*, commandant, etc. Every time any of them passed the gates we expected to hear the orders for the first division to march. Christmas at last made its annual round, but was not respected the same by us as heretofore. Our minds at this critical crisis were engaged entirely on the worldly pleasures we hoped daily to enjoy. However we passed the day quite comfortable and tolerable, peaceable when we consider the unsettled state of the depot.

December 26. In the evening, Daniel Howlett came to the gate and gave orders for the 1st division to be all in readiness to march at 8 o'clock in the morning.

'Now my boys,' says the steward, 'we are drove out of our boarding house at last, and by all appearance the next lodgers here will be Russians as their advance posts are within a few days' march of us. Tomorrow morning the first division are to leave Givet, and I give them my friendly advice, that is (as we all are fully assured of the critical situation France is placed in at the present time), let us be civil and obedient to those that have any command over us and keep still tongues concerning any political affairs. Let all this sudden overturn in the country pass our British tars the same as many squalls and thunder storms have done before; this is the way, my countrymen, for us to be well used and respected like men as we march through the country. Our orders at the present are to march to the city of Blois until further orders. This my brothers, is my friendly and sincere advice to you all.'

We all hands gave him three cheers and thanked him for his kind advice. We were dismissed, and then there was fun, one drinking a glass with his old shipmate before they part, another must pass the last night with his old acquaintance over a good glass of hot stuff. We mustered our musicians and rehearsed over the tunes we had selected for the first division's farewell to Givet. This night was kept up all through the depot. Sleep was partly banished from every eye and every man was watching with anxiety to see the approach of that blessed day we had so many long nights, weeks, months, and years been looking for, that happy morn that was to break the first link of our captive chains and restore to us the blessings of that sweet liberty we had so many years been deprived of and not permitted to enjoy.

At last the gun on Charlemount loudly proclaimed the approach of the great Jubilee day Dec. 27th 1813. At 8 am. the word was 'all the first division to muster all ready.' The gates were hove open and they all formed in a line outside the gates, were all present and in readiness. The band was then desired by the commandant to form in front and play up a march which we readily obeyed. Then the orders were to march and we struck up 'Over the hills and far away.'

December 27, 1813. The first division of British prisoners of war marched from the depot at Givet in France where numbers of them had been confined from ten to eleven years and nearly as many more were left behind never more to return. That morning being St. John's day, when all mustered we were 2,364 prisoners of war. The first division was 250 men, which left us 2,114. However we conducted them outside the gates for nearly a mile, surrounded with a great crowd of the inhabitants. Numbers of them shed tears at parting after so many years acquaintance. Numbers had formed such intimate connections that they were parting with their own children when we took our last farewell of them. For my own part I must say that my feelings were very much hurt when I took my last farewell embrace of Monsieur and Madam Perriot, their son John, and some more intimate friends of mine in town. I say when we parted there was not one of us could avoid shedding tears, and even looking back and waving our hands as long as we were in sight of each other.

Therefore it is my opinion many of my fellow sufferers had the same feeling. We returned back to the depot pretty well done over, between playing our instruments, and tasting a little cognac at times, to moisten our lips and make us play with more life, and we spent the remainder of the day in town, visiting all our most intimate friends and acquaintance. Thus we passed the day. On the 28th the prison was one continual bustle, selling off such articles as were no longer of use to us to the market women and inhabitants of the town. This day several of the French advance guard (on their retreat from Russia) arrived in Givet on their march to Challons, where it is conjectured there will be a dreadful contest, as all the reinforcements in France are to meet at that place of rendezvous. On the 29th of Dec. the second division marched with the same ceremonies as the first had done. They were 250 brave fellows, mostly merchant seamen. Left us 1,864 in the depot. This day several detachments from the Grand Army arrived in Givet, on their march to Challons, and on the 30th the same troops passing in small parties all day. They appeared greatly fatigued.

CHAPTER 11

1813-14: Driven by the Gendarmes

December 31, 1813. The third division left Givet, 250 men, all in great spirits. We paid them the same honour we had done to the other two that went before them. One thing was they had some unwelcome company to march with, the soldiers on their retreat; however they knew perfectly well that such difficulties were all forerunners of a speedy release. We shall let them march all this year, and if all turns out according to our expectations, we shall follow them on the ensuing year. We are now 1,614 men.

January 1, 1814. This day we kept as our last New Year's day in France. We eat, drank, and made ourselves contented and happy. On the 2nd the 4th division, 250 men, marched, 1,364 left. On the 4th the 5th division, 300 men marched, 1,064 left. On the 6th the 6th division, 350 men marched, 714 left. On the 7th the 7th division, 350 men marched, 364 left. And on the 8th we composed the 8th division, 364 men. This was the day I already have mentioned in a former page, when there was such floods of tears shed when we took our last farewell at halfway house. The weather was very stormy all the morning; the roads were very heavy and what made them still worse was the baggage, cannon, artillery, ammunition wagons, and all the Horse belonging to the first division of the Grand Army in front of us, and they cut up the roads to such an excess that it was almost impossible to tramp through the mud and dirt. They were very strict with us and made us walk in the middle of the road with the troops on each side of us. The general in command, an unfeeling tyrant, gave orders to the troops that if any British prisoner should attempt to leave his ranks or go off the road without a guard, such man or men were to be shot as deserters by any French soldier that might fall in with them. In this manner we had to march nineteen days successively. As for my part my fate was not quite so hard as I belonged to the band. The officer that had the command of us was a very humane good man and exceeding fond of music; therefore he took us to his quarters in Humay and had us to play before several of the officers that were attached to the army, and by this means we had a good warm room to sleep in. The rest of our party slept in the cells below, and those cells or cachots were very sorry quarters for our partners to lay down in, more particular as it was the first night, after so many years good warm lodgings and free from any fatigue whatever. But what care we for suffering a little while longer we know by the course of things our sufferings are drawing to a conclusion? We have various proofs that France is in a tottering state. One proof is the orders given by the general: not to let any British prisoner leave his ranks on pain of death (that is to prevent us from deserting to join the Cossacks) and the second proof is that all the army are to encamp on the plains of Challons, which we are in hopes will be the last push. Therefore the harder we are used the sooner our hardships will have an end. When we look round us a moment and consider what a multitude of men and horse has to pass the night in this small village we may be thankful that we have the largest mansion in Humay for our nights lodgings. (That was the gaol.) We played the band most part of the night and our own officers in company with the French passed the night in jovial harmony. On the following morning we all felt a little heavy headed after our nights carousing.

From Givet to Humay was only twelve miles and that short distance harassed some of our men to death as one may say, what through drinking with our friends at leaving Givet, and then with numbers that accompanied us to the half way house, carrying our knapsacks and instruments to ease us on our first day's journey. We had numbers of both old and young, men, women, and children, that thought as hard to part with us as they would have been at parting with their own families. They most of them took care to have a good pocket pistol with them to moisten the day as we trudged along, linked arms, some with their favourite lass, and some with their intimate acquaintance and friends, all splashing through the rugged broken path that was all tore up by the heavy wagons and artillery that passed in front of us. The troops that were on each side of us stared at the scene when we took leave of our friends and well wishers on the road, and at the halfway house; Mr. Perriot and his son John would not part with me until we left the halfway house. Then was the time (as I mentioned before) that manhood forgot itself, and for a little while gave vent to the flowing streams of affection. The tide of affection having overflowed its bounds, the sound of *'bonne voyage'* was heard from every tongue of the parting crowd, when our trumpets sounded march, march, away, and the winding of the road soon hid them from our sight. Then we in a short time resumed our former manhood and to our share of the pleasant long wished for walk on the fertile banks of the river Meuse.

We had several married women in our division. Poor souls, their fate was hard, more particular on the first day, first at leaving their parents, their home and friends, and entering into the world to seek their unknown place of rest perhaps never more to return, and another reason was the season of the year, where they were exposed to all the severities of a severe winter marching in front of a retreating scattered army. Not even the privilege for them to have a cart should they be unable to bear the fatigue of an unknown march, as all the carts and wagons were employed by the army. Nevertheless those true hearted women bore the burthen of the whole journey by the side of their chosen and dearly beloved husbands, through all the difficulties and sufferings we had to experience on our long march, of which I have as near as possible endeavoured to give a small sketch of the names of the towns we lodged in every night, their distance from each other in English miles, our treatment and principal remarks that took place amongst us, from leaving Givet on the 8th of January until we embarked in St. Maloes on the 22nd of May.

From Humay to Givet was twelve miles and those twelve miles nearly took twelve hours to march, halt, drink, and answer muster.

First mustered on the morning at the gates of the depot, second by the general and commandant outside the gates, third muster that day at the halfway house. Fourth in the square at Humay, and the fifth by the gaoler as we passed the gates of his dominions, and the sixth and last that day was in the cells under the prison at 8 o'clock that evening. This made us quite proud to find them so very careful of us. We ought to think ourselves very much honoured by so many great *Dons* speaking to every man and mentioning all our names. However we got liberty at last to lay down our poor wearied limbs on the lock of wet miserable lousy straw.

We that had the good fortune to belong to the band, being twenty-four in number, fared much better than the rest of our brother captives. The captain of the Guard that had the charge of us, being a very humane gentleman and a great lover of music, took us up into his apartment to divert him and a number of officers who he had invited to sup with him. We had plenty of the best to eat and drink and remained in the room all night. This made our situation quite different to that of our fellow prisoners, and on march we used to play on the road. This was pleasant to our people and also to the soldiers of the army. Frequently when the weather was bad and the roads very heavy we struck up the old air of 'begone dull care,' or 'o'er the hills and far away.' Such simple amusement would cheer up many a drooping traveller. Even the poor fatigued soldiers would take fresh courage at the warlike sound of martial music, and frequently would assist in carrying our bass drum. It was an uncommon large one. We got it made just to answer us in Givet when we performed the 'Battle of Egypt' and several other pieces.

On the 9th of January 1814 in the morning our trumpets

summoned us to the gates of the gaol, or town prison, where our roll was called and all found present. The troops had been marching some time before our orders were to march off. When our captain had settled his business we marched away from Humay towards Rocroi, fourteen miles. That was a very cold rainy day and after our night's carousing with little or no rest, we were a little chilly all the forepart of the day. Nevertheless we soon found a certain cure for that disorder which is reasonable to be true—march fourteen miles in the rain with a knapsack on your back; some tolerable heavy and some rendered light by tasting another and another drop of the good old sneek, and some were made quite handy to carry owing to their owners finding it most convenient to put the contents of their knapsacks either in their pockets or convert them into necessary articles for cleaning teeth etc. With this on your back and a crowd of horse soldiers or carriages on each side splashing you with good cool mud up to your knees in rugged, broken clay cut up by the continual passing of the army. At times an officer may pass on horseback; then you are sure to enjoy the pleasure of being christened over again not by the hands of a parson but by the feet of a horse and a shower of mud in your face and eyes. This we found a perfect cure for a drowsy head.

January 9. We got into Rocroi at 3 in the afternoon and were lodged in the prison with a great number of troops that were quartered there, not having room for them in the barracks nor yet in the dwelling houses; all were full. Our men were quite comfortable with the troops; they had plenty of hot soup and a good hot fire as much against the gaoler's will; however the soldiers bore the sway; they neither heeded the gaoler nor his wife. Our commandant took us to the hotel where he lodged and gave us plenty of victuals and drink. We played in the large hall until n at night then went to rest in a large room with plenty of straw and blankets where we slept warm and comfortable until drum beat next morning. Rocroi is a small fortified town on the banks of the Meuse. It has four gates and is surrounded by three walls with entrenchments one overlooking the other. It is not larger than the *citadella* of Valenciennes and is entirely a garrison, no place of any business, only what may arise from soldiers and conscripts. In the morning the drums proclaimed day and soon the whole garrison was one continual noise and hurry, with troops mustering in every direction in order to march towards Mezieres. At 8 a.m our commander gave orders for our trumpets to sound muster, As all the troops were nearly gone. At 9 we marched away.

January 10. A fine hard frosty morning; we left Rocroi and made all sail for the city of Mezieres on the banks of the Meuse opposite Charleville, another strong fortified city, the chief town of the department, and the residence of the Comissarie de Guerre General of the district. Its distance from Rocroi is twenty-five miles. In Mezieres we were quartered in the *citadella*, pretty good considering the quantity of troops that are in the town. On the 11th we reached the village of Launcy, eighteen miles, a foggy damp day, the roads very heavy, and crowded with troops, artillery, and military wagons of all description. This day the general gave orders to the troops that if any British prisoner left his ranks with an intent to go out of the road they should immediately give him *quatre sols;* that was the price of a ball cartridge. When at the half way house we wanted a little snack and a drop to drink but the unfeeling viper gave orders for the soldiers not to let any of us enter beneath the same roof where his highness took shelter. Then we prayed that his shelter might be beneath the sheepskin mantle of an inhumane Cossack up to his middle in snow, compelled to eat snow in order to quench his thirst, which really was the case.

In Launcy we were drove into an old church and the National Guard placed round us with strict orders not to let any of us pass the door, nor let any fire be allowed to enter inside, the sacred abode of night owls, bats, and very possibly robbers and murderers. We had a trifle of pork and bread allowed us, very small. The morsel of pork we eat raw, and then laid us down on a lock of rotten straw, where we very fervently all made observations concerning the cruel disposition of the old general. We then concluded with a heavy prayer not entirely for the general's welfare. We then stuck up our band and played 'dull care.' After that went to sleep like hogs in a pen, one on the top of another, all in good spirits, and on the morrow we turned out smoking like the loaves just from an oven.

January 12. Our trumpets called us to muster and found all present. We marched over the frozen road with great spirits for Rethel, only twelve miles. We had one wagon for our baggage and sick. The roads being hard we kept a head of the chief part of the army. We arrived at noon and were crammed into cells under ground like as many traitors or spies, no straw to lay down, our pillow a rock or a large bone. We had some beef and bread with a little soup served us by the gaoler. We bought a few sheaves of straw from him. He also sold us red herrings at the cheap rate of one hundred per cent prompt. We also could be furnished with a drop of kill grief at the same rate, and when evening came he told us we might have beds up in the debtors prison at one *franc* each man to sleep four in a bed. We laughed at his folly and told him to keep his beds ready for the Rusinas (Russians). They were the next visitors he would have, and most likely would sleep in his house on credit. This seemed to hurt this tender man's feelings; however it was all passed away in jest and we struck up a lively air on the band, out lights and went to rest. We were annoyed much through the night by the drops of water falling from the petrified spindles that hung suspended from the roof of our hospitable mansion. This was only pastime for us; we were certain that a few days longer would terminate our present sufferings. Two days more will take us clear of the army, then we shall be likely to fare a little better. The army has all their orders to assemble round Challons there. Bona, intends to risk a battle with Alexander.

January 13. A cold stormy morning; the snow fell fast; we mustered, all present, and off we tramped to the old favourite tune of 'Over the hills and far away' for the city of Rheims, twenty-seven miles. We had the good fortune to be on the road before the main body of the army; therefore we let no grass grow under our feet. Having the liberty of the road we made good use of it and by 4 in the afternoon we were within the gates of the city. Our guard were all well mounted horsemen and let us hurry as fast as we could. We had two wagons to take up such as were unable to bear the march. In Rheims we were put into a large *cachot* below the ramparts; they took out eight of our men to fetch us soup, which was just the thing that suited us, good soup and bread, quite hot. This greatly refreshed us. Our baggage was late before they got in. The officer of our guard was a very good man; he granted us every favour in his power. The sick that came in the wagons he put up in the gaoler's room where they had warm soup and a good fire to dry themselves by. They also had comfortable beds to lay their poor wore out limbs to rest. We left six of them in the hospital; poor fellows, we were sorry to part with them but we must submit to the will of providence and live in hopes to meet again in health and prosperity free from the oppressive hand of tyranny, in that land of freedom where dwells all that is near and dear to us, the hopes of which has caused us to overcome every difficulty that has been daily attacking us in various shapes and ways. As for my own part I can boast that thus far I have never given up the idea, but that I shall live to overcome all my troubles and sufferings in France, and return in triumph to my long absent nation and my home. This has been and shall be my guide through the rough paths of trouble and captivity. I must not forget that we are in a dungeon under ground; the officer ordered us a sheaf of straw every two men. We made our beds and went to rest quite comfortable.

January 14. In the morning at break of day we mustered in the square, snow and rain falling quite fast. We had two wagons to attend us. Our officer being ready gave the word and off we started all in good spirits for the city of Chaalons (Chalons-sur-

Marne), thirty-three miles. At 9 in the forenoon the weather cleared off, the sun broke through the haze, and we had fine weather the remainder of the day. The roads were very heavy and the artillery and wagons passing all the night had ploughed them up entirely so that it was a great chance to set a foot on solid ground. Therefore we found it was the best plan to drive on through thick and thin; we had a great many horse soldiers in company with us all day, and they are very unwelcome company where the roads are wet and bad. They splashed us terribly with mud and dirt; however we drove along and by 4 in the afternoon got into Chaalons. We left several at the half way house to ride in the wagons. They were not able to travel any longer. However they all joined us that evening. We were all lodged in a convent with very little straw, and that was quite wet and dirty. We had ½lb of bread per man and a small bucket of pease soup for twenty men. This was the time we had to go through our regular platoon exercise, that was to load, fall back, and fire, and so keep your regular rank, advance and retreat in regular order, until we had conquered and entirely plundered the *citadella* of all its shot and ammunition and then retire to our guard bed and try to get a little rest before we are again called to arms and march away.

January 14. At Chaalons we hear great whispering amongst the National Guard who are placed round our castle to protect us from thieves or robbers who they say are overrunning the Low Countries like swarms of bees. They are called Cossacks, and their whole delight is in fire, sword, and plunder. This was the tale we were happy to hear and put on a long false face saying the Emperor is only leading the Russians into France so that he may play them the second act of Moscow. This would pass off the deception, while we were rejoicing in our hearts to hear that our friends were so numerous and were so rapidly advancing into the interior of France. The city of Chaalons is strongly fortified; it is surrounded with strong walls and entrenchments and stands on a large plain that was then entirely covered with troops assembling from all parts of the country with an intent to stop the advance of their foreign invaders. We all were light hearted at the news and although we were captives in the midst of our enemies had hope.

January 15. In the morning at break of day our drum gave us the summons to muster in the yard of our lodging room, which was no unpleasant tidings to us, as we were all desirous to leave this scene of continual bustle and confusion. We were all mustered and delivered over to the charge of a stern fine old gentlemen, captain in the 27th Regiment of Foot, and a guard of fifty men to conduct us to Vitry, twenty miles. The town being in such a state of bustle and confusion our new captain thought it would be most prudent to omit the playing of our band until we had passed the lines or rather the outposts of the camp and then he said he should be very glad to have us play at our pleasure because music would give life and vigour to his men as well as us, and he himself took great delight in music! We had three carts for our baggage and sick. Being all present the word was given to march, and away we trudged helter skelter, through thick and thin, through lanes of soldiers, artillery wagons, tents etc. The fact is the whole of the country round, as far as could be seen, was one entire mass of soldiers and the main road was all day crowded with recruits all marching (*en masse*) singing and huzzaing as they went, crowding along past us with some a drum leading the van, and other parties with a bugle or an old fiddle to cheer up their drooping spirits. I well remember that day; the roads were entirely broke up, and made many a stout hearted man almost ready to give up the ship. We got to the halfway house a small village on the way to Vitry and the place was so crowded with recruits (all hurrying to the slaughter house at Chaalons) that it was some time before our commandant could make interest to obtain the liberty of a barn, where we all set down out of the rain to take a little refreshment and rest our poor mud pelters; our guard were as glad to have a little rest as any of us could be, and what makes me remark this day in particular was a laughable scene we witnessed in the barnyard; there was a whole gang of the recruits that had halted to take a little refreshment, and they had made rather free with poor old cognac, so that he set them hot for drill. They were all in small parties, in different parts of the yard practising their exercise, (raining like fury) some of them had an old musket wanting the lock, others a musket without its ramrod, and some with pikes, others with a bayonet stuck on the end of a stick, then again we would see one with an old rusty sword, no scabbard, and a great many with their staffs, all loading and firing with as much care and activity as if they had really been embodied and going through a field day. Soldiery has for many years been the principal employment of every male through France by which constant practice in the use of arms they are all soldiers before they are men or even know any other mode of gaining an honest livelihood. What was very strange to us was to see young boys at the age of fifteen intermingled with men up to sixty years of age all marching to the slaughter house and appeared in the greatest spirits; at times we met parties on the road that we heard long before we saw them, all joined in the chorus of some national patriotic song with now and then cheering every cottage they passed by. Perhaps they had an old drum that used to take a part of the oratory. Our commandant called our band together and he very kindly requested us if we could make convenient to play a march as we passed through the next village (as the rain had somewhat abated), and that little village was the place where he first drew the breath of life and where at the present time many of his relations and old acquaintance were still living and he was determined to try what they had in their cellars. We informed the commandant that we were ready at his pleasure to obey him in any thing he requested that we were able to perform. He than called for sergeant of the Guard and informed him to call his men together and tell them they must all say that we were a party of the Cossacks that they were conducting towards Vitry where we were to be kept in confinement until further orders and that they were compelled to treat us kindly for fear that we should turn resolute with them and all desert on the road; also that we were very submissive and obedient when we had plenty to eat and drink and that the band was our greatest delight as it drowned all our cares and roused us from all reflections. This the commandant contrived so that we might all take some refreshment before we reached Vitry as he was well aware our fare would be very poor there. As he desired, so he was obeyed; we all halted outside of the village (its name is St Blanc, seven miles from the city of Vitry). Our band led the van; the rest all fell into their ranks and the guards on each side. The commandant gave the word to march, we struck up a very celebrated French rondeau, or quick step, and up we were conducted by the commandant to the door of the mayor surrounded by every soul that *levée en masse* had left in the village. The mayor was inn keeper of the village, and brother in law to our commandant. The orders were to halt and go into a large barn, the guard and band into the mayor's parlour and lodging room. It was with great difficulty our guard could keep the peasants from crowding in at the doors and windows; they, hearing such horrid tales of the Cossacks, were all anxious to see what sort of wild beasts we were. Many of them that were close to us as we discoursed to each other in English would start and rush back into the crowd exclaiming that they heard us speaking Cossack and perhaps we were laying some plan to rise and massacre them all. We soon were served with bread, cheese and wine ordered by the mayor. Our captain and his men had their refreshment upstairs. We all eat and drink hearty for we had really plenty left; then we played a favourite French air and by this time our baggage joined us. They halted to partake of the good old mayor's hospitality. We all formed our ranks as before and left room for our women and sick comrades that were with the baggage. Made our obedience to the gentleman the mayor, struck up our music and bid good bye to the hospitable little village of St Blanc. Our captain made us laugh all on the road afterwards when he related the story of his brother and all the poor peasants in the place, how they enquired of him how we had been caught, and if we had committed any depredations since he had been with us, whether or no it was true that we eat those whom we conquered and all such simple questions. Our captain told them there was no fear of any such outrages being committed as long as we had plenty to eat and drink and if he had his desire, he would choose to convoy us to Vitry equally as soon as he would so many British prisoners. And he said on leaving the village he informed the mayor what nation we were, and his reason for thus alarming all the old women in St Blanc. This caused many a hearty laugh that day on all sides; we then began fast to approach our place of residence for that night. The weather cleared up and the day being far advanced we were not pestered with so many troops passing us on the road. We reached Vitry about 5 in the evening. We were put in a small barracks, had plenty of straw and in a short time were served plenty of good soup and white bread all hot. All those favours were bestowed upon us through the generous humane intercession of our good commandant. We had plenty of fire wood and made good fires in the barrack rooms to dry our wet clothing. Our baggage arrived about 7 in the evening, all quite comfortable. They were taken care of and we all went to rest.

Next morning January 16th we had orders to halt and wait that day for orders. This was very good news and was much needed amongst us, owing to us having for several days back had bad weather, heavy roads, and long marches. This had in a great measure harassed and partly cut up several of our bravest men. However thank our good fortune this day's rest, and good warm soup, over a comfortable fire, set most of them on their legs again. We sent three to the hospital. Poor fellows, we are sorry to part with them but it cannot be avoided. (May they and numbers more live to return again to their native land.) We hear great whispering round that the Austrians have crossed the Rhine into France and that the British have besieged Bordeaux. This is all working together for our good; we are sure if all we hear be true France must be in a tottering state and certainly must shortly have a fall. This decisive battle at Chaalons must decide it all.

January 16. Halting in the city of Vitry in a small barracks entirely for lodging strangers that pass and repass. It is also supported by voluntary contribution, has old people to live and attend as nurses, cooks etc. (a noble institution). We had two good meals per day, plenty of fire and wholesome warm lodgings, which very possible was the means of saving many of our lives. Several of our men began to fail fast owing to the long marches, bad roads, and continual wet cold weather, miserable lodgings, and scanty poor rations, and what was a great disadvantage to us was some of our people had been laying upwards of ten years in the depot of Givet and during that period had little or no exercise, then drove as it were from town to town in front of a retreating army, made our fatigued limbs unable to support our poor feeble bodies through every laborious day's work we have to encounter. Should we turn faint hearted and lurk by the way we know what would most certainly be our destiny. That was what the French soldiers call *quatre sol*, the price of their ball and cartridge, and those orders we knew had been given to all the troops on march but we may hope all our greatest sufferings are past. The army has halted and we are daily marching away out of their reach. It is true we are at this very moment in a city full of soldiers but they have no concern with us.

In the evening our commandant reviewed us in company with the *commissarie de marine*. He then informed us that we were to march in the morning for Chaumont, and he with his men must return to Chaalons. This part of his story we were very sorry to hear. He was so kind and attentive to see us well treated as far as it lay in his power, but we must do the best we can and strive to surmount every obstacle we meet with the reviving hopes that a few days longer will put an end of this wandering unsettled way of regaining our dear purchased freedom.

January 17. A foggy, rainy morning. At daylight we had hot soup and at 8 o clock our captain and an officer of the Horse mustered us, the captain of Horse took charge of us. Our former captain spoke greatly in our favour to his brother officer, he made a low bow and retired. The general of the city ordered us two carts and two wagons to take up any of our people that could not march. Our Guard of Invincibles, twenty in number, being ready, off she goes.

We left Vitry and marched across the country to the village of St. Dizier, twenty-seven miles. Rain fell all day and made the cross roads horrid dirty and heavy. Our guard were very patient feeling men. They gave the men every chance to choose their footsteps, and made their horses take the worst of the road or rather foot path. In this kind of marching we at last reached the village of St. Dizier and were locked in a large tower formerly some ancient nobleman's residence. We had a large room to lodge in and the peasants brought us plenty of straw, and wood, two very welcome articles, and in a little while our baggage arrived, then they brought us bread and milk, Soup, potatoes, and some stewed mutton, all very good. We had some invalids to do duty over us, very good men. They passed the night inside the room with us out of the rain and cold, and those that were inclined had a plentiful tuck out of brandy and wine which the old soldiers furnished them with through the night. We got our stockings, pantaloons, and even our shirts dry having plenty of fire all night. Some sat by the fire all night singing songs. As for me I buried myself in straw and slept all night.

January 18. In the morning our bugles gave us an invitation to prepare for another day's journey. The weather was fine but the paths were wet and muddy. We had two large wagons to attend us and our captain must have a tune at leaving St. Dizier which was readily granted and we struck up the quick step in the battle of Marengo. This was the very thing that placed us in the highest esteem both by the captain and his men. They being all old veteran soldiers were much gratified with the complement we had conferred on them. At the half way house the captain made interest to get us a snack of bread and cheese, also each man a dram. We halted an hour and then started off to the tune of 'Paddy Carey,' the old captain shaking his sides with laughing when we explained to him the name of the tune and part of the words, where it says:

> *His brawny shoulders four feet square*
> *His cheeks like thumping red potatoes* etc.

The old captain after this was constantly repeating poor Paddy. etc. This day we kept our baggage in front all the way and in the evening by sun set we reached the town of Joinville, twenty-five miles from St. Dizier. In this place the mayor was a great enemy to the British, so that the good will of our captain could render us very little service. We were put in a large cashot under the town's gaol and in a little while we were served boiled beans, and one thing I can say of it is a real factotum. Jack Mclagan tore the top off his loaf and hove it against the wall of the dungeon where it stuck fast and there we left it sticking for a sign when we left the place in the morning! We had a little dirty straw, and with it and our own clothing we made out to pass the night tolerable warm and comfortable, no thanks to Mr. Mayor. At daylight in the morning the rattling of keys and creaking of bolts and rusty hinges was our alarm drum, and then the old gaoler hoarsely grunted, 'All hands to muster in the court of the prison.' The mayor and several *gendarmes* waited at the door, to take particular care of us, lest any intruders should (like Paul Pry) pop in and run off with some or perhaps the whole of us! We may all of us ever thank those careful keepers for their unlimited care they took of us in the ever to be esteemed town and gaol of Joinville, also its mayor and gaoler.

January 19. After being mustered in the court yard of the prison and found that none of us had either sunk into the rock or vanished through the iron barred air holes that shone like two stars through the vaulted roof of our sleeping room, or rather condemned cell, the place of deposit for murderers, traitors, and lice, we were counted through the large iron gate and then very carefully turned over to our former captain and guard. Indeed we were all of us very happy to have our old friend once more to rule over us. 'Come my sons,' says the captain. 'Revive us all with Monsieur Paddy as we leave this depot of misery. We have provided three wagons and they shall keep in front of us so that those who wish can ride by turns and this I know will greatly ease any man that feels unwell or any way fatigued.' The morning was fine, our wagons and guard all ready. The captain took the front of the band, drew his sword, gave the word, and off we went to his favourite air, 'Paddy Carey!'

From Joinville to Vignory was eighteen miles; this was only a flea bite! We reached the half way house in good time. The half way house was a blacksmith shop where we all halted and the captain gave each man a dram. We played the old blacksmith and his family a tune. The good woman gave us a large kettle full of boiled potatoes and a bowl of milk, which was very kind. Those amongst us that had any money bought bread, butter, cheese, eggs and herrings so that we all made quite a good dinner. The soldiers gave their horses a small bait, then we again struck up a tune and bid adieu to the jolly old blacksmith. We then met a large reinforcement of horse and foot on their march to Chaalons. They retarded our progress greatly because we had to halt in a field by the wayside nearly two hours so that they might pass undisturbed. We got into the village of Vignory about five in the evening. The captain halted us at the entrance of the village and then he addressed us as follows: 'My sons, this is a small place and the people are good disposed Christians. The mayor is a good man and an acquaintance, therefore I shall use my whole authority and interest in your favour. This is not the Mayor of Joinville!' We made our obedience and struck up his favourite air, marched up to the door of the mayor and he appeared and saluted the captain They past a few words and we were ordered into a barn, where we soon had plenty of straw and the peasants prepared some of them soup, others brought bread, some brought wine, and some brandy, so that we wanted for nothing they had to spare! In the evening the captain, mayor, and several more old gentlemen paid us a visit. They enquired if we had plenty to eat and drink etc., which we undoubtedly answered in the affirmative with respect! The captain then said it was the desire of the mayor and gentlemen present that we would go into the mayor's house and play a little while for amusement and to this we readily consented, and mustered up our tools, books etc., in order to spend the evening. The mayor also informed all hands that he would have something hot prepared for breakfast before we started in the morning. We then went to the house where we were treated with every civility.

We had plenty of wine, brandy and cider, bread and cheese or cold ham at our pleasure, and you may believe me we made that old mansion tremble that night. We did not break up until 4 o clock in the morning; then they made us a field bed in the parlour where we took a short nap until 8 in the morning then we were called up to breakfast in the room where we slept. We had hot *fricassee* soup and bread.

January 20. A hard frost. We all mustered to the sound of our bugle, fresh, lively, and ready. We had two large wagons started in front as before! The word was given to march and the music struck up, 'o'er the hills and far away,' for the city of Chaumont twenty-three miles. We had heard several whisperings amongst the gentry at the ball in Vignory that if our captain did not look out the Austrian Army would reach Chaumont before we did! This we took as a romance amongst old soldiers over a glass of wine. Poor John Mclagan has said two or three times, through the course of the morning, that he hopes the Germans or Cossacks may fall in with us and then perhaps he may get clear of the wearisome marches that are daily killing him. We often advised him to ride but no! Jack had a heart that would sooner die than shrink. His word always has been that he is a man and never was afraid of any man; therefore he should scorn to give up marching sooner than any other man.

At 1 p.m. we reached the halfway house, halted half an hour, and got a little refreshment. We met the corresponding *gendarmes*; they told our captain that is was in vain to think of going to Chaumont. It would be running into the fire. They told our captain that the troops had all left the city and marched towards Chaalons and left no other guard in the place than a few invalids, and by some means this news had reached the vanguard of the Austrians with an account of the weak state this strong garrison was left in. The Austrians immediately dispatched a division of the army to take possession of the city and our captain in his funny manner of discourse made answer that his orders were to Chaumont and in spite of both Germans and Russians he would endeavour to fulfil his commands; at least he would try very hard to do it.

'Never mind, my men,' says the captain to us. 'We have all seen both Germans and Russians before now; they are only men and they know how to treat prisoners of war, particularity you that are British and their allies! Therefore courage! We will always hear them before we see them.'

We struck up a lively air and cheerfully tripped along; about 5 in the evening we entered the environs of Chaumont, marched up to the grand square and there we were ordered by *prefecture de la police* to lodge for that night in the *citadella* and on the morrow they would make fresh arrangements for us. Up we tramped to our castle, strongly fortified but weakly inhabited. We lodged in the barracks. The barrack master served us boiled beans and a morsel of salt pork per man. We had plenty of old straw and with what little wood we collected round the *citadella* we rose a tolerable good fire. Some went to their Irish feather bed and others sat by the fire reflecting on the curious tales that has been passing all the day. At last fire wood falling short, and fatigued limbs requiring natural repose, nearly all hands were lulled in the arms of sleep, when lo! What alarm! The thundering of artillery outside the city walls gave the unwelcome tidings that some strangers on a visit wished to gain instant admittance into the city! Damned rough visitor! We wished they had kept silence until daylight, when a hue and cry ran through our part of the old barracks commanding all the British prisoners of war to muster immediately; then there was hurry scurry, *gendarmes*, sword in hand driving us out of the barracks. They never stopped to count us over, all were drove out of the *citadella* at the point of the sword. They drove us up to the *gendarmes'* horse barracks, where the *gendarmes* mounted their horses and conducted us out at the West gate of the city in order to shun the besieging army that lay on the east side of the place. The night was dark and rainy and they took us across the country over fields and commons, through ploughed fields and broken ground, neither road nor foot path, nor even light enough to choose our steps if we had been allowed time enough to pick our road, because those infernal horse *gendarmes*, being well mounted, drove us before them, sword in hand, with now and then a horses breast against one or another's back followed with a heavy stroke across your back or shoulders from the sword of one of those cruel monsters. In this inhumane manner they drove us until daybreak presented to our view a small village. All the time we heard the continual roaring of the besieging cannon against Chaumont. We got into the village where we were in hopes to have a little refreshment, but no! Not even a drink of water.

'*Marche! Buger, Marche*!' was our our tyrannical conductors' cry.

The people in the place asked what meant that continual rumbling in the air and the old Dutch brigadier told them it was the guns in Chaumont rejoicing for a victory gained over the British Army at Bayonne. We got into a country road that led from the little village we just left to the city of Bar where we were to stop that night. Bar is twenty-seven miles from Chaumont and having no wagon or cart to help us through the fatigues and sufferings of this torturing night and day's march, several of our strongest men began to fail and one in particular that I shall never forget, one of my very intimate acquaintance while in Givet and on our journey, a brave, brave fellow, a Man! This was the very same man that yesterday said if the Russians or Austrians did not release him the march would soon put a period to his troubles. We had left the village nearly an hour when we came to a part of the road where on each side lay heaps of stones for the repairs of the roads. John Mclagan chanced to be near me and kept dropping behind more than he commonly used to do. I in our free way of talk says to him,

'Come Jack, they won't keep us much longer, so cheer up your heart; you heard their guns and almost smelt their powder. Perhaps tonight we may see their faces.'

In this manner we used to cheer up each other in midst of our severest trials.

Mclagan says to me, "Wetherell, it is not in my power to walk any further. I am chafed entirely raw and it is death to me every step I take so I will sit down on this heap of stones until I recover a little."

I begged him to let William Crown and me take hold of his arms and help him along telling him it was only a few miles more to the town and them savage *gendarmes* would most likely beat and ill use him! But no. Every entreaty was in vain, he sat down, and we had to proceed on. We had not left him twenty yards, when up rides one of those butchers, sword in hand.

'*Allez chein*,' says he to poor Jack, at the same time gave him a heavy blow on the head with the flat of his sword.

We all halted to look and Mclagan sprang from his seat presenting his naked bosom to his murderer. The fiend of hell at that instant plunged his weapon in the unfortunate Mclagan's breast and laid him a lifeless corps on the high way. When the rest of the *gendarmes* (they were mostly in the rear driving us along) saw the bloodthirsty deed and we all halting they rode up to us full gallop, sword in hand and told us that was only a beginning and the first man that halted again should share the same fate. This was very galling but what could we do in the midst of a squadron of horsemen all well armed, and equal in number, and us a set of poor moving skeletons with no other weapon to defend ourselves that our tongue, and that was of very little use in supplicating mercy from a set of inhumane, bloodthirsty monsters, in humane shape. In short we grinned and bore it, and at last we reached the city of Bar. They drove us up to the municipality where we were counted and crammed into a dungeon underground, with very little dirty straw to keep our wearied bodies from the cold wet stones that composed the bottom of the cell where we were lodged for the night. When we were alone then we had an opportunity to pass our various reflections on the strange overturns that one night brings forth:

In the first instance we are routed from our confinement by our friends, at the same time they were not aware of us being there. If they had, no doubt we had been all demanded before one single gun had been levelled on the city, or had they had any idea of us being drove out of the place when they first arrived before its walls, one of their out pickets could have secured both us, and our cruel unmerciful bloodthirsty, inhumane, savage, tyrannical cowardly guards, because experience has taught any man who has been exposed to the ravages of war, that he is a real coward that will slay a poor worn-down prisoner of war in cool blood, he not even offering any kind of resistance nor yet has he any means of defence. Let me see that murderer placed before one of the German Hussars that were not far distant at the time; although he be cased in his steel armour and his sword and pistols about him, his first attempt will be to try if horse flesh cannot make the hussar run which he is most sure to do, but in what direction? Why, pursuing the warrior that likes to try his skill in war over an innocent wore out unarmed prisoner of war, a man that had been shown mercy and quarters already by the man who first made him prisoner. That was a man and warrior, no cowardly villain that would inhumanely rush upon a vanquished being that was already in his power! Mclagan was captured by Jerome Bonaparte's squadron. He was quarter master on board the Hon. East India Company's ship the *Lord Nelson*, on her passage from the Indies to England where they defended their ship with the greatest courage against a frigate and a ship of eighty guns until the rest of the French squadron came up: then, overpowered by numbers, they were compelled to surrender when nearly two thirds of their men lay dead on the decks. The *Nelson* Mounted fifty guns and when she engaged the squadron had 147 men all told and when surrendered only fifty-two souls left alive. Mclagan was one of those men worthy the title of men. Having described the manner this unfortunate man first became a captive I shall next hint on the treatment he found on board the *Jumbar*[1] of eighty guns after being taken on board as a prisoner of war. The first sight was her decks were all floating with blood and mangled bodies occasioned by their determined resistance. Nevertheless the instant they were all on board they had wine bread and cheese served to those that were able to take any, and those that were wounded were carefully taken down the sick bay and placed amongst the wounded men that had been wounded in the action, where every possible attention was paid. They had the same attendance as the crew of the *Jumbar*. The captain gave strict orders to every officer and man on board the *Jumbar* to treat the prisoners like men as they had defended their ship to the last moment with extraordinary bravery. They were now their captives and had given themselves up to the mercy of their vanquishers; therefore he considered that the greatest honour that crowned the head of a conqueror was to conquer and save, and those that were well were distributed amongst the ship's crew, so many in each mess, where they were treated like brothers, and no longer considered as enemies. Those are the men that I spoke of in the latter page that would have shrunk at the idea of killing a man in cool blood unarmed and wore out with fatigue. This account of the treatment that the crew of the ship *Lord Nelson* received on board the French ship *Jumbar* I have heard several times related over by my own messmate William Crown. He was armourer of the *Nelson* and slightly wounded in the action.

When I reflect on this and then look at the barbarous murder of this brave fellow after being shown mercy by the very men he a few minutes before had been striving to kill and they to kill him; but at the moment they struck their ensign as a token of craving mercy, they mercy craved and mercy found!

'Quickly man all your boats my boys, they are no longer our foes.'

This was the language of that gallant pillar of France who had the honour to command His Majesty's ship the *Jumbar*

---

1. *Jumbar—Jean Bart.*

under the flag of Jerome Bonaparte or rather under his orders. Napoleon at this time was king in France. William Crown and me sat most of the night repeating over such circumstances as those already mentioned.

January 22. The sound of the gaoler's key gave us warning that day had again broke its way through the east but not through the huge rocks which surrounded our cell. The creaking of the iron doors on their rusty hinges summoned us forth to the fresh air, there to answer our muster. Served us a loaf for every three men, our day's ration, and would not allow us any wagon. The morning was rainy and cold; we had a fresh guard of Horse Grenadiers and off we started for the village of Vendeouvre, only fifteen miles. Our bass drum was the most troublesome baggage we had, yet we stuck to the old drum and took our turns two and two to carry it along as we had done the day before. We got along as well as could be expected when we consider the weather, the poor country road, and worse than all a surly proud disdainful old Flemish officer. He was very strict with us and would not suffer any of us to leave the middle of the road. This we were no strangers to so that we gave no cause of any displeasure to our officer nor guard. We reached Vendeouvre by two in the afternoon where we were put in the guard room of the gaol.

In Vendeouvre in the guardhouse, municipality town hall, court house and place of safe deposit for conscripts, at times a dance house but this day converted into a depot for prisoners of war, or rather a British barn where gypsies hold their nightly meetings; however we were lodged in this large room within the walls of the gaol; on the limits poor Janet Carter was taken quite ill and the mayor had her and her husband lodged in a room in the gaoler's house. This good young woman has stood firm through all our hardships and always been the first to assist any of us that might be sick, or at different opportunities she has stood interpreter on the road for the sick men in the wagons. She very seldom rode but would walk alongside the baggage. She was our trusty guard over any thing we left with the wagons. Every man in the division greatly respected her. The mayor's wife hearing she was sick sent her some warm herb tea and other restoratives necessary for a woman sick with fatigue, and in the morning she was quite smart again, which we were all glad to hear. That was the only woman we brought from Givet that any of us took any thought or care about.

I shall now turn back to ourselves and try to get something to kill that that surely would soon have killed us. The keeper of the prison had *fricassee* to sell made of liver, besides a horn of brandy, but he was mistaken in his market because *l'argent* was scarce, therefore he made a poor speck of his liver and lights. In the evening the mayor visited us in our council chamber and he asked us if we had been served any rations. We told him no, but the kind gaoler had offered us fricassee for sale. The mayor shook his head and said something to a brigadier of *gendarmes* that was with him. The mayor then asked us if we had got any clean straw; we told him no. Him and the brigadier left us and presently in steps two men with a large tub full of boiled horse beans and a little pork all made into soup exceeding comfortable and very acceptable. This was ready on our first entering the place, but the lousy thief of a gaoler kept it back so that he might make his market out of us, when we were hungry, with his liver, lights, red herrings, and other trash, such as butter, cheese, bread, and *eau de vie*. We eat hearty of our bean soup. Ah! Hunger is sweet sauce! and after supper the same brigadier again returned; he took ten of our men out and in a little while they came back with five large baskets full of good white bread which was divided a loaf to every two men and one small flat cheese called *fromage de Marolles*, very good with bread. Thus the kind gentleman of a mayor found means to sell us cheaper bread and cheese than the thief of a gaoler. The mayor entirely under rated the monopolising merchant. The mayor presented us the bread and cheese as an act of charity; the bloodsucking imposter sold his trash for the sake of filthy gain. He kept our allowance of rations from us as long as possible entirely with an intent to cause us when hungry to buy from him. We then had a wagon load of straw to fetch in and this finished our night's adventure. We all went to rest quite comfortable and after a few remarks on what curious overturns we had experienced since we left Givet the story of poor J. Mclagan closed our parliament in the Council chamber until about four o'clock in the morning we were alarmed by the drums through the town beating to arms.

'Rouse, my boys,' cries Thos. Johnson one of our men, a merry soul, 'Come my lads, the Germans are haunting us again. Rise and let us clear out of this. They want this place for their head quarters.'

'Go to h—l,' says one, 'with your news.'

'Damn you and the drums too. You wont let a fellow have a wink of sleep!' mumbles out a third, 'God strengthen their arms. I hope they won't let us run out at the back door the same as they did at Chaumont in the middle of the night.'

In a little while all hands were awake. We heard a continual beating to arms. What can all this mean? No person seems to interrupt us nor even to come near us. We listened all with various conjectures till day began to peep in the eastern windows of our castle. We at last heard footsteps approaching our door. This proved to be William Carter who had been upstairs in the gaoler's house all night with his wife. He told us she was much better. Then he told us all the troops, *gendarmes*, National Guard, and every man that could carry arms were all marching away to the city of Troyes. An express had arrived in the course of the night with orders to the mayor that the Austrians had taken Chaumont, and were on their march towards Troyes and he must dispatch every man that can make use of arms immediately to the city of Troyes and that our guard had gone amongst the rest. Good, good, this was a pleasant morning's bitters. Well, let them go. We will follow them and see that none skulks behind.

'Now boys,' says Jack Waddel, 'We shall have a chance to fall in with the boys that will send us home in short order!'

'Why, you damned fool,' says Walter Jones, 'they will make you help to fight their great guns!'

'Damn their kindness,' says Charles Jones. 'To hell with them.'

Some one opens the door and looks out. 'Whew!' says he. 'What a snow storm!' And in he pops his head, shuts the door, and again crept into his burrow of warm straw. 'Let us keep warm when we can,' says he, and down he lays.

'Well, shipmates,' says Carter, 'I will go in and see if Janet wants anything. The drums are all gone; we no longer hear their warlike sound and the town seems all silence. He is a good dog that barks when he is told. It is soon enough to rise when we are desired or when we are wanted.'

About 8 o'clock our friend the mayor visited us in company with an old officer, an invalid who the mayor informed us was going with us as a guide to the city of Troyes. We should have soup and soft bread to breakfast, then we should have as many wagons as we required to help us through the snow. He also recommended us to be civil and act like men on our march and we would be respected and well treated wherever we went. We eat our breakfast and mustered at the door. We had five wagons; two of them we started a head and three in the rear to pick up lame ducks! The mayor sent Janet in a carriage after us.

Chapter 12

1814: To the South

January 23, 1814. We left Vendeouvre for Troyes by the main road, thirty-two miles, and by the country road, which is not very good, only twenty-four miles. This we chose. Our wagons being started, the old gentleman gave a signal with a twirl of his cane, and to his great astonishment our two bugles struck up a favourite French bugle quick step and the two trumpets took the trumpet part. The old gentleman halted and shook his sides with laughing, declaring he was never more agreeably surprised in his life than he was at the present moment. He was happy to hear that we had such good courage at the first onset in such a heavy snow storm. The mayor sent a boy after the captain (our shepherd, as we styled him); the boy brought him a horse to ride on but he sent the horse back, saying he rather wished to walk and keep in company with the men under his charge. We got along wonderfully. The wind was mostly in the rear so that it helped us along through the snow. The road mostly was clear of snow as it laid quite above the level of the land on each side, and no fences to stop the wind from blowing all the snow off the road, and as for cold we kept warm with bodily exercise.

About 2 in the afternoon we came to an old castle which must have been once in its splendour the residence of some August family. At present it was the residence of a number of old invalid soldiers and their families where they lived retired and quite happy. They kept a tavern in one wing of the building. On our first turning the corner that leads up to the gate of this asylum our captain smiling said we would alarm the garrison. He desired our bugles would sound a charge, and we all full of mischief our bugles readily obeyed! Then believe me if a man had but half life in him he would have laughed then, to see the old fellows hobbling out at the hall door neck over heels with intent to protect their castle, some of them only one arm, others with wooden legs, then a blind man with his staff of defence, followed by a cripple with his crutches ready for action. Each individual showed fully determined to protect their comfortable habitation. The captain advanced up to the gate and saluted the person at the bar. He then informed the tavern keeper what we were and the gate was hove open. We were all kindly invited to go in and take share of their little stock which was at that very time hot and good. What they termed their little stock was some of their stock pork and bean soup smoking hot! This was very wholesome just at that very moment. Our captain took a part in the repast and after that a can of good wine was handed round. Janet Carter was taken away by the women and had something comfortable made for her in quick order. We now found we had nine miles farther to go and it had abated snowing. Our baggage horses had eat their mouthful and it was three o'clock, therefore we were determined to please our jovial friendly old warriors. We mustered our band privately behind the wall and as soon as the captain thought of moving we had a big drum and all ready, and as they wished us a good bye the band struck up 'Mal-Brouk,' a well known French air. The old lads stood some time as in a trance. At last they gave us three cheers and wished us a *bonne voyage*. We then placed our drum and instruments in the wagon again and off we trudged all healthy and merry! In a little while we saw the lofty towers and steeples of Troyes raising their majestic heads above the white extensive plain that surrounds them. The sight of the towers in our intended port gave us fresh courage and we then put the best leg foremost to try and gain the harbour with daylight, which we did. When within about three miles of the walls of Troyes we saw numbers of tents and temporary buildings in all directions on the plain round the outside of the walls and sentinels within hail of each other in every direction. When we advanced nearer the lines we were met by a large picket guard and as we were considerably dispersed along the road the officer of the guard desired us to halt, it being his positive orders not to let a mortal pass until they gave a satisfactory answer what they were etc. At this moment our old captain came waddling along.

'What!' says he. 'Have you got some of my men prisoners?'

With those words he presented our *Felle (feuille) de Route* to the officer of the Guard!

'There, sir,' says the captain 'That will pass my men to the gates of Paris,' and when the officer was satisfied what we were and from whence we came he ordered us to pass. He also sent a sergeant along with us to the city gates which were shut. We soon were admitted in through the gates.

January 23. We arrived in the city of Troyes and we halted in the Faubourg until we all had got gathered together, our baggage included; we then were marched up to the grand place. There we got billets to be lodged and victualled on the inhabitants. Very happy tidings; this was certainly a healing balsam to many of us. The good people of Troyes will never be forgot as long as one of our division draws breath. They nursed us the same as their own relatives, neither sparing time nor trouble to get every thing they thought would nourish us and restore us all to our natural cheerful spirits. The city was full of troops but they were mostly all quartered in the *citadella* in barracks and in the suburbs. After we had got warmed and began to feel good our host, a fine gentleman who kept two large bakehouses, sat down and called the three of us to take a glass of wine along with him and give him a small idea of our captivity etc. We sat down and accompanied our kind host until we were all called to supper which was exceeding good. We eat and drank! What more could we require? Well I will tell you. We wanted rest, and that we soon found, good and comfortable. I forgot to mention that when our old captain served out our billets he requested us to meet in the same square tomorrow morning at 9 o'clock for further orders. In the morning we had a good breakfast, then went over to the square, were mustered by the *commissarie de la ville* and *Monsieur le Mayor, la Commandant de la place* and we then were ordered to our last night's billets as the gentlemen wished us to halt so that we might take some rest and nourishment for a day or two. This was again glorious tidings. Why, it appears almost too good. However we have latterly experienced severe hardships enough, therefore our fortune has taken a contrary turn. We went back to our billets every one praising their good treatment. Our orders were muster tomorrow morning at 9 in the square. We sent seven of the sick to the hospital, which is quite moderate after such severe fatigue and sufferings. Our host was happy to see us return. He told the girl to fetch up some wine and some bread and cheese to take our eleven o'clock and sit down by the fire.

January 24. Halting day and very cold. We kept close quarters all day, laid snug in a good harbour where we repaired damages, recruited our men, sent our sick to the hospital, took on board what provisions, wine we could conveniently stow away and made our shattered hulks all in readiness for the first fair wind or the first orders from our commander-in-chief.

Our landlord the baker informs us that the most of the inhabitants would desert the city and leave their all, their houses homes and all they are possessed of in the whole world to fall into the hands of the Austrians. They have left Chaumont and are on the road for this city.

'But why should we leave the home we have to go look for another we know not where? As for me and my family we will stick to our home until we are drove away by force. Numbers have shut up their houses and suspended business, terrified out of their senses at the thoughts of the enemy. They want to abandon the place of nativity but the orders are proclaimed by the general and mayor this morning that not one soul of the inhabitants shall be allowed to pass the gate of Troyes under its present expectations of a siege.'

The mayor also advises every person to proceed as usual with their different occupations, as he was well convinced the Austrians were far from distressing the inhabitants of any place. Where e'er they had been they only wanted the command of the garrison forts and magazines belonging to the present government of France. This was the most part of the mayor's proclamation; not one word of defence! Indeed that would be folly and madness. With only troops enough to relieve the posts round the city what could they pretend to do or attempt, offering to stop the advance or even refuse the admittance into the city of an invading army?

'Let them come,' says the baker. 'I will give them what bread I have to spare and then bake more. This is my creed, let who will be ruler of the roast, I must be baker.'

We drank round, had a good laugh, and went down to dinner. We had a grand dinner and plenty to drink, which brought on evening. We had several remarks on the wonderful progress the Russians were making; also the British Army were victorious in the south.

Our discourse soon brought bed time. Our host being extraordinary partial to cognac and water, I thought perhaps it arose from the dry spark that frequently prevails amongst bakers! However the old lad was quite merry and was quite hot to hear a song in our English language before we parted. This was granted and William Crown favoured the company with Bonaparte's parley with John Bull. After the song we interpreted the heads of it to the baker and his family. This caused great laughter through the house and his family. This also brought another round of old cognac. One of the young men, a baker, favoured us with a voluntary French song, and this closed the evening. The host was pretty well so, and we had quite plenty, so that we all found bed the best place, made our obedience to the family and crept to our warm nests where we slept till day light shone bright through the windows. We rose in order to march away this morning. Certainly we got a good hot breakfast, then buckled on our knapsacks, took leave of our generous benefactor and family, thanked him for his kind treatment and departed! The old man hollowed after us beseeching us if ever we came that way again to make our home at the bakehouse in Troyes.

We all assembled in the square, were mustered by the mayor *commissarie*, general, and our old shepherd. They found us all present; the *commissarie* then informed us that our *felle de route* mentions four in particular that had been writing in the bureau at Givet. Those four he wished to see. Accordingly we four were presented to his highness, William Crown, Tho. Johnson, William Aplen, and me; his honour informed us that we all must remain in Troyes this day, and tomorrow morning we were to march to the village of Aix; that we should have four wagons for our accommodations, and he requested two of the four interpreters to start quite early in the morning with a passport that he would have ready for them. This they must present to the Mayor of Aix in order to prepare billets for the division when they arrived and then the Mayor of Aix will sign the passport and the other two interpreters can take their early turn to the next place—only be sure that two remain with this gentleman who has very kindly volunteered his service to conduct you to the city of Sens as your guide and protector. We then were dismissed until 8 tomorrow morning.

January 25. Halted again in Troyes, every man ordered to return to their former billet and four interpreters to meet at the municipality at 4 in the afternoon, to get the passport. We went to the good old father of a baker, who was sitting in his parlour when we passed his window. He saw us and up he rose, ran to the door and very friendly shook hands with us.

'Welcome, Welcome, my sons. Come in to my house and be seated.' We followed him in, told him we had one day more to stop with him. 'Thank God,' said he! 'A little rest will be of infinite benefit to you all! Catherine,' says the good man, 'fetch us a cruise of wine and a luncheon of bread and cheese. Then make ready a good dinner for my children.'

In fine, we eat, drank, and sung until ten in the evening, except, about half an hour, when we went to the city hall to obtain our passport. The old man told us he had two sons in the army, but had no tidings of them lately; one of them was in Spain last news he heard from him, and the other was in the army of the north.

'Perhaps,' says the old father, 'they may have been captured, and may fall into the hands of some humane Christian that may feel for my poor boys the same tenderness I feel for you.'

Thus we passed the evening discoursing on the serious overturn that was likely to take place in France. At last we felt inclined to take some repose. The old man gave the girl orders to rise early and prepare some hot breakfast for us in the morning before we marched away.

As for William Crown and Wetherell we had to take the first morning's early start for the village of Aix. We therefore appointed 4 in the morning should be the fixed hour for the two that had the turn that day to go ahead and obtain billets ready for the party when they arrived. Thus we made our arrangements, the other two interpreters to remain with the guide and the party so that if any thing strange should take place on the road they would be at hand to speak for any of their comrades should it be required. We all retired to rest for the night where we slept until 4 in the morning, when to our astonishment the old gentleman brought us a light, roused Crown and me, telling us that it was Just 4 o'clock and the girl had made some hot coffee. We rose and took our morning—that was a stiff horn of cognac mixed in a bowl of strong coffee, hot bread, and a hunk of Pellona. That was our morning's bitters before we left the hospitable mansion. We left our host with something more than a natural adieu. He shook hands and bid us farewell, wishing his blessings might restore us safe home to our native country in health and prosperity. Thus we parted and left him.

January 26. A fine clear frosty morning we passed the gates of Troyes by producing our passport and there we had a corporal of the Guard to conduct us to the outer pickets etc. William Crown observed to me that if we should chance to meet any of the British, Russian, or German scout parties we must immediately deliver up ourselves to them to remain under their protection. Thus we passed our conjectures as we tripped along until daylight placed us in the midst of a small village ten miles from Troyes. We halted here nearly half an hour, then proceeded on our journey and at ten in the forenoon we reached Aix, found the mayor and presented our passport to his honour. He perused it over then gave orders to his secretary to make out the billets for the party immediately in order to have them ready when the men arrived. As for Crown and myself, the mayor took us up to his own house and treated us very politely. In a short time the billets were ready and we took them, went to the entrance of the place where we waited a few minutes. Then we heard our well known bugle sound: 'Fall in!'

There was a hill outside the village which hid them from our sight. At the sound of the bugles and three thundering blows on the big drum, the villagers flocked round us, all eager to know what was the meaning of all those sounds they had just heard like martial music. We smiling told them that a division of British were falling in on the other side of the hill and would be in Aix directly. Then we had a grin to our own cheeks when up the hill they marched with the old captain and the band in front, the peasants all standing thunderstruck as they descended the hill. We addressed the captain and presented him the billets.

'Let us proceed,' says the captain, 'to the door of the mayor, so that they may all have a fair chance to hear what I delight in—martial music.'

We marched up to the mayor's door with a lively French quick step then halted, and distributed the men to their respective billets, Janet Carter and her husband were taken to the house of a rich lady where they were well provided for. Tho. Johnson and William Aplen, also the captain, all joined us at the mayor's table. We eat a good dinner, took a look round the place amongst our comrades until night warned every man to your tents all Israel! We past the evening quite comfortable, slept in good beds at night, and gave Henry Alms a hint in the evening that if they might sound the bugles at sunrise we would start early in the morning and get through our day's march in good time. Aplen and Johnson took their turn at 4 in the morning. At 7 our bugles gave warning and at 8 we marched with four wagons in front for the little compact village of Villenetive (Villeneuve-sur-Yonne), only fifteen miles. Our band led the van and although the weather was very cold we counted this day's journey only a morning's recreation. We reached the place at noon where we had a large warm barn for our depot. We deposited our knapsacks there, then we took a look round the place. Some that had money purchased victuals in the taverns and others not overstocked with *vino* returned to the depot where they unexpected were provided with plenty of good soup bread and meat all hot and ready for their use. The captain visited us in our humble habitation to see that we were all satisfied. He told us that the village was so small we would not have been half so comfortable at billets as we were in our present habitation. There was plenty of wood so we kept a roaring fire at one end of the château, and we had oceans of straw to roll amongst. The poor people also brought us blankets to cover us through the dreadful cold night as they termed it, but our men all slept warm and happy. Crown and me went with Aplen and Johnson to the tavern to sleep, but we should have fared better in the company of all our country men rolled in straw. For my part I was glad when 4 o'clock struck so that I might warm myself with walking which we actually did.

At 7 in the morning we reached a toll bar and a draw bridge with a tavern blacksmith shop. Here we took breakfast and a good dram. Small rain beginning to fall made the roads rather heavy. We rested a while took a draw of the pipe and we took another twist of *eau de vie* and then mounted shank-naggy and away we went through thick and thin, stopped for nothing (because we had nothing to stop for) until we ran close on board the city of Sens, seventeen miles from Villenetive. We then made our first enquiry where to find the municipality, then we were introduced to the mayor and the Comissarie General. They looked at our passport, pronounced it good, signed it, and gave the clerk orders to fill up billets for 343 men and one woman. (I have neglected to mention the other six women that we brought from Givet in my former pages.) We left two in Mezieres not very well and four in the city of Rheims to follow us as soon as they were able. We got our own billet which proved to be at the house of a priest. We went to the mansion of the holy Father in order to wait the arrival of our party. The good old gentleman ordered us plenty of victuals and good champagne to wash it down. He said he felt sorry for us poor unfortunate young men that had laid so many years confined not even allowed the happy sight of a line from your unhappy parents who perhaps may have entirely given up all hopes of ever seeing you again.

'This present circumstance, my dear children, is a clear proof to you that we should always have our anchor fixed on hope, because at the very last hour there still is hope, and my present hopes are that the Lord may see fit to restore you and all captives safe to your aged parents, your friends, and your country in peace to rest your heads at the last moments in the arms or on the bosoms of those that are near and dear to you. May peace and reconciliation spread their banners o'er the universe and all the inhabitants of the earth join in one sacred song of praise to the great architecture of the universe. This, my children, is my wish and earnest desire towards you and all unfortunate captives.'

By this time we thought our people would be drawing near the city. We informed our kind host what our business was and took our leave for the present. When we reached the gates of the city we saw no signs of our comrades so we went into a guardhouse and stood talking with the old gentlemen that kept the gate. In a little while we heard Mount Meg (a name we gave our big drum). They passed the gates and marched up to the square, served billets, and conducted five of our men from the baggage wagon to the hospital, an elegant place for them under the superintendence of sisters or nuns. We then returned to our fatherly old gentleman's habitation where we were tenderly and kindly treated. The old lady gave each of us a clean shirt and told the servant to show us our room that we might change our linen. We did all that with pleasure and the servant took our foul linen away. We then were invited to supper, eat a good supper and after a fatherly blessing went to our comfortable place of repose.

We arose quite early in the morning with intent to march, took some hot breakfast, and got orders to halt that day in Sens, to remain at our former billets. Johnson and Aplen were informed the night before by the mayor that we should halt one day to refresh our men, therefore they both laid fast in their beds laughing at us. However we passed the day quite comfortable and happy. We had a fine pleasant day which gave us opportunity to walk all round the city. Night at last summoned all Israel to their tents. We partook of our kind host's well provided supper and after his usual blessings all repaired to our comfortable lodgings. Good night. In the morning Johnson and Aplen started early. We took breakfast and a good hunk of bread and ham in our pouch for the half way house, took leave of our charitable Christian, and away we jogged to the old tune of *'Monsieur de Moulin.'*

The morning was dull and rainy. Our old captain left us and we had two invalid soldiers, fine old men, as guides. We had two wagons and two carts, and the distance from Sens to Ferrieres is only fifteen miles, so that our day's work was soon over. Our two interpreters met us at the end of the village with billets, which were soon distributed and every man soon found shelter from the rain. In Ferrieres we found good quarters and plenty, had all our clothes dried and all quite comfortable and ready for march, and in the morning, being the 30th of January, fine and clear weather, we mustered to the sound of our well known bugles. We had three wagons and our two guides all ready. The bugle sounded and away we started for the town of Courtenay, seventeen miles. We then went on ahead of the party and found we had the billets ready in Courtenay equally as well as to start so early, on a cold winter's morning. We therefore after this all left together in the morning (two men will march a great deal swifter than a large party). However we drew billets and met the party on the entrance into the town, marched up to the hall, served out billets, and discharged our baggage wagons by 2 pm., got our papers signed by the mayor, and had four carts ordered to be in the square at 8 in the morning, our usual hour to march.

January 31. We left Courtenay, very cold, and marched to that miserable lousy hole, Montargis, only fifteen miles. We counted that only a morning's recreation. On the road we were passed with several large carriages guarded by Horse *Gendarmes* driving in full speed. However on our reaching the town our orders were to take up our quarters in the gaol as there was some great personage in the town and the mayor could not attend us.

'Who the devil can it be,' says Crown, 'that we must be neglected?'

We took possession of this public hotel and those who had a *franc* or two in their pocket were the best provided for. The old rascal of a gaoler took his opportunity to make hay while the sun shone. He charged for a bed one *franc*, supper of fried liver one *franc*, a seven *sol* loaf one *franc*, and for a six *sol* measure of brandy one *franc*.

'Why, you damn'd old rascal,' says Jack Waddel, 'do you think we are all *francs*? No Sir! My name you shall know is Jack Waddel and to hell with you and your *francs*.'

At this time our two guides came in and told us the town's people were fetching us bread and soup or what they had ready prepared for us to eat. This was a sad disappointment to Mr. Gaoler after all his frankness. He had bought up most of the spare bread in the place, also all the liver and offal to make us a *franc* feast, but we were so frank, we kept our francs, and left him very frankly to try some other method to gain our *francs*. We also wrote on the wall (with charcoal), *We are not franks but true blooded Johns!* This we wrote large in English and left Belshazzar to send for a Daniel to interpret the writing on the wall. Our guides sent us plenty of straw and the people gave us plenty to eat, and as for drink we could do without. The mayor signed our papers ready for the morning.

February 1. We were not permitted to leave our hotel until the company had left the place in their eight coaches and four horses to each, also two guards to each of the coaches. All we can learn or make out is that they are some characters worth more care than we are. At 9 we were at liberty to proceed. The morning was fine and we had four carts for our baggage. We left the place with no other music than a solitary tap on the big drum. This day's march was only fourteen miles. We arrived in the small village of Loreux (Lorris) quite early, drew billets, and were all quite comfortable. We passed the remainder of the day amongst the peasants and the mayor signed our route. Thus we finished the day.

February 2. Weather frosty. We had three carts and all marched together for the city of Chateauneuf, thirteen miles. We reached the place by noon, got our billets, and spent the remainder of the day looking round this ancient residence and place that gives the title to the Prince of Newcastle or *la Prince du Neufchateau*. Got our pass signed and four carts to be ready in the morning.

February 3. Fine weather. We left Chateauneuf for the city of Orleans. Part of this day's march was through the forest of Orleans where the people in a small mill by the road side informed us that they heard this morning by some *gendarmes* of a body of Cossacks having been seen by several people to enter the forest yesterday evening, and this we took as a hoax on the poor miller and his family by the *gendarmes*. However we heard afterwards that a party of Cossacks on that same night plundered the miller's house and mill, took his cattle and hogs and what they could not conveniently take with them they destroyed. They cut the ham strings of two oxen and one horse, ripped open several sacks of flour and grain, took what they wanted, and left the remainder on the road by the house, set fire to the mill and disappeared! At that time we must have passed not far distant from Jackey.

We pursued our rout for Orleans and being an ugly cross country road we did not get along very quick and the distance being twenty-five miles caused us to be rather later than usual when we got to the city. We arrived and marched up to the city hall where we had good warm lodgings ready to go into. This was a convent and every care possible was given to us by the kind sisters that had the superintendence of this charitable asylum. We had several sick men in the baggage carts. Those were taken to the hospital with the greatest care and attention. We had the liberty of the city and were as comfortable as kings. Our orders were to halt next day and take a little nourishment so that we might be better able to reach Blois.

February 5. We halted and were happy to meet seventeen of our old prison mates belonging to the other divisions that left Givet before us. They had been left sick in the different hospitals on their march and having recovered strength were sent to Orleans in order to join the first prisoners of war that passed that rout. We learnt by them that they all took a quite different rout from Vitry that we had taken. The seven first divisions were sent to Nancy and Luneville and they also informed us that many of our fellow sufferers had dropped off in the different hospitals on their march from Givet. We have left in hospitals on our road to this city twenty-one sick and one murdered; that leaves 342 arrived in Orleans and those nineteen men that has joined us makes our number for billets 361 men and one woman. In this city we enjoyed all the pleasure our hearts could require in our then present circumstances. We had plenty of good victuals, comfortable beds, and each man a new shirt, shoes and stockings. We also were paid up our arrears of marching money from leaving Troyes to the present date which amounted to the enormous sum of 77 *sols* per man, at that time to us a good round sum! The *commissarie* general also appointed another interpreter to have five in case of one being taken ill or unable to attend his duty. He also fixed their daily pay at thirty *sols* each interpreter per day, so that he might find himself on the way independent of any billets. This passport was addressed to the mayor of every town and city where we might have orders to from Paris to lodge or halt in according to the various routes we might be obliged to take at this critical serious instant. Our passport was delivered to us in the municipality of Orleans signed by the prefecture the *commissarie* general, mayor, etc., of the city of Orleans, department *le Loiret*. This ceremony having passed our next visit was to the bridge where we saw Jean d'Arc trampling the soldiers under her feet. We then visited the grand museum of France where we saw a splendid variety of curiosities. We also saw *le duc de Montebello* bleeding on the field and the Emperor weeping over him etc. In the evening we had an invitation to the theatre. We went and were very much gratified with the music and the performance. We then returned to our mansion and took share with the rest of our companions in part of a good night's repose. In the morning we all arose and partook of a good breakfast, milk thickened with flour, and good bread washed down with each man a gill of good wine. We had four carts and two wagons to help us on our journey after the mayor had given us his friendly admonition to leave all national politics entirely on one side, to be civil, obedient and honest, to fulfil our stations and maintain our character as prisoners of war.

'Then let what overturns in France you are likely to find daily be what they will; you will always be protected and respected as prisoners of war. This, my sons, is my advice to you all! Farewell.'

We made our obedience to his honour, our band struck up a lively air, and off we went baggage and all.

February 6. We left Orleans for Beaugency, twenty-one miles. The morning was mild with a light fall of snow and at 3 in the afternoon we were in the village of Beaugency where our appointed abode was an old church fitted up entirely for troops or any body of passengers that stopped there during the night. It was on the same principals as our lodgings in Orleans. We wanted for nothing to eat or drink had good field beds. The mayor signed our papers and appointed six carts to be in readiness next morning by 8 o'clock.

February 7. We took our breakfast, started our baggage on before us, then we marched off to the tune *Paddy Carey* towards the city of Blois, twenty-seven miles from Beaugency. The weather fine and good road made the march quite light; we halted nearly on hour at a large castle ten miles from Blois where the English kings in former days used to reside while on their hunting parties round the borders of the forest of Orleans. The present duke of Blois was then living there retired from the court and present administration of Napoleon. We halted at this ancient structure where we were requested to eat and drink the health of a friend and well wisher to the British, not to mention any names. We had a lunch of bread and cheese and several large cruises of wine were handed round by the domestics of the duke until all had been served. We then mustered our band, and played 'dull care.' The Duke having been some time in England in his younger days spoke good English and was greatly elevated on hearing his favourite air. We then struck up '*lee rizs*' and away we went. We reached the environs of Blois, before sunset, where we were met by several British officers, and amongst them Mr. Pridham, our first lieutenant on board the *Hussar*. They directed us up to the city hall, where we were directed to a large building called the hotel for strangers; there we lodged our baggage etc.; being evening we had not an opportunity to have any discourse with our officers. We therefore attended on the mayor and had our papers signed; he also gave orders that we should halt next day in order to receive some distributions that was to be served us according to our need of them. We has a good supper and went to our welcome repose.

February 8, 1814. Next morning we all arose in good spirits knowing, in the first instance, that we had a day to rest our wearied bodies and nourish ourselves by the side of a good fire, Secondly we knew the mayor was going to serve us clothes, shoes, etc., and thirdly we were given to understand last evening by our officers that they had orders to assist us on our march through Blois. By sunrise Mr. Pridham, Mr. Leftwidge, Mr. Reynolds,

Doctor Lawmont, and my friend Mr. Smithson all visited us. They were happy to see us and very desirous to see all the *Hussars* we had in our party. We all mustered and made out eleven of the old ship's crew. We gave them a list of all the *Hussars* that were left alive when we left Givet, which only amounted to 95. Mr. Pridham shed tears when he heard so many of that gallant crew had fallen beneath death's fatal sting within the fatal walls of Givet. He then told us that he wanted us all to be present at 2 in the afternoon as he wanted to see us, his shipmates, in particular, and at 4 he wanted all the rest of the party. They enquired if we were well provided for in our present quarters. We told them we had plenty and good. At ten the mayor visited us, paid up our arrears, and served each man a pair of woollen pantaloons, stockings, and shirt and he then told us we should halt again tomorrow in consequence of the British officers having to make some arrangements in our favour. We had five of our men taken with the ague and they went to the hospital where they would be well taken care of. My interpreter's business being partly done for a little while, Mr. Smithson, my friend, visited us. He wanted me a little while if I could make convenient to leave my partners.

'Yes, Sir,' says Crown, 'I will answer for him should he be wanted before he return.'

I have neglected to mention the name of the fifth interpreter that was appointed by the prefecture of Orleans. His name was Andrew Smith my young friend and pupil. I went along with Smithson and took Andrew along with me. We went to a tavern, took a bottle of wine, and had a great many old stories. He told me how Captain Alexander shot my old friend Lieutenant Barker and he also told me that the allied armies were before Paris, and that the British Army under Wellington were at Bordeaux. Smithson said we might daily expect orders for Morlaix, St Maloes, or some part of the sea coast to embark for England. He also said Louis was embarking in England to embrace the crown of France (*Louis dix-huit*). All those tidings we kept privately locked up in the secret coffers of our hearts.

The hour of two drawing on, we took our steps towards the

camp of our countrymen. We met Crown, Aplen, and Johnson in the street. This caused us to take a small horn. I gave them a hint of what Mr. Smithson had revealed to me, and had we not been required to Meet Mr. Pridham at two o'clock, we should have washed that horn down with a second and perhaps a third, on the strength of our welcome tidings, but our time at this moment must be put to a different use. Mr. Pridham and several officers passed the door taking the road to our habitation. We followed at a little distance and all met at the mansion appointed. Pridham desired the *Hussar's* men to stand together and then addressed the rest of our men.

'Fellow country men! At 4 o'clock I shall be here again and give you what assistance our present funds will allow to help you through your toilsome journey, which I have great reason to believe is near an end! God send it may!'

We all went down to the British agent's office where each man signed his name and received five French crowns in part of his wages for the *Hussar*, and one *louis d'or* per man from Lloyd's coffee house which we also signed for. Mr. Pridham informed us that we were all ordered to Tours to wait there for fresh orders, and they had contrived means to have us all taken down the river Loire to Tours in boats at the rate of two *livres* per man, the distance being thirty-nine miles by the main road. We then returned to the camp as they had to serve each man a *louis d'or*. My stars how wonderful rich we all are! Plenty of Money, plenty of cloths, plenty of victuals, and plenty of rest. All we want is plenty of freedom in our own native land which we hope will very soon be our happy fate. We mustered our band in the evening on the green in centre of the square, where we had all the officers and principal people in the city around us. We played several favourite airs, French and English. Young girls and boys were hopping around the square like as many poppets. The British officers were very much gratified to see us so friendly used by the citizens of Blois. When we left Givet we had seven new heads in our baggage for our bass drum, and it happened that evening, Jack the drummer being a little lively, made rather free with his 'logger head' as he used to name his large stick. He drove in the last head he had left and this put an end to our evening diversion. Mr. Pridham talked some time with us after we left off playing. He was very happy to find we had devoted our time in prison to learning. He was desirous to know in what manner we first rose money to purchase so many fine instruments and how we gained our instructions etc., etc. When we told him how we purchased our instruments he smiling said:

'Well you are worthy the title of musicians, you that can fill your bellies with music and sell your rations to purchase instruments! However in the morning I shall make enquiry after some new heads for your drum and tambourine.'

We enquired if any of our people had passed through Blois lately; he said three divisions from Givet had passed through Blois, since they had been sent there to inspect the prisoners that passed through the city on their march towards Tours, where all the British prisoners from the North were ordered to meet and wait fresh orders. I enquired how many of the *Hussar's* crew had passed. He said he believed about twenty-seven but if I called at the bureau in the morning I should have all their names and what day they left Givet etc. We then took our leave and away to our tents where we slept without rocking all night, and having got permission from the mayor to halt another day, and then make two days' stages in one, by going down the Loire to Tours in boats we would fill our regular stages as specified on our *felle de route* from Orleans. On this account we took our time to rise in the morning.

February 9. A fine hard clear day. We visited our sick comrades in the hospital. They really looked like other men; they looked clean, lively, and contented, and they said that place was a heaven on earth, it was enough to bring a dead man to life. In short they were all on the road to recovery. We told them to make haste after us to Tours, where we were to lay some time, shook hands, and parted. We then went to the bureau and got a list of the *Hussar's* crew that had passed Blois. Mr. Pridham sent Mr. Sutton the midshipman to our encampment in search of

Jack Leversedge the drummer. Jack was soon at his side and he went to the bureau where they furnished him with half a dozen new heads, an apron, and a pair of new gloves, with a crown to drink the health of the merchant that presented the heads to us. He was a leather dealer in Blois, very partial to the British. We got our drum rigged again and that evening we gave them a real round turn after dark. The young women began to muster, and the British officers having after so many years confinement in France become quite familiar with the French mode of waltzing joined in with those lovely creatures that were left (as in other parts of France) without one single young man to join them in their simple exercise of waltzing. We played until 12 at midnight, then broke up the ball and all Israel to their tents. We went to our mansion and soon were lulled to sweet repose, where all care was entirely forgot, and the business of the day was left until we saw the light of another day or sunrise next morning.

February 10, 1814. Fine warm clear weather. This morning we were all bustle preparing for our grand expedition down the Loire. Mr. Pridham had already engaged twenty boats to carry from eighteen to twenty men each at the rate of two francs each man from Blois down the river to Tours. Our detachment at this time amounted to 356 men and our only young Nurse Janet Carter. She stuck true to us! Never was seen nor even heard in the greatest of our sufferings, to murmur or in the least to reflect on her rash step she took in marrying a prisoner of war. She was beloved by every one and often would drive away melancholy reflections from any of us that appeared to be low in spirits. At 9 a.m. we embarked. The key or quay was crowded with people and our officers were all present. We embarked the band in the two first boats, to lead the van. All hands embarked. We gave three cheers, which was answered from the shore. Our band struck up 'O'er the hills and far away.' We had a fine breeze down the river and the strong current in our favour soon wafted us out of the sight of friendly spectators. We had a fine passage down the Loire. Had it been in the summer season the beautiful villas and seats on the banks of this large river must have presented to us a beautiful romantic landscape.

At 4 p.m. we arrived at the large quay, near the bridge in Tours where we met numbers of our countrymen ready to direct us to the *citadella*, where the secretary of the mayor attended in the bureau. William Crown and Johnson went to the bureau and presented our *felle de rout*. They returned with orders to proceed to the *citadella* where they would find barracks all ready for us. We discharged the boats and proceeded up to the dwelling appointed and placed twenty in each room. In this place we had the happiness to meet many of our shipmates, prison mates, and countrymen flocking round us, all happy to have the band join them again. We found our seventh division had been in Tours ten days. They were taken a quite different rout to that we took, from Vitry. They had left a great many brave fellows in the different hospitals on their rout. They mentioned several of the first divisions that left Givet had (word missing) through fatigue and perished with cold in the miserable cold cachots where they were drove for security through the night. All those sufferings we were no strangers to; dear experience had made them known to us. We had every thing comfortable, both victuals and lodgings, also liberty in the city from 8 in the morning till 8 in in the evening. The drawbridges were drawn up all round the city at gunfire, 8 o'clock, and opened in the morning at 8. We sent twelve men to the hospital, none of them seriously ill, but fatigued, and severe colds were most of their ailments. This reduced our party to 344 men. On the third day after our arrival we were joined by a detachment from Bitche consisting partly of those men that were sent there from the different depots in France for punishment, desertion and being taken again. Amongst them were many of our old companions in Givet, and particularly their interpreter, no other person than Robert Smith my old messmate and Andrew's brother, and with him his wife the late Madam Gammant. Young Andrew was happy to meet his brother. Madam Smith was also very glad to see us both in good health and spirits. The Bitche division were 273 strong. Their route was from the city of Chateauroux to the city of Angers, in *Maine et Loire*, so that they only halted with us one day, got some refreshment and proceeded their march towards Angers, that evening being the 14th of February, Valentine's day! And my day! The mayor sent for the interpreters of the 8th division prisoners of war, British from Givet to Tours. The five of us attended his worship the mayor at the bureau where he presented us our *felle de rout* for the city of Richelieu to march on the succeeding day; also three other detachments were ordered to the towns of Chinon, L'Isle Bouchard, and Loudun, all in the same direction with Richelieu. We warned our party and on the following morning we had two carts and after being mustered by the Comissarie de Marine, mayor, etc., we marched from Tours on the 15th of Feb., 344 men, for the village of Axay, eighteen miles. The cross roads were frozen hard so that we soon performed this day's journey. We had a large room in the town hall to lodge in and seven *sols* per man paid us by the mayor to find our own rations. This village afforded plenty of bread, milk, cheese, eggs, also excellent cider. This suited us. We had plenty of straw allowed for those who chose to sleep in the camp and those who chose to hire lodgings had beds at six *sols* each man.

February 16. Fine weather. The mayor had two carts prepared for us. He signed our rout and we took our departure for Chinon, seventeen miles, which was only making game of us. By the time our joints got limber we were in Chinon, drew billets, and all quartered safe by two in the afternoon. Next morning we met and the mayor had three carts ready. He signed our rout and we have made a general rule that where the mayor acts like a gentleman and gives us billets, we always give them a tune on leaving the place. We therefore mustered to the call of our bugles.

February 17. We travailed to L'Isle Bouchard, only fourteen miles.

Our band in front by turns did play
'March on my boys make no delay.'

At 12 noon we landed on the island. The river Vienne runs on each side of this curious little town. Rain began to fall shortly after our arriving. We drew billets for 344 men, served them round, and all took shelter from the storm. In this place we lived on fish, a rare treat. The people were remarkable clever liberal folks. They kept us employed relating old sea-faring adventures in which they greatly delighted. They reckoned themselves partly sailors as they lived by fishing although they had never seen the sea-shore perhaps in their life time. We had plenty of wine at three *sols* per bottle and other things cheap in proportion. We slept well that night and on the 18th of February we had four carts and marched early the morning. Being fine we gave them a tune and took the woods leading to Richelieu.

February 18, 1814. At 3 in the afternoon we arrived in Richelieu about half an hour before the party reached the gates, William Crown, Andrew, and your humble servant. We went to the mayor in the municipality, presented our *felle de rout*. He looked at it and smiling said to some of the gentlemen sitting at the desk:

'We are going to be honoured with a party of foreign visitors. They intend to stop some little time with us. They are near the gates at this present time and request our advice to find them lodgings. Those three gentlemen are their interpreters. What must we do in this case? Shall I give them billets or what do you prefer or wish me to do?'

'What nation are they?' says an elderly gentleman.

'British prisoners of war' answered the mayor.

'How many of them are coming to visit Richelieu?' says Monsieur.

'The *felle de rout* says 344 men and one woman,' answered the mayor.

'Well then, let us divide them amongst us and our friends through the city. As for me I should like to have eight or ten,' says Monsieur.

'Well,' says the mayor, 'I should like to have the like number.'

A third gentleman says, 'If you begin to take so many you will not leave any for those that are not present! Numbers of our friends that perhaps might have a desire to share their generosity with that of their fellow citizens on poor captive prisoners of war will be disappointed. Therefore my advise is to let them all march up to the square; then we can divide them through the city to those that are able to use them like men and brothers!'

As he finished his decision, we heard three strokes of the big Drum. 'Hallo! What is that?' says the mayor in amazement.

'That, Sir, is our big drum, warning us that our party are at the gates of your city' was our reply to the mayor.

'Go, go quick,' says the mayor, 'and conduct your brothers up to the square.'

We were leaving the room when old Monsieur says to us, 'Please to favour the citizens of Richelieu with your music on entering our small but humane city.'

We made a bow and parted and went to the gate, the mayor in company with us. Our men were all ready; we gave the signal and in one moment the streets of Richelieu were thronged with astonished spectators. Our band had a grand effect in the street. We made the windows and doors all rattle, at every stroke on the big drum. The air was a trumpet tune, with a trumpet solo, which had a grand effect. We then changed to a French *rondeau* with a bugle solo; this was grand! The mayor and several gentlemen marching in front, we got into the square, halted, and then we were surrounded with gentlemen. Some took eight, some six, others four, and so on, until the square was entirely clear of our folks. As for us five interpreters we were taken to the house of the mayor's brother, at the prefecture of the city, named Monsieur Blanchard, a fine young gentlemen, and a great musician. We had clean stockings and slippers first thing, and then the servant conducted us to a large room where we left our knapsacks, and instruments. We then were invited to take some refreshment. After a while we walked out to see the place. We found Leversedge, and Henry Conolly our octave flute player, Frederick Taylor the bandmaster and Henry Alms the first trumpeter, were all at the mayor's house. In fine, we soon found all our comrades well taken care of. The whole of our men all declared that this place ought to be called paradise, and no longer have the name of Richelieu. Aplen said if it was possible for happiness to be found on earth that was the place!

CHAPTER 13
1814: Perfect Paradise

February 19, 1814. Richelieu. Rain and cold in the morning. We all kept close quarters this day, repairing damages. On the 20th, fine weather, we began like snails to creep out of our nests and look round our city of Paradise. We also visited the ancient castle of the renowned Cardinal Richelieu. Four of our men were sick and went to the hospital. Many of our people were so contented that they kept close quarters to their houses, and as for Janet and her husband they were at the house of Monsieur Beaumont, a very rich respectable gentleman, where the old lady treated Janet the same as her own daughter. In the afternoon Monsieur Blanchard would have us sit down and give him some information, how we were captured and how we were used in France, etc. We had wine, cakes, and fruit in abundance. We gave him the outlines of the loss of the *Hussar*, our sufferings in the boats, and we also gave him a sketch of our march from Brest, our sufferings in Givet upwards often years, our march from Givet in front of the army, and several trials we have gone through to our arrival in Richelieu. Those heads or outlines were the subject of his discourse whenever we sat down on an afternoon or evening, which gave him great satisfaction to understand the whole of our narrative. In the evening he brought out an elegant clarinet to hear what we thought of it. Crown took it and played '*Monsieur de Moulin*' in style. He looked and smiling said:

'If I mistake not Sir, you play on the horn when you arrived in Richelieu.'

Crown told him he played any instrument that he fell in with occasionally. He then took the clarinet and played a waltz very masterly. He desired us to muster our instruments and try out one of our tunes. He should like to accompany us which he did and in a short time he could run over our music quite correct, and made his large front room the band room and invited all our musicians to meet there every afternoon and rehearse. We had ten or twelve gentlemen belonging the city joined us, and attended regular every afternoon. Our host Mr. Blanchard kept the decanter always ready to wet the instruments; in fact we had far too much wine. One or the other continually were having us at their houses. The mayor and several other gentlemen requested us to play a little while every evening (when the weather was fine) in the grand square. This greatly amused the inhabitants. They made it their business every evening to meet in the square and pass an hour in mirth and friendship. We became so far acquainted with the young ladies that we gave them a ball every Sunday evening on the green outside the gates. We were also invited to play in the theatre and we had our fishing, shooting, and all sorts of simple amusement with the gentlemen of the city. We got so habituated to them that we could go out to the field or the vineyard as regular as any old farmers and assist in what ever was doing.

The word would be, 'Where are you going tomorrow?' and the answer, 'To our farm or our vineyard to work.' What ever was the property of our host was ours. Monsieur Blanchard would say to us: 'My children, we will visit our farm, or our vineyard tomorrow.'

This was the manner we amused ourselves daily. We constantly found some diversion or exercise so that the time passed away like a dream. We have even gone over to L'Isle Bouchard on visits to our countrymen that were quartered there. We also heard various reports such as the Russians were at Paris, the Germans at Fontainbleu, the Prussians at St Dennis and the British at Bordeaux, but we left them to settle all disputes. We gave up the notion of troubling our heads with national politics and diverted that part of our leisure hours in the lovely company of our female companions, where we found more comfort in the tender tales of love in one evening, yes, more than we could, or had found, in ten years debating on politics. Mr. and Mrs. Blanchard called us their children and treated us the same. We were counted as their own family in regard to washing, victuals, or any thing that was to be done in or out of the house. We had three of our men went into the hospital during our stay and four on our arrival. One of them named Henry Stevens, formerly of the *Lord Nelson* Indiaman, died, and we buried him with all the honours our circumstances would afford. We had no other misfortunes worth relating; all was friendship and harmony with us in Richelieu.

The month of February stole away. March crept along unnoticed, except on a Saturday afternoon we used to go out to the brooks and pick watercress. This warned us that spring was hastening towards us with rapid speed. We used to say that when spring came we would do this thing, and when summer came we would do the other thing, but no more of that building castles in the air; the scene is changed. Preparations are making to restore us to our own nation, but by a long tedious round about turn. Such strange overturns took place in the administration that our happiness began to tremble. The shattered government contrived a plan. In order to keep us from falling into the hands of any invading enemies they gave orders to have all the British prisoners of war in France marched with all speed to the south clear of all the allied armies. The mayor got some hint of this but not any particular account nor yet any orders in particular. In the latter end of March, Monsieur Blanchard, at the prefecture, our generous land lord (or supporter) desired us to write him the music of some favourite English pieces that he had taken a great fancy to. At the same time he observed he was rather suspicious that the minister of war was inclined to drive all the unfortunate prisoners of war into some remote place of security, to prevent their falling into the power of the enemies of France, and we amongst the rest would be tore from our friends and well wishers to wander and suffer every sort of hardships that some tyrannical, inhumane rulers art very apt to inflict, on a poor unfortunate prisoner of war. And afterwards boast of their brave exploits when o'er their cups, thinking it does them great honour to say:

'I have had my satisfaction out of such a nation, I made their prisoners remember me, when I had them under my jurisdiction etc. I took my revenge out of them, by confinement, starvation, beating them, defrauding them of their rations, and confining them in the cells of a dungeon, to sleep on the bare ground without any straw or covering.'

Perhaps he can boast that he ran one or two of those poor unarmed captives through with his own hand or gave orders to some of his followers to shoot that damned Englishman if he don't march quick etc! or keep the middle of the road, or keep his place, or something to find a reason for their barbarity. This is the treatment that has been, and I am afraid will again be given to prisoners of war when under the tyrannical government of such inhumane unfeeling monsters!

This was the character that this worthy gentleman gave of his own countrymen. He observed he was sorry to have such a character to give his own nation, but all those acts of cruelty and oppression that he had just mentioned he heard his own dear father say, that he in the time of the tyrant Robespierre was a soldier in the army and had seen all those acts of tyrannical cruelty put in execution both on French men prisoners and also other nations that fell beneath his displeasure.

'However,' continued Monsieur Blanchard, 'we will not point this out to be so, only it has been so. I hope and pray your fortune may be quite reverse to what we have conjectured. It is the humble request of all the citizens in this our small city that you may remain with us until some arrangements are made to restore you all home to those that are near, and dear to you. Therefore hope for the best, keep up your spirits, and like men undertake and perform the second part of your long fatiguing pilgrimage. Come, my sons, take a glass of cognac. Then we will have a tune and drive all care away.'

We played a while and then took our evening's walk, each to their choice, some to see their heart's delights, others to join in a song, or a dance. I shaped my course to the mansion of Pierre Collordo the vintner. That was my usual retreat; on any evening there was a load-stone under his roof that had very great attraction over me, and frequently caused me to make night, day, and day, night. I told the old gentleman what was the apprehensions of Monsieur Blanchard, but the old gentleman would not hear a word of our leaving Richelieu until the orders were for us to march to the sea coast in full express to embark for our native country. On the 28th of March three of our men came out of the hospital, quite smart.

On the 30th of March the ladies gave a grand ball. This ball was in the city hall, and our band was invited to attend and take parts in the music in concert with the violins. They had some very grand performers on that instrument, all of them gentlemen of the city. The house was very much crowded and the evening was passed in friendship and good order. The gentlemen that frequently played along with us would come and relieve one or the other of us so that we all had an opportunity to take a few round turns round the room with our little load-stones that had been all invited to attend, and when the gentry and their ladies had danced then the master of the ceremonies called the young men and young women to fall in and go round with a dance. We had a variety of dainties both to eat and drink and kept up the sport until past two in the morning, when we closed the ball with an English hornpipe danced by young Andrew Smith. We left our instruments in the Orchestra until next morning, and all retired home to rest.

On the following morning, March 31, we mustered and collected our instruments, went through our rehearsal in the Theatre, then to the music room in our house (as we then termed the house of our host Mr. Blanchard). When our band were all present, French and English, playing some of the favourite marches, rondeaux or waltzes the city of Richelieu would echo from corner to corner. Our band consisted of twenty-four men and we mostly had from twelve to twenty French, mostly performers on the clarinet and horn. We now considered our selves in perfect paradise!

But stop! Look to the first of April. What fools! The sudden change that this fool's day made with the young girls that had been dancing to our music the night before. They were heard in various parts of the city performing music of their own composition which had an entire different effect on both the hearer, and the performer. The solos were pensive and solemn. The chorus or *forte* parts were like the dead march in *Saul*, and those active limbs that had so gracefully beat time to the music were seen trembling beneath the heavy load of grief. Even those enchanting eyes that had been an illumination to the room where they shone were like stars shrouded in a cloud which turns into rain. Those bright orbs were also shrouded with sadness and bathed in tears, and that member of the body that expresses the sentiments of the heart and by the least turn can give ease or pain, joy or grief, was by this sudden stroke of unexpected separation entirely for some time deprived of its usual utterance, only able to vent its grief by sobbing, sighing, and inward lamentations. This was the effect this grievous first day of April had amongst the young females in this blessed asylum for the unfortunate captives, that had the fortunate change from hunger and cruelties, into the hands of good humane friendly affectionate Christians.

I shall endeavour to explain the cause of this sudden revolution that took place amongst us in Richelieu on April fool day. William Crown and myself were busily employed in the music room writing out a book of marches from various selections that we had collected in Givet, which we intended for Monsieur Blanchard, when we heard a noise in the street, looked out at the window, and saw a horse *gendarme* in great haste, ride up to the municipality. We left our music, being jealous that this messenger bore some orders concerning the prisoners of war. Numbers like ourselves crowded round the square, both citizens and prisoners, all desirous to hear what hasty tidings this messenger bore to Richelieu! We were however soon given to understand his mission.

The mayor sent for the British interpreters; we answered his call. He desired us to let our bugles call all our men to muster immediately; he also said the messenger was the bearer of dispatches from the Comissarie General in Tours, Signed by orders of his highness *Monsieur le Duc de Feltre*, Minister of War in Paris, to march all the prisoners of war under his orders in Richelieu from that place on the third of April. That he had also received a *felle de rout* of every day's stage we had to make from Richelieu to Orillac on the borders of the Pyrenees, ready to fill up with our names. He therefore desired all the men to muster in the square and give them timely notice. We immediately went to our trumpeters; they took their bugles and sounded the old call to muster. That was the time, and that the very cause of the sudden change that took place amongst the young girls, and, I must tell the truth, many of our own young countrymen.

However all hands were mustered and warned to make themselves in readiness to leave Richelieu on the third of the month. This caused a great bustle with all those who thought to fulfil the scripture, by leaving tomorrow to provide for itself. Many were sorry to leave their only comfort behind, but the orders are given and we must obey. We went home and found Mr. Blanchard, his wife, and his aged father, all quite down cast at the news of our having to leave them and march such a long distance entirely from the sea shore. Madam Blanchard provided each of us with a new shirt, new stockings, and shoes. Mr. Blanchard made each of us a present of a jacket and pantaloons and the old father presented us each a *louis d'or* to help us on our journey.

April 2. In the morning we made a general muster to see that all the names were correct in the new *felle de rout*, or, in English, the list of the towns we had to pass through and the day of the month we had to sleep in each town, also to have our rout signed by the mayors of such certain places on such particular dates, and that we are to victualled and lodged on the inhabitants of the towns appointed on our route to sleep in. The next thing we had to know what was to be done with our six men in the hospital. We visited them and found them all willing to join us as they were quite smart. We have lost one man by the fever and ague which leaves us at present including the six in the hospital 343 men on the list and one female. We have lived in paradise upwards of six weeks where we have become robust healthy looking men and make a quite different appearance to that we made the day we arrived. In the evening I visited my happy retreat and passed part of the night in the charming embraces of one that proved faithful and true, as will be found in the following numbers. I took a little rest towards morning and then arose in order to attend my business in leaving Richelieu at 8 in the morning as proposed the night before. We had four wagons and two covered carts to attend us to Loudun, seventeen miles. The morning was very heavy rain which made the march quite unpleasant, yet we jot all ready to start and were detained some time in the square by our friends and well wishers pouring their blessings and good wishes on us.

Shaking hands, embracing, taking a farewell glance across the square at the lovely beauty that waves her handkerchief for the last time and retires leaning on the assisting arm of an elder sister. At that moment we gave the signal, and our large drum made the square echo with three thundering strokes. Mr. Blanchard, and the mayor, and the old father's last request of me was to be sure and write on the first opportunity. They bowed their heads and drew back. Our band then struck up the French farewell quick-step, 'Farewell Sweet Maid'! And away we marched crowded on both sides of our friends, one carrying our knapsack, another with a bottle of kill grief. All this time the rain fell in torrents. Nevertheless we had both good inside and outside lining to defend us from the severity of the weather. We got clear of the city by ten o'clock, kept slowly pursuing our journey, and by twelve we had nearly parted with all our company. We secured our drum in the cart appointed for the band and thus proceeded along.

April 3. Marched from Richelieu for Loudun where we arrived about 4 p.m., still raining. We had sent Andrew Smith and Aplen in front to prepare billets for the party. They had our billets all ready when we arrived so that we soon all found shelter from the rain. We were very kindly treated by the inhabitants. Several of them had frequently visited our happy residence on business. The mayor was a kind old gentleman where we, the five interpreters, lodged. He was a great friend of our protector Mr. Blanchard in Richelieu. We were in discourse concerning our next day's march and, looking over our *felle de rout*, our next day's march was to Argenton (Argenton-Château), in the department of *Deux Sevres*, nineteen miles. The mayor was signing our route when a rap came at the hall door. The door was answered and found the visitor to be a courier from Tours with orders from the *commissarie* to alter our route from Richelieu to Chatellerault and Poitiers on the main road to Niort. This caused us to return back to Richelieu next day.

For my own part I should rather have proceeded our route to Argenton than to have another parting with Richelieu. Still at the same time there was a sort of wavering in my unsettled mind that almost caused me to think I should like to have one more glance at my greatest treasure. Morning came; still rain falling incessantly, but the idea of returning home drowned and overcame every obstacle either in regard of rain or roads with the greatest part of our company. We had the same wagons and carts back again. We took breakfast and then left the town of Loudun.

April 4. At 3 p.m. we entered the western gates of Richelieu. We dispersed as quick as the mayor could reach us, every man to his former home! We five were welcomely received by our worthy benefactor, had our linen changed, took a little refreshment, then took two of our men to the hospital. They had taken severe colds through being wet the two days following; we then had a long talk with Monsieur Blanchard. He said he was certain that our confinement in France would not be long, owing to the tottering state the country was placed in at this present moment, entirely through ambition. He said France was entirely overrun by her enemies and their determination was to reinstate the Bourbons on the throne of France, Louis the 18th.

'Therefore make the best shift you possibly can a little while longer; a few more weeks will restore you all to your native country. Therefore, my children, bear your hardships a little longer with manly courage and you will find my words verified, then you will remember that those were the predictions of your old father Pierre Blanchard.'

We then began to make a move to our separate parts of the city where we had to enjoy the pleasure of one more evening's company with those that made our captivity the happiest part of our lives. As for my part I visited my old father the vintner. He always saluted me. He was very happy to see me returned once more to his house and the sound of a favourite voice soon was answered from the room above with the enchanting words of 'Father, is that my dear.'

The old gentleman kindly answers, 'Yes, my child. Come down and make him welcome and happy and drive away your melancholy sadness. Be cheerful and let us pass one more happy evening together in the same manner that we have passed numbers before.'

There certainly was something whispered in each fluttering heart that whispered, 'We will never be parted.'

We were at last aroused from a lovely trance by the oldest sister entering the room. 'There, Louisa,' said the father, 'I have the happiness to see Mary once more roused from her melancholy dream.'

Louisa was very happy to have the pleasure of saluting her favourite Lincolnshire hero, and once more the house of sadness was by chance transformed into the abode of momentary gladness and cheerful smiling faces once more enlivened the aged spirits of the affectionate father, Pierre Collardo.

We sat, loving and beloved, repeating our little tales concerning our various changes through life and the old father was at last inclined to go to his bed. He wished us all a goodnight and shaking the hand of his young English son says, 'Ah, my child, would to God you were a Christian. You should not leave my daughter in Richelieu to mourn your absence and never more to behold your presence.'

'Father,' answered Louisa, 'John is a good Christian.'

'Yes father,' says Mary, 'he is no heretic like the other English men. We can soon instruct him in our mode of worship.'

'Ah, my child, the laws and rules of our church will not grant you permission to stray beyond the bounds of your holy church by joining hands with any man unless he be baptised in the faith of our holy Virgin.' He then retired to his bed.

Mary smiling says, 'Well, Louisa, you are much older than me. Can you advise me what is the best course to take, because I am convinced that I cannot live if my dear boy must be tore from my arms never more to enjoy his lovely presence?'

'I can tell you, sister,' says Louisa, 'what my advice is. Take part of your cloths in a handkerchief and I will assist you to leave Richelieu early in the morning. Take the road to Chatel-lerault and boldly venture to try your fortune with the only man you adore.'

'What say you brother?' says Louisa. 'Won't that be the best way Mary can do?'

My answer might easy be known, it was sure to be, 'Yes, and we will be married the very first opportunity. We cannot be separated. Yesterday I suffered more than my tongue can express, and if I have again to part with my lovely Mary I might as well part with my life, because death is far preferable to a life of misery and woe. I will protect her by night and by day. I will travel by her side and make the fatigues of march slide softly away by my presence and affectionate conduct.'

'Yes, my dear,' says Mary. 'I will take the advice of my sister, and trust myself under your loving protection. We will enter into the world together and when that happy, day does arrive that you are restored to your native country I shall also be restored to you. Your happiness will be mine, your parents will be mine and you shall be mine until separated by death, our fortune shall be the same.'

'Sister,' says Louisa, 'let us begin to prepare your articles most required on a journey. Father is fast asleep, therefore we have nothing to fear, and we must leave this house before daylight so that the neighbours may have no suspicious thoughts.'

Being all prepared for our elopement the clock struck five, Louisa and Mary both took their bundles and as old father never rose early they were not under any apprehension that he would find out our departure until we were some miles from Richelieu.

When we left the house Mary and her sister passed out at the north gate and walked round to the road that leads to Chatellerault where they were to join us at the halfway house, and our hero took the road to his lodgings to prepare himself for the bold stroke for a wife. Crown rose on my entering the room and we awoke our other three partners. I informed them that we had a frosty morning to start this time from our homes, therefore we would be better able to perform our day's work of twenty-three miles than we had been to perform yesterday's that was only seventeen. Daylight began to make its appearance through the windows so we got our traps all ready and in a little while Henry Alms saluted us with the old mornings bitters on his bugle which said, 'Rise and march away.' We left our noble benefactor's dwelling, having before observed that we would not disturb the family again to take our leave; once was enough.

April 5. Being all present in the square we counted over and made 341 men all included and two left sick in the hospital made the old complement 343. We now waited for his honour the mayor to see the men counted over and to sign and make a little alteration in our *felle de route*. He soon was with us and in a little while was satisfied with the number of men, went to the bureau corrected our papers and with our six carriages in front we again took our last farewell of that heavenly abode of humanity, charity and true Christianity. Our band played up a fresh quick step called 'My honour calls me from thee,' and for the last time passed the gates of Richelieu. We were again crowded with our friends and acquaintance. Several of our boys had heavy heads all this day's march; our day's march being twenty-three miles caused our company to part with us soon so that we might proceed on our journey. They gave us three cheers at parting, which we answered with three times three and three rolls of the big drum: we then marched on all in good spirits and William Crown, Andrew Smith, and his honour went ahead as usual to have the billets ready for the party on their arrival.

The ground was hard and we let no grass grow under our feet. They had no idea that I was in chase of a beautiful French frigate, but believe me every corner we passed and every movement I saw on the road I thought was the prize I looked after. We reached a small village twelve miles from Richelieu; we called at a tavern and took a mouthful of bread and cheese, a bottle of wine and off we tramped. We had many little rigs on each other on account of the girls in Richelieu. Crown was resolved in his mind that if peace took place and he was released he would shape his course direct for Richelieu (which he really performed). Aplen said (as we heard at Chatellerault) that the three of us had gone back to Richelieu after our girls. However they found the contrary on their arrival in Chatellerault, because Crown and Andrew met them with the billets.

For my part I went in search of my only treasure, and not more than two minutes after I left them with a pretence to find out what sort of a billet we had allotted us I heard a tap at a window, looked round and there stood the two young adventurers. I rushed into the house perhaps a little bewildered. However they told me I never spoke until I had taken a bite at each of their faces. We then sat down and discoursed a little while Mary told me she had taken a cart at the halfway village; her bundle was too heavy for her and her sister, and they gave five *francs* for a carriage; that was the reason we could not fall in with them on the road. Louisa says:

'Brother, where do you sleep tonight?'

I answered, 'At my billet most likely'

'Well, she said, 'that will be best. This lady of the house has promised Mary and me lodgings for the night and I shall want to see you early in the morning as I am going back with the same carriage we came in.'

'Why, sister,' says Mary, 'Father will be sure you have been with me.'

'Yes, I shall tell him I have been striving to take you back, but finding my entreaties were all in vain, I was under the necessity of returning without you, and by that time you will be far distant from Richelieu. You know what I did when I married Francois. Father would not hear a word of my leaving home to travel with my darling husband, to join the army in Germany but all his talk was mere folly. I mounted the baggage and like a brave Amazonian followed my heart's delight in troubles. I comforted him in sickness, I lulled his poor aching head in my bosom, and on that unfortunate day he fell at the battle of Wagram I bathed his dear bleeding wounds with my tears. And then I for the first time felt what it was to be robbed of my heart's delight, I returned home with the wounded or at least I came with the wagons to Strasbourg and then travelled home to my father. Mother was no more. Father had only you, my dear Mary, left to comfort him; you were then young and found the loss of our dear mother. I returned to my father and he was happy to see his lost Louisa return, and he ofttimes has said he believed nothing except death could prevent a woman from following the man she has placed her affections upon. This, my dear brother and sister, is the reason of my trying every effort to have you both made happy. I have seen and am fully convinced that you dearly love each other, and with my consent you shall never more be parted. God bless you both,' kissing us while the tears ran plenteously over her downcast cheeks; poor Louisa Francois.

We were in a neat little parlour. I called the lady of the house to know if she would provide dinner or supper which we may please to name it.

She said, 'Certainly, with pleasure.'

I called for two glasses of ratafia for the ladies and a horn of cognac to my own cheek. Then I went to our billet which was near at hand and found all my messmates at dinner.

'Where the devil have you been?' says Johnson.

'We thought you were in Richelieu by this time,' says Aplen!

'Ah,' says Crown, 'I rather think he has been looking out for another sweetheart on purpose to kill the thoughts of his Mary in Richelieu in the wine house.'

We had our jokes all pass in friendship. I made an excuse that I fell in with a man that was a soldier sick in the hospital at Givet the same time that I was nurse in the 4th ward and that he was a tanner and lived in the environs of the city etc. This proves that a lover is never without an excuse. I sat down and took a glass and made excuse as to eating, because I had promised to take supper with my particular friend, the tanner (but that friend was Mary).

Supper being over we then went to the mayor after our papers and to hear the orders for morning, how many wagons etc. Our next day's march was to Poitiers, twenty-five mile, and to have four carts. We got our papers and returned to our lodgings where I left them in order to fulfil my engagement to sup with a particular friend. I was soon in the arms of that particular friend. Supper being ready we sat down and enjoyed it with comfort. I repeated over their different jokes and my story of the tanner which made a hearty laugh and kept us cheerful all the evening after supper. Mary begged her sister to excuse her a few minutes as she wanted to speak to me. We went into the yard and my lovely girl gave me a small locket containing ten *louis d'or*.

'This locket and its contents, my dear John, was presented to me by my poor mother on her death bed and I present it to you as a sure pledge of my love and faithfulness towards you. From this moment I willingly leave myself entirely under your protection. I give myself up to your advice and directions as to what you may imagine for both our welfare and by this embrace! I will never leave you nor forsake you in whatever situation you may be placed, but will in trouble be your comforter and in sickness I will heal you with tenderness and affection, and should we live to reach your native land your mother I will love as my own, your friends shall be mine and when death calls us to leave this world and fly to the realms of bliss may we go hand in hand, loving and beloved.'

My reply was very easy made and easy signed and sealed with the impression of her sweet ruby lips, and one moment of silence locked in each other's arms signed our definitive treaty for life!! We then returned to sister Louisa; she was uneasy at our long absence, but we told here what was our real business. She rose and embraced us both, saying she was now contented and could return home with pleasure being fully convinced of our regard for each other.

The evening was far advanced and I must repair to my billet and take some rest so as to be ready to start early in the morning for Poitiers; therefore it was proper for me to provide conveyance for my sweet girl to Poitiers. She proposed to walk!

'No, no! That won't do. I will find a carriage in a little while.'

I called the man of the house and told him I wanted a carriage in the morning to take that lady to Poitiers. His answer was that his horse and light covered wagon was at liberty. If that would do we could have that, and his boy to drive, for the sum of ten *francs*. I sealed the bargain and was quite contented. I then addressed Louisa, desiring to know how I might address my letters to her. This I soon understood. Next was to know what time she intended to return back in the morning. She said the cart would be ready at 7 o'clock, therefore she wished to see me by 6 if possible, unless I could make arrangements to stay with them all night, but this would not be prudent at present, therefore I thought best to retire, I took my leave of my charmer and Louisa and then made all sail for my destined port. I arrived in time. My messmates were all quite merry over a game at cards. They had two or three bottles of wine to come in, and we sat chattering with the old landlord, a butcher by trade, a great royalist. At last the clock struck twelve and all hands immediately fled to their nests. We had good beds but sleep was far from me.

My thoughts on what steps I had already taken and what I was about to undertake occupied my mind until I heard the clock strike five. I rose and dressed, walked the room a few minutes, then called on Andrew, my only confidential friend. He soon dressed himself. We left the house; Andrew wanted to know where I was going so early and I soon convinced him. On entering the mansion where all my comfort lay, Mary was the lovely porter. Andrew drew back. Mary flew to my arms and with her lively turn says:

'What, Mr. Smith, are you afraid of me? You were not so in Richelieu.'

He then entered and saw Louisa. They as usual saluted him. He then turns round to me. Louisa and me made our excuse for a little while and left Mary to unfold the whole secret to Andrew. Louisa advised me to get married in Poitiers as there was a Protestant Church and ministers established in that city since the reign of Edward the black Prince who lays buried in the church.

April 6. Louisa also requested me to write her word from Poitiers how circumstances were with us and every particular that might occur, to direct to Louisa Francois; her father would not know any thing of it, until his pursuit would be vain. She also made me promise if ever we got our liberty that Mary and me should pay them a visit in Richelieu, all which I sealed on her lips with a faithful promise to perform, and at parting her last request was not be ungenerous to Mary nor act beyond the bounds of honour until the laws of God and man had united us together in lawful wedlock which she hoped another night's sleeping apart would terminate. I faithfully promised Louisa to take her kind advice; we then entered the room where Mary and Andrew were very busy, Mary relating our intentions, and he listening.

'Come, Wetherell,' says Andrew, 'we must go. Our bugles sounded some time ago.'

I advised Mary not to start until after breakfast with the wagon, so that she might overtake us at the halfway house.

We took our farewell of poor Louisa never more to behold her lovely grief worn face. Tears fell on all sides; I took my leave of my young adventurer and we parted. We went to the square where our men were nearly all present. The morning was quite hazy and soon turned into a rainy day. Never mind; the two sisters have each a covered carriage, and as for me I can back off a little moisture. The mayor saw us count the men and all being correct signed our papers and off we started with our four baggage carts in front. The rain prevented the band playing but our bugles made a very good change, and took us clear of Chatellerault. William Crown and Johnson took their turn to start ahead. We all proceeded on with speed.

Owing to the rain nothing particular took place until we were close up to the halting place, a beautiful little village. I began to look back for my young adventurer and on entering the village I, being nearly the head-most man, heard some one call my name. Looking round saw a wagon driving up towards me with a horse *gendarme* on one side, and an old gentleman riding on the other side. Ah, I was thunder struck!! All the fiends from the infernal regions could not have struck me with such unexpected terror as those unwelcome visitors at that present moment! I stood, my heart fluttered within me! I gazed, and Oh, cruel fortune; what was worse than a dagger piercing my breast. I beheld what nearly deprived me of my reason—My dear Mary waving her white handkerchief to me and beckoning me to go to them. I was young and robust and in fact could bear more than the general run of young men. They stopped the wagon and the two horseman sat by it. I plucked up every grain of courage that was to be found in my possession. Towards them I went, casting a side glance at the fountain of my joy, or grief. She was bathed in tears. Father Collardo rode up to me; he looked sorrowful at me.

At last he says, 'My son, give me your hand,' which he held fast in his. 'Be not the least daunted my child. I lay nothing to your charge, nor yet to my own child. She has already confessed to me that she followed you entirely for the love she has for you and that you did not delude her away from her home with any carnal intentions. Things appear to me that you do love each other but you must be parted at present. Perhaps,' continued the father, 'the day is not far distant when you will have free liberty to return to Richelieu where you shall both be united in one and until that time you must be parted. My daughter must return with me to Richelieu and you must pursue your journey. This, my dear young man, is the only advice I can give you. Wait with patience, be true to your country, and perseverance may restore my daughter lawfully to your arms once more. This is all the chance you can have to gain your prize. Therefore we must return. The rain is too heavy to delay. If you wish to speak to her and take your leave I will wait with the greatest pleasure.'

He rode on one side and I flew to the arms of my lovely angel. His utterance was nearly past comprehension owing to her sobs and sighs.

'Ah, my dear John, this will soon terminate my existence. I shall never live to see you again! Let me feast my eyes on you for the last time. My dear John, my last request is keep my medal and what it contains, and when you look at it think of your faithful Mary, and she will always love and pray for you. Farewell, my darling boy, farewell.'

I descended from the wagon; the old man took my hand, shook it, and put five crowns into it.

'There, my son, take that and my blessing, farewell.'

They turned round their horses and back they drove and left me standing a living statue, worse than I should have felt had I fallen into the hands of some banditti of robbers that took from me all the treasure I had in the world, then stripped me of all my apparel and left me like Adam naked; I stood and gazed after them reflecting on cruel fortune etc. They vanished from my sight.

'She has gone. My all, my only hope is tore from me; what shall I do? It is folly to pursue her, she is safe guarded and cannot be regained, God bless her, I will follow my companions; their lively romances and cheerful discourse perhaps may drive away part of my ponderous burden of trouble and sorrow.'

My young companion Andrew waited on the road for me; he joined me, and he himself was very much hurt with the unfortunate circumstance. Him and Mary were always great friends in Richelieu. We waited a little while in the village, took each a little brandy and water, and so proceeded on to Poitiers. We had a heavy shower of rain as we drew near the city, went into a tavern in the environs of the city, waited near half an hour until the rain abated and we entered the gates of Poitiers.

I felt a little apprehensive that Crown or Aplen might have some hint of my disappointment but they had not taken any notice of my being called and stopping behind. I put the best leg foremost as we passed through the streets. We soon met Crown, Aplen, and Johnson. They took notice of me not being so cheerful as usual. Andrew said I had felt a little unwell and he staid by me in a tavern on the road till I felt a little better. Aplen said yes, he supposed I was fretting about the girl in Richelieu. I utterly denied that story, being certain she was a considerable distance from Richelieu. However when supper was over my only study was to get to my bed, which I had a good opportunity to do. My messmates all went out to see fashions. I embraced the opportunity and off I went to bed where I lay meditating on the sad reverses of fortune that had that unfortunate day tore from my arms, my sweet lovely Mary.

I slept a little towards morning and that greatly refreshed me. I considered that she was gone, and were I to give vent to grief I should make myself continually unhappy all to no purpose. It would not bring back my lost treasure nor do me any good whatever. I therefore determined to form a resolution and drive all melancholy thoughts out of my mind. In the morning I arose, took a walk on the ramparts and being warned the night before that we were to halt that day in Poitiers I did not return home until breakfast was over. The good lady of the house made me a bowl of strong coffee which gave me great relief. I had been very sick all the morning owing to my not eating any thing since the morning before when I took a cup of coffee at Chatellerault at 12 noon.

We mustered in the grand place and were all called over by the *commissarie* mayor, etc. We were all correct according to our *felle de route,* 341 men and one woman. Two men went to the hospital left us 339 Men. The day was fine and clear. We were greatly amused, looking round the ancient works and curiosities that were once the pride and dwellings of the King of Great Britain.

At 4 p.m. the bugles sounded to muster, which was answered. The mayor's secretary brought orders from the bureau that the *commissarie* and mayor thought proper for us to halt again tomorrow as the roads between Poitiers and Louisgnan (Lusignan) were very bad owing to the late heavy rains. This muster was soon over. We had nothing to do, only eat, drink, and sleep. Crown, Andrew, and myself took a walk round the suburbs of the city and returned home owing to some snow beginning to fall. We passed the evening with our landlord; he was a doctor, a fine old fellow, one of Louis's party. He made himself certain that before another week passed round Louis 18th would be king of France; he also told us that Paris was taken by the Allied armies and Bonaparte was made prisoner by his own officers. This all helped to cheer our spirits, and give us fresh courage to continue our march a few days longer. He then caused us to wash this down with good cognac.

We passed the remainder of the evening in discourse on various subjects. The old gentleman spoke his mind freely as to his opinion regarding the present state of France and its Imperial Government. I begged to be excused from the company owing to not having much sleep the night before, neither did I at that time feel very smart. My absence was granted, and bed was my most agreeable company at that time. I retired to my room and when alone by myself my past disappointments began to crowd on my mind; nevertheless I diverted trouble with the conquering delusions of sleep and it was daylight next morning before any thing troubled me, excepting silly foolish dreams.

I found myself greatly refreshed after my good night's rest, got up, went down to breakfast, eat quite hearty then we all took a walk round the ramparts. We visited the English Church (the church that was to have sealed all my joys) and we also were admitted into the burying place of the English Kings that in former days were laid within the vaulted walls of that ancient mass of magnificent architecture. We also took a turn round the grand horse barracks and should have visited many other curiosities in this ancient city, but a heavy fall of rain caused us to repair home and take shelter under the doctor's roof, where we passed the remainder of the day. In the evening Aplen went up to the bureau for the mayor's orders, Our route was signed, wagons ordered, and all ready to march at 8 in the morning. He returned with his message and we all went to rest early, that we might rise early.

April 9. We rose early in the morning and found the ground all covered with snow. We should have chose to be excused starting that morning, but the decree was passed and we must proceed; we all met in the square, were mustered by the secretary, had two large covered wagons, secured our drum and instruments with our baggage, mounted Janet as a guard in one of the wagons, and marched 339 men for Louisgnan, eighteen miles, snow falling lightly all day. However the wind blew quite fresh, which kept the roads pretty well clear of snow. We got to the town of Louisgnan about 2 pm. and met Crown and Johnson on our entering the town. They had no billets but what we found afterwards was equally as good: we were quartered in a church that had been converted into a sort of hospital or asylum, for those that passed through the place. We arrived at the appointed place, and found every thing clean and comfortable, cradles with straw beds and two good blankets for every two men, a large fire at each end of the ward, and several women to attend and prepare victuals which we soon had the opportunity of tasting, because they served us soup and bread, for eight in a mess, then beef and potatoes, etc., all good and clean. We got our route from the mayor and went to rest early (no brandy enters those doors).

April 10. The morning was quite mild, made the roads a little sloppy under foot, but we were all pretty well shod, and met, all present, had three carts, and started, for the village of St. Maixent, nineteen miles. We soon got through this day's journey, arrived, were billeted, and all to our quarters by three in the afternoon (fine people in this little place).

April 11. A fine warm clear morning. We mustered early and had our route signed. We had one wagon and three carts, 339 all present. We made the happy little village all ring when Leversedge gave his arm a swing. We gave them a parting tune and by the good character they had given us of Niort and the news we had on the road we were all eager to get there. The roads were good and we had twenty-five miles to march. Aplen and Johnson were left with the party while Crown, Andrew, and his honour, made the best of our way ahead, to get the orders ready when the party came up to the city!

On our way we met several peasants, some of them quite mellow, waving their hats and shouting, '*Vive Louis dix-huit!*'

Crown first took notice of what they said. He turned round to us took off his hat and cheered danced and capered round like a mad man. I stared at him. The peasants began to draw near us; we then heard them distinctly proclaiming Louis the eighteenth king of France!! What glorious tidings!

'This cannot be true,' says Andrew. 'The news is too good!'

By this time the smock frocks were up to us. '*Vive Louis dix-huit!*' says a merry old farmer.

'What are you?' says another.

We answered them that we were British prisoners of war.

'No, no,' says the old grasscomber, at the same time tugging out a bottle that he carried in the bosom of his frock. 'Come my friends, drink, long live Louis the 18th. You are no longer prisoners. You are our friends and brothers! Your liberty is restored and Louis is Proclaimed king of France, this day in Niort. Napoleon is dethroned and peace is once more restored to our distressed and depopulated country. Come, sons, take another swig, and we will make our village ring with the happy tidings we are bearing to our families and friends. *Adieu* my brothers!

Vive Louis dix-huit,' says the hearty old cock, and away they trudged towards their homes, and we towards Niort.

It is easy to think what effect those glad tidings had amongst us. One moment we thought it could only be a delusion and perhaps what was the desire of the peasants. On the other hand we said it was possible enough as we had been frequently told by people that were the most experienced and able to form some idea of the state their country was in. We kept wandering along as quickly as we possibly could to be convinced whether or no; we soon came near the gates of the city and seeing nothing more than usual we began again to be doubtful but this silly notion was soon banished. On entering the city some of the soldiers in the guardhouse between the walls fired a musket out at the window and displayed a large white flag with the following inscription on it: '*Vive Louis dix-huit*' Now what ought we to say? Thank kind fortune this must be true.

We had not gone many steps farther before an elderly lady looked out at a window, 'Stop, young men,' says she. 'You look like strangers. Step in a moment!'

We did; it was a large gentleman's house. The lady enquired our nation, what we were, and she then made us welcome to what we pleased, to drink the health of Louis. She also gave us each a white ribbon for our hats, informing us that we were no longer prisoners! Our captive chains were burst asunder that moment Louis was proclaimed king.

CHAPTER 14

1814: We Meet the British Army

April 15, 1814. A snowy morning. At 7 a.m. our bugles sounded, 'Up and march away.' We mustered in the square at 8. The mayor and *commissarie* were present; our number was 332 present (and seven in the hospital). Janet Carter had been so much kept among the ladies of the city that I have not had a sight of her in Niort until this morning. Poor girl, she has been very kindly treated by the ladies. They have furnished her with a very handsome new cloth habit, laced boots and every thing comfortable for the road. Janet was as usual ready to take charge of the baggage but the lady of the house where she had been living in sent her chair and horse with a servant to drive it and requested the little heroine to be seated in the chair; that his orders were to take her to Melle. Away goes Janet. The mayor presented us the *felle de route*, and we started. Aplen and Johnson off to Melle mounted on two mules to have our billets ready on our arrival. All being ready the word was given to proceed, and Leversedge set all hands in motion by a stroke on his drum. Our band struck up the favourite old air of 'Britons strike home.' Thus we left the city of Niort.

April 15. We marched from Niort to Melle, a double stage twenty-seven miles. Light snow fell most of the day. Our party towards the latter part of the day must look something like a gang of gypsies changing their abode. In one place there was a horse or mule with two or three Quixotes mounted waddling through the snow; in another place one mounted, another leading the poor creature by the bridle, dragging him along with his head and neck stretched out in a direct line, and three or four dodging along under his lee, and as for the wagons they were the head quarters and towards the latter end of the day's march well manner both within and outside under their lee.

We reached the village of Melle about 4 p.m. Our partners had billets ready on our arrival. We took our baggage from the wagons and to our quarters with all haste out of the snow. We had very good billets in this small place amongst the farmers. Milk and eggs were chief of our diet, then to bed, as it was the best place after our fatiguing day's journey.

April 22. A fine dry morning; we left the city of Limoges for the village of Pierre Buffierre, eighteen miles. Aplen and Johnson went a head. Crown, Andrew and me remained with the party. We passed along quite cheerfully nearly half way, with many of us wearing the white cockade, when on turning a corner of the road we saw a whole body of soldiers meeting us. At this place the road was cut through a hill and the foot path led above on each side the road. Crown was driving a head, never took any thought about his white cockade, nor did he notice their tricoloured flag on their helmets. One of the officers rode up to him and gave him a blow with his sword and iron scabbard that laid poor Crown sprawling on the grass.

'There you English rascal. Take that, and strike your white cockade in a moment or I will sever your head from your body.'

At the same time two or three soldiers dismounted and ran up to Crown tore the cockade off his hat and they all danced on it exclaiming, 'Down with the Bourbons and long live Napoleon!'

We that were behind and saw how the game went had our colours struck in an instant. They left Crown and passed through the midst of us looking for more game but we took the hint on the first onset and until they had all gone past put on quite serious tricoloured face but still kept a heart as pure as a lily sheltered by a British rose.

As we passed those ill minded fellows they passed a great many malicious threats on us. We were this, that, and the other, and if they had their will they would send us where they had lately sent some of our countrymen at Toulouse (that was to grass with our mouth downwards). We made no reply but proceeded our route. We then came up with Crown. He was very angry at the mean spirited fellow that struck him in such a cowardly manner. We proceeded on towards our destined village. When we got there our two comrades gave us the hint that those were not our kind of folks. We therefore halted on the entrance of the place, served out billets, took each man his baggage and to our quarters. Those who had not enough to eat and drink contrived to buy what they needed and we passed the evening and night as well as we could. We learnt also that those troops we had passed were part of the army that Wellington had beat near Toulouse through their not acknowledging Louis as their King. They held the city in the name of Napoleon until they were compelled to surrender after a horrid slaughter when the British took the city in the name of Louis the 18th.

April 23. A fine hard morning. We had three carts, got our papers signed, and marched through the place with the march. Played *Louis Returned.* Outside the place we made the best of our way to St Germain, sixteen miles, and got there quite early. Our boys were ready for us. Andrew and Johnson preferred the task to go a head and draw billets, which I cared very little about. I mostly remained with the party and Andrew being the fifth interpreter mostly took my turn to start ahead. They gave us to know that we were all right. We soon awoke all the children in the village with a volley or two from our travelling two gunned battery. We entered the village and set their windows all dancing to our electrical instruments. At the mayor's door we saluted the old gentleman with three rolls and then served out billets and dispersed every thing good, and free, in this little paradise. Next morning it rained hard, however, we all met at the mayor's door, had four carts, and on the 24th of April we marched for

Uzerche, twenty-three miles. We had a sorry day of it; however we got through and arrived, got billets and took shelter.

April 24. We anchored in Uzerche after a very disagreeable day's journey, eat our victuals and soon looked for bed. Hung our wet things in the corner and started to our rest. The mayor was a horse so we let him rest in the stable. He is three colours and might kick, so we leave him and start away in search of the Mayor of Tuolle, only eighteen miles. We had four carts and a fine morning to march through Uzerche to the rap, tap, rap, pap, tap, dumb march. We soon reached Tulle.

April the 25th; 325 men. My friend William Crown was quite out of order all the day yesterday and this day he gave up, unable to proceed any further on foot. At the halfway house we fixed him quite comfortable in a covered baggage cart in the charge of our trusty young Nurse Janet. We reached Tulle and were directed to a convent, a real fine place, an asylum for travellers. Here is also an hospital on the same principals, attended entirely by the ladies of the veil. We had every thing good, clean, and plenty: clean linen for every man and good comfortable beds. We lodged Crown by his own request in the hospital or rather in the nursery.

The mayor visited us and told us to ask for any thing we wanted, and the ladies would get it for us. He also told us that we must halt in Tulle tomorrow and those who wanted shoes should have them on the new constitution in the name of Louis the 18th. This was happy tidings to us having to halt tomorrow amongst our friends where we can speak our mind without deception, nor false faces. We took a look round this beautiful city, and at sunset our band played a tune in the yard fronting our castle. We passed the evening very comfortable and on the 26th in the morning, fine weather, we took a tour round the market. We then attended breakfast. After this was over the mayor sent word that he wished to see the interpreters at the bureau by ten o'clock. We attended his honour, and his request was for our people to muster and be at the bureau by 2 in the afternoon. This was also done, and all who were badly shod, got new shoes and stockings. Then we got an order to admit two more of our men that were taken very ill to the hospital. This was granted and we returned to our castle well shod.

We then took our sick to the hospital and saw Crown. He was rather low. We did not trouble him much but passed on. The ladies said he required to be kept as still as possible in his present situation. We left them and called at the bureau. The mayor expressed a great desire to have our music play in the square that evening at 6 o'clock. We told him that the musicians were dispersed all round the city and the only way to gather them together was to let our bugles sound a general muster, then all hands could be counted over and the band have their notice to attend in the square, and thus dismiss again. This was his wish; we therefore sent young Andrew to look for alms or Mr. McNally, the two leaders of the bugles, and warn them to sound general muster. It was not long ere we heard our bugles rattle through the streets in all directions. The mayor attended the muster. We counted heads and made 322 men, gave the band their orders and broke up; at 6 we met in the square where all the heads of the city were met to hear a specimen of our abilities.

April 26. This evening we played two hours in the square, then we were sent to the Hôtel de la Ville where we had what ever we chose to drink and five francs each man a present from the ladies of the city. We played them the new rondeau, 'Louis's return,' and returned to our castle.

May 1. Marched from *Aurillac* and left Tho. Johnson and Andrew Smith with the party. Aplen and me, having fine weather and, more than that, light hearts, were wide awake this day. We came to the first village on our way, took a little refreshment, and away we tramped for the next place to halt in. We reached that village at the same time some of the British officers entered the place, being some of the officers belonging the British troops that were on their march to Aurillac. Some of them halted at the small tavern where we were. They seemed not to take any particular notice of us, as we were in our French dress and were speaking French to the landlord; however one of the the young fellows, I suppose a captain, steps up to the landlord.

'Well, my old daddy,' says he, 'have you any cognac brandy?'

'Oui Monsieur,' says the landlord. He presents the officer a bottle and a glass, as customary in that part.

'No, no, old man, I don't want this thing, give me a tumbler and some water.'

The old man shook his head, not understanding what he said. Aplen and me sat by the window grinning to see the farce.

One of the officers that stood near the door says, "Come captain, I believe the old gentleman and you are making that grog,'

'Why damn it, I am waiting for a tumbler.'

Aplen spoke to the old man and told their wants; and he gave them a tumbler and a jog of water.

The captain then looked round at us. 'What? Do you understand English?'

'Yes, Sir,' said I, smiling, 'I ought to.'

'Why, what the devil are you, in that gaol bird's dress?'

'We are English men and have suffered nearly eleven years confinement in the cause of our country.' He looked in amazement at us.

'My God,' he exclaimed. 'Gentlemen, look this way,' says he to his brother officers. They all gathered round. 'Here is two of our countrymen that has been confined all the war in this country by that infernal Bonaparte and his cursed crew.'

Then was the time that I wanted half a score tongues to answer each person's questions. They wanted to know the whole history of our captivity at once; however we gave them to understand our present business. Then we must drink and eat and talk all at one breath. They wanted ham and eggs, but for want of time had to put off with bread and cheese. They said their men were two leagues behind, and we calculated our party about the same distance. They asked us how the Bonaparte's followers used us since Louis was proclaimed king. We mentioned the affair of the officer that struck Crown and trampled on the white cockade and how they made us all strike our white colours, threatening us what they would do.

'Stop!' says the captain. 'What was their number?'

'They were the 7th regiment of Invincible Guards,' says Aplen, 'on their march to Fontenay in La Vendee.'

'Damn me!' says the captain. 'Those were the very same fellows stopped our baggage guard on the road from Niort to Limoges. They made all the guard halt in a small village and ordered them to strike their white ribbons that they wore in their button hole. The sergeant answered them that the men in that little village had just given them the white cockades to wear as the emblems of Louis the 18th. This sergeant of ours is a Guernsey man and spoke French fluently. His name is John Bray. He knew that our men were close at hand—so they were; however this valiant Egyptian hero, as they style the invincibles that were in Egypt, he ordered them to strike their white colours; if not he would be at the trouble to do it for them.

"'Well Sir," says Bray, "and supposing we were to strike the colours of Louis the 18th, what will be the consequence? By whose authority am I to inform my general that I was ordered to do so? Certainly when we arrive at our place of destination my officers will require an account for such cowardly conduct as this will be, if I were to do it, to strike the colours that we are sworn to defend, and not know who it we have struck them to, nor by what authority you have given those orders"

"'I tell you, Sir, I order you and your men to strike them in the name of our Emperor Napoleon."

"'Ah, ah, ah," says Bray, "now you mention your master, I shall have to consider a moment. Pray, Sir, have you seen your Emperor lately to give you those orders?"

'The great and valiant hero drew his sword, and swore if he was not obeyed instantly his men should obey him and use such means as he would not wish to do, but as words appeared to be useless he should try what the sword could do.

'"Now Sir," says Sergeant Bray, "you are jesting. I know you are more of a gentleman than to use any rash means on such a silly affair. We are only eleven men and you are a regiment strong, as appears by your men that are coming up. Suppose you take us back to the next village; there you can lodge our two wagons and I shall save my character. There in presence of the mayor I give you my honour we all will strike."

'But Sergeant Bray knew the detachment of his division was near at hand; this was the mayor he meant.

'"Well then return back before us," Says Monsieur Steel Jacket.

'So Bray and his small party, with their two heavy wagons turned about, and like a decoy duck, let Monsieur into such a snare that he would have given all the tricoloured cockades in his regiment to have passed Bray; and as he could not bear the sight of the Bourbon cockade, he might have shut his eyes and rode along. But to return to Sergeant Bray: He, and his few men counter-marched the road about a mile, when turning round a corner of a wood, that lay on the side of the road, there the whole body of the British troops were close at hand. Bray proceeded on towards them.

'Monsieur looked, then halted, then conversed with some of the officers, then halted the regiment. He was struck with astonishment.

'"What shall I say to those fellows when they enquire my reason for insulting one of their officers and making prisoners of their guard and baggage?"

'By this time the party were up with Bray.

'"What the devil is the matter now, Bray?" says the lieutenant colonel. Bray, smiling, repeated the business in a few words. He told the colonel that he came back to strike Louis's colours, as he made sure they could not be very far in the rear and the Man of Steel was there waiting to see him fulfil his verbal treaty. "Yes," says the colonel, "you shall strike and that damn'd hard."

'He then halted the whole division, formed eight deep and then advanced with the drums and fifes playing *Louis's Return*. Monsieur sent six or eight of the Steel Jackets ahead to hear what news. They were riding past very civil, but Bray, by the colonel's orders, commanded them in French to halt. They obeyed. He then ordered them to strike to the honourable flag of Louis the 18th by order of his highness the Duke of Wellington, Commander in Chief of the British forces in France.

'"Strike immediately that tricoloured cockade from your helmets or they will be immediately struck for you."

'The colonel ordered the twelve men to advance up to them with charged bayonets but not to touch one of them. The moment this was done, Bray, being the interpreter, asked them if they were going to strike the tricoloured cockade. They looked round to their commandant (he was observing their motions at a distance).

'"Well," says the sergeant, "it is useless to resist any longer," so he very tenderly took his blue, white, and red from his helmet and the others followed his example. Sergeant Bray stepped up and took the sergeant's cockade, hove it on the ground and set his foot on it.

'"There Monsieur," says Bray, "I told you I would strike when we got to the village, but we have not reached it yet, therefore you have to strike to me for not taking me there undisturbed."

'The colonel then told Bray to tell them they might pursue their journey, and the colonel advised them not to interfere any more with any British subjects on their travails through the country. They passed on and the British marched on towards the commandant and his men of steel. They remained in their position the same as at first only with this exception: they had every man taken off their cockades. We marched past them with the same tune as before *Louis's Return*. When we passed their commandant, Bray saluted him with "*vive Louis dix-huit*," and in this manner we left them.'

This tale took our time nearly an hour, which made both us and the officers think about moving. We took our road towards Argental and they towards Aurillac. We hurried along nearly four or five miles when we met all the troops and their baggage. We spoke to several officers who enquired what we were and where we were going and many other questions. We answered them all as quick as we could with civility and respect and kept on our journey until we had seen the rear of them. Then our discourse was entirely about those lousy invincibles and poor Bill Crown until we reached the town of Argental, went to the mayor, got our billets, and met our men in good time at the entrance of the town. Served the billets and marched up to the square to that very hateful tune (to those folks) 'Louis's return.' We dismissed to our quarters, small rain beginning to fall quite fast.

May 3. Hazy weather. Took breakfast and made ready to start. Crown came dancing in and halloed out for something to eat and drink We then met together in the square. Had four wagons, started them off under the charge of our female guard. His honour the mayor visited us and bade us a long adieu. We then started the wagon with 'o'er the hills and far away,' and on passing the gates struck up *Louis's Return.* Johnson and Smith took their turn to provide lodgings at night. Crown, Aplen and his honour remained with the party. After we had got well started we began to have a little pastime with Crown about the length of the steel jacket's sword and how heavy he thought it was.

'Well, Crown,' says Aplen, 'Wetherell and me can tell you a little ditty that will make you treat at the halfway house,'

'You can?' says Crown. 'Well then, go on with it and we will leave it to the opinion of Wetherell who shall pay the piper.'

All agreed. Aplen related over the tale of Bray and the Man in Steel. He got to where Bray turned back to see the mayor before he liked to strike his white cockade.

'There, there,' says Crown, 'it is my treat.'

'Wait a moment,' says Aplen, 'till you hear how he struck.'

'Well, proceed,' says Crown.

He then got to where they met the whole division of British that Bray was attached to, and indeed them he was looking for. Crown was fully satisfied, but when he heard how Bray took their three stripes and stamped his foot on them and the commandant with all his invincibles had to dowse their stripes, Crown leaped and halloed like a wild man.

'Now,' says he, 'I will treat twenty times at such a curious way as this is to hear how things will round. Makes the French word prove true that says "never mind, John, your day today and mine tomorrow." Now I am contented,' says Crown, 'and freely forgive the fellow that took such a pleasure in laying a snare to take himself.'

We arrived at the halfway house, took our treat and then travailed on for Uzerche, only eighteen miles, a light day's journey. We are in no great hurry to this three coloured mayor. We know him before; however in our present circumstances we regard him no farther than in civility. We reached the town, got our billets, marched in to the tune of *Louis's Return*, discharged our baggage, and to our billets, much of the miserable (says poor Thomas Crisp). However we made crooked places straight and brought morning.

May 7. We left Limoges for the village of Bellac, twenty-six miles. This was only a morning's promenade for us. We were at the village in a jiffy. In this small place we all turned farmers, eat fat bacon and beans. We also drank small wine by the jug full as a substitute for tea or coffee. Some of our men were billeted, they said, three miles from the village. Aplen, Crown, Andrew, and me were at the mayor's house, a good mile across the ploughed fields from the main road.

It was in this village that we took possession of a farm house from the whole family merely through harmless pastime. Crown and me took our bassoons along with us into a cottage near the mayor's house. Our errand was to look for a drop of brandy, which we found. We sat down talking to each other in English. The old man, the old woman, their son and daughter all stared at us!

'What are they saying?' says the son.

Aplen winked at us.

'Now,' says he, 'we will have a little fun.' He turns to the master of the house and says in French, 'What nation do you think we belong?'

The poor man shook his head and said he could not tell unless we were English or Germans.

'No, no,' says Aplen.

The son steps to where we had set the two bassoons. Taking up one of them he says to Aplen, 'What is this thing to do?'

Bill starts at the poor fellow.

'Oh, my God, take care—you will kill some person. She is loaded.'

'What!' exclaimed the old father. 'Loaded, is it a gun?'

'Set it down, Louey, set it down and go away from such dangerous engines as them. You might have blown the house and all of us in it into the air had not this good gentleman been fortunate enough to have noticed you in time. He most likely has saved all our lives.'

'Yes,' says the old woman, 'I have often cautioned you, Louey, not to meddle with things that did not belong to you. A pretty story would have been to tell. Perhaps you might have shot me, or your father, or even your dear sister, with your curiosity. Do, my good gentlemen, put them instruments of death in the barn, where they will be quite safe until you go away.'

'Now you shall see some sport,' says Bill. 'No, Madam,' says he, running to the bassoons and took up one of them holding it out towards the son and snapping one of the long brass keys, 'we are Cossacks.'

The son set up a roar and fled into the barn, where his sister was already concealed. The old woman fell speechless across the table; the old man down on his marrow bones, praying us not to take their lives nor terrify them out of their senses and we should have the best of all he had in the house. Aplen returned his gun into the corner and told the man we wanted some bread and milk made hot.

'Yes Sir, yes Sir,' says the old man, 'in a minute, in a minute.'

The good old dame arose from her dream and tottered

across the room to a large chair in the corner. She looked very hard at the two guns, then at us. At last the old man came puffing in from the milk room with a large brass kettle full of milk. He soon made it hot and put plenty of bread in it, then set it on the table, gave us bowls and spoons, and at it we went, more for the sake of devilry than for the want of bread and milk. When we were engaged with the bread and milk the good man enquired of Aplen if we were the Cossacks that kill people and eat them and destroy every thing they fall in with. We now thought we had carried the joke far enough and must wind up a little.

'No, no, Sir,' answered Aplen, 'we are quite a different nation. Our greatest pleasure is to prevent the shedding of human blood and this is our motto—*we conquer to save*—so that you nor your family has the least cause to be any ways jealous of us. I suppose,' says Aplen, 'you know that your neighbour the mayor directed us to your cottage?'

'Yes Sir,' answered the peasant. 'We always lodge the people that are billeted on the mayor; he has a large family and no room for strangers etc. I suppose he informed you that my beds were straw but clean, and clean warm bed cloths to cover you. This is what we give all our own troops that pass and repass through Bellac.'

Night drawing on we went to bed quite comfortable and in the morning quite early the old man and woman were up they had a good fire and another kettle of milk hot ready for us. We arose, took our poultice as the doctor had prepared it, and mounted our knapsacks, shouldered our muskets and just as we gained the top of a little hill outside of the barn Aplen looked back and saw the farmer's son and daughter peering out at the barn door. Aplen snatched my bassoon and pointed it at the two poor terrified prisoners; they quickly hid themselves again by slamming to the door. Again we made a start across the wearisome ploughed fields; the morning was charming and the small birds saluted us from each bush as we passed along. Our bugles also invited us to pay our morning visit to the rest of our countrymen who were mustering together from all direction. We being all ready and three wagons for our baggage, made sail for the village of Lusac, all in great spirits etc., distance, thirty-four miles.

May 8. After a long day's journey we arrived at Lusac, got our billets and found all things plentiful and good, went early to bed, and took our rest etc.

May 9. We all met quite early to start off for Poitiers, twenty-nine miles. Fine morning and four carts to attend us. We gave the mayor (a fine young gentleman) three rounds from our two gunned battery, and a taste of *Louis's Return* etc., then steer away for the city of Poitiers. We got there by 4 in the afternoon, Johnson and Smith met us with the billets. They found a new mayor in the city, a good sort of a man. We served our billets and repaired to our various lodgings, after we got settled and took our dinner, Aplen went to the hospital with two of our men that were sick, and brought back the two that we left on our march to the south; I went along with my bosom friend Andrew and took a look at the English Church that was once to crown all my happiness, but, no, it was not to be, therefore I must take my farewell of both the church and the treasure that it was to have bequeathed to me. However I can yet have a glimmering spark of comfort, that is of fulfilling her last request—that was, to write every opportunity!

Accordingly we went to our lodgings and I took my pen and wrote in my usual style. I addressed old Pierre Collardo as father, and Louise, as sister etc., and as for the grand address! That is left to myself. I told them I should write again on my arrival in St. Maloes which would be in about twelve days' time and to be sure and have a letter ready for me when I get there. I gave them my address etc., to be left in the post office until called for yours etc., J P W. I then took it to the post office and finished my day's work, went to bed not to sleep but lay and think what to do.

May 10. Fine morning, We had three carts and marched to Marebari, twenty-five miles, we had good billets and on the 11th of May we had four carts and travelled to Airvault, thirty-three miles. Fine weather good billets, and on the 12th of May rainy etc., we arrived in Chatillon (Chatillon-sur-Sèvre), thirty-one miles, had grand usage and plenty. On the 13th we reached the village of Mortagne (Mortagne-sur-Sevre), eighteen miles, good lodgings etc. Next day the 14th we got into the city of Nantes, twenty-nine miles, good quarters, left three in the hospital, and on the 15th of May we marched to Blain, seventeen miles. Poor billets, left Johnson sick. May 17th we reached Balm (Bain-de-Bretagne?), thirty-four miles, good billets, and on the 17th we arrive in Rennes, twenty-nine miles. We had a large room in the city hall and plenty of everything. On the 18th we halted to have our arrears paid up, and new shoes etc. May 18th we were paid twelve *francs*, each man had shoes where they were wanting, put three men in the hospital, and on the 19th, fine morning, Aplen, Andrew and myself left Crown with the party, and at 4 in the morning we left Rennes and walked to Becherel, twenty-seven miles. By ten o'clock took some refreshment and walked to Combourg seventeen miles by 3 in the afternoon halted at the mayor's left our orders and made the last Push.—to St. Survey (St. Servan), twenty-three miles, where we took lodging in a tavern for that night. Now my boys we once more beheld the salt water and vessels etc. We were determined to call this a day's march, only sixty-seven miles.

We being at last arrived on the sea coast, it was time to leave off keeping any more journal of our land travels. I therefore took an opportunity at the time my messmates were sleeping I was employed writing a few incorrect lines that chanced to strike my intention at that present time therefore I sat down in the bed chamber and wrote.

ALSO FROM LEONAUR
AVAILABLE IN SOFTCOVER OR HARDCOVER WITH DUST JACKET

THE JENA CAMPAIGN: 1806 by *F. N. Maude*—The Twin Battles of Jena & Auerstadt Between Napoleon's French and the Prussian Army.

PRIVATE O'NEIL by *Charles O'Neil*—The recollections of an Irish Rogue of H. M. 28th Regt.—The Slashers— during the Peninsula & Waterloo campaigns of the Napoleonic wars.

ROYAL HIGHLANDER by *James Anton*—A soldier of H.M 42nd (Royal) Highlanders during the Peninsular, South of France & Waterloo Campaigns of the Napoleonic Wars.

CAPTAIN BLAZE by *Elzéar Blaze*—Elzéar Blaze recounts his life and experiences in Napoleon's army in a well written, articulate and companionable style.

LEJEUNE VOLUME 1 by *Louis-François Lejeune*—The Napoleonic Wars through the Experiences of an Officer on Berthier's Staff.

LEJEUNE VOLUME 2 by *Louis-François Lejeune*—The Napoleonic Wars through the Experiences of an Officer on Berthier's Staff.

FUSILIER COOPER by *John S. Cooper*—Experiences in the 7th (Royal) Fusiliers During the Peninsular Campaign of the Napoleonic Wars and the American Campaign to New Orleans.

CAPTAIN COIGNET by *Jean-Roch Coignet*—A Soldier of Napoleon's Imperial Guard from the Italian Campaign to Russia and Waterloo.

FIGHTING NAPOLEON'S EMPIRE by *Joseph Anderson*—The Campaigns of a British Infantryman in Italy, Egypt, the Peninsular & the West Indies During the Napoleonic Wars.

CHASSEUR BARRES by *Jean-Baptiste Barres*—The experiences of a French Infantryman of the Imperial Guard at Austerlitz, Jena, Eylau, Friedland, in the Peninsular, Lutzen, Bautzen, Zinnwald and Hanau during the Napoleonic Wars.

MARINES TO 95TH (RIFLES) by *Thomas Fernyhough*—The military experiences of Robert Fernyhough during the Napoleonic Wars.

HUSSAR ROCCA by *Albert Jean Michel de Rocca*—A French cavalry officer's experiences of the Napoleonic Wars and his views on the Peninsular Campaigns against the Spanish, British And Guerilla Armies.

SERGEANT BOURGOGNE by *Adrien Bourgogne*—With Napoleon's Imperial Guard in the Russian Campaign and on the Retreat from Moscow 1812 - 13.

AVAILABLE ONLINE AT
www.leonaur.com
AND OTHER GOOD BOOK STORES

ALSO FROM LEONAUR
AVAILABLE IN SOFTCOVER OR HARDCOVER WITH DUST JACKET

WELLINGTON AND THE PYRENEES CAMPAIGN VOLUME I: FROM VITORIA TO THE BIDASSOA by *F. C. Beatson*—The final phase of the campaign in the Iberian Peninsula.

WELLINGTON AND THE INVASION OF FRANCE VOLUME II: THE BIDASSOA TO THE BATTLE OF THE NIVELLE by *F. C. Beatson*—The second of Beatson's series on the fall of Revolutionary France published by Leonaur, the reader is once again taken into the centre of Wellington's strategic and tactical genius.

WELLINGTON AND THE FALL OF FRANCE VOLUME III: THE GAVES AND THE BATTLE OF ORTHEZ by *F. C. Beatson*—This final chapter of F. C. Beatson's brilliant trilogy shows the 'captain of the age' at his most inspired and makes all three books essential additions to any Peninsular War library.

NAVAL BATTLES OF THE NAPOLEONIC WARS by *W. H. Fitchett*—Cape St. Vincent, the Nile, Cadiz, Copenhagen, Trafalgar & Others

SERGEANT GUILLEMARD: THE MAN WHO SHOT NELSON? by *Robert Guillemard*—A Soldier of the Infantry of the French Army of Napoleon on Campaign Throughout Europe

WITH THE GUARDS ACROSS THE PYRENEES by *Robert Batty*—The Experiences of a British Officer of Wellington's Army During the Battles for the Fall of Napoleonic France, 1813.

A STAFF OFFICER IN THE PENINSULA by *E. W. Buckham*—An Officer of the British Staff Corps Cavalry During the Peninsula Campaign of the Napoleonic Wars

THE LEIPZIG CAMPAIGN: 1813—NAPOLEON AND THE "BATTLE OF THE NATIONS" by *F. N. Maude*—Colonel Maude's analysis of Napoleon's campaign of 1813.

BUGEAUD: A PACK WITH A BATON by *Thomas Robert Bugeaud*—The Early Campaigns of a Soldier of Napoleon's Army Who Would Become a Marshal of France.

TWO LEONAUR ORIGINALS

SERGEANT NICOL by *Daniel Nicol*—The Experiences of a Gordon Highlander During the Napoleonic Wars in Egypt, the Peninsula and France.

WATERLOO RECOLLECTIONS by *Frederick Llewellyn*—Rare First Hand Accounts, Letters, Reports and Retellings from the Campaign of 1815.

ALSO FROM LEONAUR
AVAILABLE IN SOFTCOVER OR HARDCOVER WITH DUST JACKET

CAPTAIN OF THE 95th (Rifles) by *Jonathan Leach*—An officer of Wellington's Sharpshooters during the Peninsular, South of France and Waterloo Campaigns of the Napoleonic Wars.

BUGLER AND OFFICER OF THE RIFLES by *William Green & Harry Smith* With the 95th (Rifles) during the Peninsular & Waterloo Campaigns of the Napoleonic Wars

BAYONETS, BUGLES AND BONNETS by *James 'Thomas' Todd*—Experiences of hard soldiering with the 71st Foot - the Highland Light Infantry - through many battles of the Napoleonic wars including the Peninsular & Waterloo Campaigns

THE ADVENTURES OF A LIGHT DRAGOON by *George Farmer & G.R. Gleig*—A cavalryman during the Peninsular & Waterloo Campaigns, in captivity & at the siege of Bhurtpore, India

THE COMPLEAT RIFLEMAN HARRIS by *Benjamin Harris as told to & transcribed by Captain Henry Curling*—The adventures of a soldier of the 95th (Rifles) during the Peninsular Campaign of the Napoleonic Wars

WITH WELLINGTON'S LIGHT CAVALRY by *William Tomkinson*—The Experiences of an officer of the 16th Light Dragoons in the Peninsular and Waterloo campaigns of the Napoleonic Wars.

SURTEES OF THE RIFLES by *William Surtees*—A Soldier of the 95th (Rifles) in the Peninsular campaign of the Napoleonic Wars.

ENSIGN BELL IN THE PENINSULAR WAR by *George Bell*—The Experiences of a young British Soldier of the 34th Regiment 'The Cumberland Gentlemen' in the Napoleonic wars.

WITH THE LIGHT DIVISION by *John H. Cooke*—The Experiences of an Officer of the 43rd Light Infantry in the Peninsula and South of France During the Napoleonic Wars

NAPOLEON'S IMPERIAL GUARD: FROM MARENGO TO WATERLOO by *J. T. Headley*—This is the story of Napoleon's Imperial Guard from the bearskin caps of the grenadiers to the flamboyance of their mounted chasseurs, their principal characters and the men who commanded them.

BATTLES & SIEGES OF THE PENINSULAR WAR by *W. H. Fitchett*—Corunna, Busaco, Albuera, Ciudad Rodrigo, Badajos, Salamanca, San Sebastian & Others

AVAILABLE ONLINE AT
www.leonaur.com
AND OTHER GOOD BOOK STORES

NAP-1

ALSO FROM LEONAUR
AVAILABLE IN SOFTCOVER OR HARDCOVER WITH DUST JACKET

A JOURNAL OF THE SECOND SIKH WAR by *Daniel A. Sandford*—The Experiences of an Ensign of the 2nd Bengal European Regiment During the Campaign in the Punjab, India, 1848-49.

LAKE'S CAMPAIGNS IN INDIA by *Hugh Pearse*—The Second Anglo Maratha War, 1803-1807. Often neglected by historians and students alike, Lake's Indian campaign was fought against a resourceful and ruthless enemy-almost always superior in numbers to his own forces.

BRITAIN IN AFGHANISTAN 1: THE FIRST AFGHAN WAR 1839-42 by *Archibald Forbes*—Following over a century of the gradual assumption of sovereignty of the Indian Sub-Continent, the British Empire, in the form of the Honourable East India Company, supported by troops of the new Queen Victoria's army, found itself inevitably at the natural boundaries that surround Afghanistan. There it set in motion a series of disastrous events-the first of which was to march into the country at all.

BRITAIN IN AFGHANISTAN 2: THE SECOND AFGHAN WAR 1878-80 by *Archibald Forbes*—This the history of the Second Afghan War-another episode of British military history typified by savagery, massacre, siege and battles.

UP AMONG THE PANDIES by *Vivian Dering Majendie*—An outstanding account of the campaign for the fall of Lucknow. This is a vital book of war as fought by the British Army of the mid-nineteenth century, but in truth it is also an essential book of war that will enthral.

BLOW THE BUGLE, DRAW THE SWORD by *W. H. G. Kingston*—The Wars, Campaigns, Regiments and Soldiers of the British & Indian Armies During the Victorian Era, 1839-1898.

INDIAN MUTINY 150th ANNIVERSARY: A LEONAUR ORIGINAL

MUTINY: 1857 by *James Humphries*—It is now 150 years since the 'Indian Mutiny' burst like an engulfing flame on the British soldiers, their families and the civilians of the Empire in North East India. The Bengal Native army arose in violent rebellion, and the once peaceful countryside became a battleground as Native sepoys and elements of the Indian population massacred their British masters and defeated them in open battle. As the tide turned, a vengeful army of British and loyal Indian troops repressed the insurgency with a savagery that knew no mercy. It was a time of fear and slaughter. James Humphries has drawn together the voices of those dreadful days for this commemorative book.

AVAILABLE ONLINE AT
www.leonaur.com
AND OTHER GOOD BOOK STORES

www.ingramcontent.com/pod-product-compliance
Lightning Source LLC
Chambersburg PA
CBHW031625160426
43196CB00006B/278